0·00

D0762141

FURNISHING
DOLLS' HOUSES

FURNISHING DOLLS' HOUSES

by

AUDREY JOHNSON

LONDON: G. BELL AND SONS, LTD

745.5923
JOH
(2)

ISBN 0 7135 1691 7
Printed offset in Great Britain by
The Camelot Press Ltd, London and Southampton

☆ CONTENTS ☆

☆ PHOTOGRAPHS ☆

between pages 96 and 97

☆ INTRODUCTION ☆

This book came about as a result of my own experience and interest in dolls' houses and their furnishings. Although some research and historical background is involved, it does not set out to be a history of the subject. It could perhaps, be described as a practical handbook for those who are interested in such matters, collectors, enthusiasts, teachers and those who have to care for and renovate their properties. I am conscious of a growing and surprisingly widespread interest in such miniature furnishing, perhaps due to a feminine urge for home-making that is not entirely fulfilled in everyday life.

I have limited any description of old and valuable dolls' houses to a minimum and dealt more fully with the later Victorian and early 20th Century dolls' houses because these are so much more likely to be the concern of the reader. In fact, the collector of dolls' house furniture need not have a dolls' house at all for there is a very long tradition of housing such collections in cabinets that open to reveal rooms full of miniature furnishings. The oldest and best are probably those of the 17th Century Netherlands. Their magnificent inlaid cabinets, standing on richly carved and gilt stands, display room after room so fully furnished that some of the items exist now only in miniature form. Such splendour must inevitably be beyond the reach of almost all of us today, but the idea of using a cabinet to form rooms full of furniture is worth emulating.

I have a large mid-Victorian dolls' house but I acquire more furniture than it will hold and so I have converted a late 18th-Century cabinet into a dolls' house by the simple addition of a shelf and two central walls that in no way alter the original. There are alternative possibilities; glazed wall cabinets, medicine chests, bedside cupboards that once held chamber pots, and all kinds of cupboards.

I would like to acknowledge the help afforded me whilst I gathered material for this book from Patience Arnold of Ambleside, The Bethnal Green Museum, London, Mrs. & Miss Garnett of Kendal, The Kendal Museum, The London Museum, Rossana Mellor, The Harris Art Gallery & Museum, Preston, Kae Smith of Coniston, The Salford Art Gallery & Museum, and the Tunbridge Wells Museum.

8

PART ONE

THE RESTORATION AND CARE OF
OLD DOLLS' HOUSES

✩ THE RESTORATION AND CARE OF
OLD DOLLS' HOUSES ✩

There is a lot of pleasure in collecting dolls' houses and in the acquisition of more and more appropriate things to put in them. There is probably even greater pleasure in actually putting them in good order and in making for yourself furnishings that are otherwise unobtainable. There immediately arises the old problem of how much should be done in the way of restoration, an argument that creates an astonishing degree of dissension and fury. My instinct is to be practical rather than doctrinaire. Old dolls' houses are like old furniture, and if they are old enough and of a sufficiently high quality they are called antiques and valued accordingly. In fact, their scarcity gives them an added value in terms both of money and esteem. It would be unwise to strip and repolish or repaint antique furniture unless it was hopelessly damaged and a similar restraint would appear appropriate to a dolls' house. Therefore, if you are so fortunate as to acquire a dolls' house of the 18th or early 19th Century you might as well be advised to take it to either a firm of professional restorers or to a museum before doing anything for yourself. If you do this, then it would be well to remember that all such authorities are not necessarily either well informed or free from collectors' mania. I would suggest that you consult several such authorities and keep a firm grip on your parcel. Inevitably, with the years, and with the pressures of fashion, scarcity and inflation, dolls' houses made since the beginning of Victoria's reign are regarded as antiques, but the majority of them never attempted the high standards of craftsmanship of earlier years and were made, almost always, as toys for children rather than as pseudo-toys for rich parents. Nevertheless, every effort should be made to keep them as near their original state as is compatible with essential repair. Of course, broken pieces should be mended and missing pieces replaced, but the whole should not be so thoroughly rejuvenated as to lose forever the patina and charm of its age. There will be a lot of small but awkward decisions, particularly with regard to the main fabric of the house, but in the case of furnishings, which can always be removed, such decisions are not very important and if you cannot find an old piece of furniture then you might as well make it yourself, and move it on if the real thing should ever come to hand.

The actual making of miniature things is so real and rewarding an experience, common to so many different times and cultures, that it seems worth while to provide a setting for the things themselves, and what better than a dolls' house, old or new. There are some things that cannot easily be made at home, such as metal castings and ceramics, although even they are not wholly impossible, and they are, fortunately, just those things that were made in the greatest numbers commercially, and so remain the most readily obtainable.

The older pieces of furniture, such as chairs, tables and beds are now very difficult to find, but in the past some of them were very often made by amateurs so that there is almost a tradition of furniture making, such as a bed made from a box with the lid up-ended, and it is very rewarding to continue this tradition.

I begin this book with a description of the treatment of an old dolls' house; the care of its woodwork, paintwork, wall-coverings, furniture and fabrics, and some consideration of possible renewals and additions. This will inevitably demand some knowledge of a variety of minor crafts, such as woodwork, painting and decorating, and needlework. I do not believe that a very high standard of skill is essential to begin with, but that a feeling for the right material should be acquired. By this, I mean that one should get to know, instinctively, what kind of paint or fabric or degree of finish will be appropriate for the job in hand. This understanding will come from a study of objects from the past, together with an experience of the tools and materials of the various crafts.

CARE OF THE STRUCTURE

Woodwork

Dolls' houses have all too often been stored away for many years in damp places and when they are brought into heated rooms they shrink, panels crack and joints fall apart. Changes of humidity and temperature are so primary a cause of damage that ideally a dolls' house, like other antique furniture, should be kept at a fairly even temperature, about 65°F, and away from direct heat. Immediate repair should await the effect of any such change.

The other major enemy of antiques is woodworm. This is a beetle that lays its eggs in the cracks and joints of woodwork, where they hatch into larvae. The little grub bores on into the timber, eating as it goes, until it changes into a pupa and finally emerges as a beetle, to begin all over again. Active woodworm shows itself by small, pale-coloured holes on the surface of the wood, together with very fine sawdust on the floor beneath. If the holes are dark, then they are old ones, perhaps vacated years ago. There are several proprietary brands of woodworm killers on the market and Rentokil is the one I have used. This liquid has to be injected into each of the holes, a long and wearisome task, and it is advisable to paint it over the base of the doll's house to deter any new infestation.

Do not overclean an antique dolls' house. The surface dirt certainly should go, but leaving the patina of age.

First remove the dust with a soft brush and a duster, and then with a soft cloth clean it with the following mixture:

2 dessertspoons of turpentine
2 dessertspoons of linseed oil
2 dessertspoons of vinegar
1 teaspoon of methylated spirit.

When thoroughly clean, the house can be polished with a good beeswax polish of the kind sold in antique shops. This you can make yourself by melting 1 part of beeswax into 3 parts of genuine turpentine. It is essential that you remember always to leave untouched the original polish, and with it the patina, unless it is in a truly horrible condition.

Paintwork

Painted dolls' houses acquire with time a quality not dissimilar to polished wood and this patina should be particularly cherished. The choice of colours reflects the fashions of the time and their mellowness would be difficult to imitate in new paint. Creams have become a golden honey or biscuit colour and the browns and reds are pleasantly muted.

Such paintwork should be cleaned in the same manner and with the same materials as polished wood. Similarly, cracks and holes should be filled with slivers of wood, 'plastic wood', or Polyfilla, the choice of material being dictated by their size. This repair will have to be painted to match its surroundings and I propose to deal with the choice of paints in the section dealing with crafts (see page 23). The common mistake is to use those all too readily obtainable tins of enamel paint. Such glossy paint may well already cover the older paint and it can sometimes be removed by careful chipping with a sharp blade.

Wall-coverings

Many late 19th Century and Edwardian dolls' houses had their roofs and even their walls covered with paper that simulated bricks or tiles. Varnished, this material often stayed in remarkably good condition, but if it is so widely affected as to be beyond repair, it can often be replaced, either by new papers similarly painted, or by a paper copied by yourself—a last resort that might demand superhuman patience.

Inside walls are more often papered than painted, for it gives a better finish, and sometimes layer upon layer of paper has accumulated. Unlike real houses, the paper beneath might well prove to be in better condition than the one above. Happily they usually respond to being thoroughly wetted and left for a little while, although stubborn bits might demand picking with the fingernails. Such wallpaper strippers as Polystrip are rarely needed.

Do not despair about damaged wallpapers, for they respond remarkably to techniques of restoration. The common brown streaks of damp can be disguised by using artists' pastels that simply cover them up. If you haven't exactly the correct shade of pastel they can be 'mixed' on the wall by fine strokes of appropriate colours, like painting a picture. They should finally be fixed with a P.V.A. fixative, now sold in aerosol form.

Should the problem be one of missing pieces of an otherwise acceptable wallpaper, then new pieces can be made by exactly copying the old pattern on to suitable paper, using watercolours, inks, gouache, poster paint—whatever gives the closest copy. The effects of age can be copied with the pattern, to match the old, rather than applied afterwards, which is difficult to do effectively. Often enough, quite old wallpapers are only dirty and will respond to a gentle rubbing with breadcrumbs or a soft gum rubber.

Hinges & Locks

Those hinges or locks that are jammed with rust can be readily cleaned by the application of penetrating oils sold especially for that job. A more awkward problem is loose, ill-fitting hinges where the screws have worn great holes. Refill the holes with bits of wood and glue and refit, if necessary, with new screws.

Fortunately, small brass hinges, knobs, catches, hooks and locks can still be bought from the better stocked ironmongers. Of course, only the same, or very similar fittings to the old ones should be used and, in the case of the older hand-made fittings, they should be repaired or made anew.

CARE OF THE FURNISHINGS

Fabrics

This usually means carpets, curtains and upholstery.

The upholstery of chairs and sofas is usually best left as it is, apart from brushing away dust and dirt. All these fabrics have had the advantage over those in a real house for they have rarely, if ever, been exposed to strong light, let alone sunlight, which is the most powerful destroyer, apart from moth, and they have had little or no wear and tear, or smoke from fires and cigars. The greatest enemies have been moths and the dirt that attracts them and the years when this has been allowed to go undetected. Recently I found moth grubs in a moleskin rug in my dolls' house and had to destroy the rug and treat everything in the house with crystals sold for the job. Really old and valuable carpets should be cleaned rather than washed and specialist firms exist for the cleaning of such antique fabrics.

Curtains may usually be washed, especially cottons and linens, but old dyes are often fugitive and can be tested in the following way: wet a piece of white cloth and squeeze a corner of the curtain in it, so that any loose dye will show and oblige you to use dry cleaning. If all is well, soak them in several changes of lukewarm water to loosen the dirt, but do not rub them unnecessarily. Then wash them gently in warm water and Stergene (a very mild detergent) and rinse them finally in cold water. At Uppark, where there is a famous dolls' house, the life-size curtains are the original 18th Century ones and they have been washed regularly in a liquid made from the very pretty pink carnation-like plant called soapwort. A solution made from this plant can be had and is called Saponin.

Lace curtains can be washed in warm water with a little Stergene, floating them about in the water rather than rubbing them, to avoid tearing the fragile threads. After a thorough rinsing they should be dried flat on absorbent paper so that they retain their shape.

When the threads of fabric are breaking with age, the curtain or carpet should be mounted on to nylon net, a process known as *tramming*, where it is sewn from the back with small stitches in even rows, so small as to be virtually invisible from the front.

Wooden Furnishings

If the house and its contents have been for long in a damp atmosphere, the animal glues will have lost their hold and joints will open and things will literally fall apart.

Fortunately, this condition may be remedied fairly simply with glue. More difficult is the problem of missing pieces, for these will have to be made. The first and major problem is to find the right kind of wood and when it is found or an alternative chosen, it will have to be so stained, coloured, painted, varnished or polished that it matches the original. This will inevitably lead to a great deal of trial and error with the different materials described in the next section and others that may occur to you to use.

Metal Furnishings

There is a long tradition of metal furniture in dolls' houses. The 17th and 18th Century houses will occasionally boast whole sets of silver furnishings, whilst the 19th Century abounds with a startling variety of cheap metal castings of even the most unlikely objects.

Old silver that is tarnished can be cleaned by immersion in liquid silver dip. This is both magical and safe, providing that the instructions are faithfully carried out. A lacquer can then be applied, of which a reliable make is

Frigilene, and this will keep the silver bright for a year or so. Such lacquers are usually applied with a soft brush but, as in the case of the silver dip, it is essential to follow the makers' instructions with great care.

Brass objects can be cleaned in a strong solution of washing soda in water, and lacquered.

Tinned objects suffer from rust and this can be removed with patent rust remover. Lacquer will, to some extent, prevent further rusting.

Metal furniture is very difficult to repair, for it is usually very delicate and made from soft metal so that a soldering iron is all too likely to melt the whole object. Each problem must therefore be considered afresh and a solution can usually be found, even if it involves recourse to the shadier forms of camouflage.

For example, a missing leg might be replaced by a wooden one covered with metal paint or foil, or a broken one joined with a collar that is repeated on the other leg to balance the whole. Legs at the back can, if all else fails, be lost to sight if the object is stood against a wall in a dark corner.

A useful material to hold things together is the fine wire that can be got from electric wiring and this is often more effective, even if it shows, than the glues sold especially for metal. The problem is not the lack of adherence of the glues, but the lack of surface and the excess of leverage.

Other Materials

Glass, marble and pottery are all difficult to repair without some evidence of the break remaining. Great strength is rarely essential so glass and pottery can be effectively repaired with the thin transparent glues such as Durofix. The broken pieces should be very carefully cleaned and dried before glueing. Marble is best repaired with such glues as Araldite. First it should be cleaned with soft soap, ammonia and water and thoroughly dried. Then the Araldite is mixed and applied as advised by the manufacturer, and awkward pieces can be held into place with Sellotape until everything is thoroughly hard.

PART TWO

TOOLS, MATERIALS & CRAFTS

☆ TOOLS, MATERIALS AND CRAFTS ☆

WOODWORK

Tools

The small scale of a dolls' house demands small tools, but these need be surprisingly few and the following list should meet most needs. Most households will already have many of them.

A fretsaw and blades
A small tenon saw
A ruler
A light hammer
A 'craft' knife which has replaceable blades that are exceedingly sharp
A variety of sandpapers
A range of glues
Scissors
Tweezers
Pliers that will cut wire

Wood

The timber chosen should be well seasoned, free from knots and easy to work. Such small quantities are needed that most of it can be culled from waste rather than bought new. Timber is of two major kinds, hardwoods and softwoods, and although the latter might appear the easier to use, they do have certain disadvantages and much doll's house furniture has, in the past, been made from hardwoods, particularly birch and beech, close-grained, pale-coloured woods that can be cut into very fine shapes without splintering. Oak and mahogany were used for elaborate 18th Century furniture, presumably because the full-size furniture they sought to portray was itself made from these woods. Oak was used at the beginning of this century for the Edwardian and mock Tudor furniture then fashionable, but it was not very suitable as it is hard to cut, the grain shows overmuch, and there is a tendency for small projections to break off. Most of the wood that I have used has been taken from old cigar boxes and from the wooden frames of honeycombs, a particularly beautiful smooth white wood. Fortunately, most old households can provide a supply of broken bits of furniture, well-seasoned, and free.

The soft, almost spongy, balsa woods are probably most suited for the inside structures or padding of pieces of furniture that will be covered with cloth, although the very thin strips and slices that are stocked by most craft shops are convenient and useful, particularly as trimmings.

Obechi wood, also sold in these shops, is harder and very useful indeed. The varieties of dowelling stocked are obviously of the greatest value for rails and posts.

Sandpaper

Sandpapers can be bought in a variety of grades but only the finest will be needed for such small work and these are the O's. These grades are of a different colour from the coarse papers, greenish rather than gold coloured, but must be used in the same manner, which is essentially the following of the grain. Rubbing across the grain will leave fine scars that are accentuated by subsequent coats of paint. Damp sandpaper can be brought back into usable condition by simply drying it off on a radiator.

Nails

Remarkably few nails are used in dolls' house furniture for they do not fulfil any very useful function and they are very difficult to insert into such small objects. The smallest $\frac{1}{2}$-inch panel pins are the ones to use, but more often dressmakers' pins, cut to the right length, do the job better, particularly in the very soft woods like balsa. Almost always the many efficient and varied modern glues will do the job far better than screws and nails: and even the old animal glues were preferred in the past.

Glues

The old animal glues that had to be kept warm in a double boiler are no longer to be considered when there are now so many good adhesives available. A good tube glue to use is Croid No. 3, which is sold in small tubes and it has the advantage over the animal glue that it is both waterproof and quick-setting. The latter quality is almost essential when parts have to be held together by hand until they are firmly joined. Such glues are fairly strong, but for a really serious bond such as is needed for a part of the structure that might be lifted, such as the roof and chimneystacks, one of the synthetic resin adhesives (such as Araldite) will be best. These glues usually consist of a resin and a hardener that are mixed together when needed and as they take a long time to harden it is necessary to clamp the two surfaces together, an awkward and difficult task that all too often demands attempts with string, Sellotape, clips and props and blocks innumerable.

Constructing Furniture

As with most things, there is a technique, or way of going about such problems, that makes everything that much quicker and better than the all too familiar pattern of trials and errors. First there should be the plan carefully drawn on paper to the exact size, and then the selection of suitable woods, sanded as smooth as you are able. The paper patterns should be transferred to the wood by tracing and marking out as economically as possible, keeping in mind the demands of the lie of the grain. For clarity and to avoid mistakes, it is a good idea to crosshatch or scribble on those areas to be cut to waste. The traced drawings can be easily muddled once the piece of timber begins to be cut into several new shapes.

Straight cuts can usually be made with the tenon saw but for curved and elaborately shaped pieces a frame saw will be needed. The most suitable frame saw is the one called a fretsaw because it has the finest blades and will cut very thin wood. It is held with the frame under the armpit and the blade vertical and the minimum of pressure is applied lest the blade snap. The wood is held by the left hand on to a fret cutting table and when a curve is required the wood, not the blade, is moved, as with a sewing machine.

When all the pieces are cut, they will again need to be sandpapered and tried for size so that further cuts may be made to ensure a snug fit. Only when everything is seen to fit and the surfaces are all smooth should they be glued together and finally stained, polished or painted.

Reducing and Enlarging Patterns (Plate 1)

As houses and flats have been built to a smaller scale, so their dolls' houses have been built to fit and it is now virtually an accepted rule that the scale should be 1 inch to 1 foot. This has not always been the case and Victorian dolls' house furniture was available in three sizes. Because this book deals, in the main, with Victorian dolls' houses, I have included patterns to different scales and the following passage describes how to enlarge or reduce the size of a pattern.

Reducing patterns can be done by tracing pattern pieces, one at a time, on to paper and drawing round each a rectangle which encloses the pattern. Divide this rectangle into smaller rectangles and mark them 1, 2, 3, etc., in one direction and, A, B, C, etc., in the other, so that it is possible to plot the key points of the pattern. Next to this rectangle, draw another of the same size, and when reducing the pattern, mark off the desired height along the left-hand vertical line and draw a horizontal line from this point. Where it intersects a diagonal drawn from the bottom left-hand corner, draw a vertical line downwards until it joins the bottom line. This gives the new size of the rectangle. Divide the smaller rectangle into the same number of divisions as the first and

PLATE I.

REDUCING

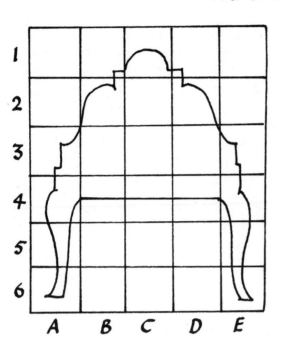

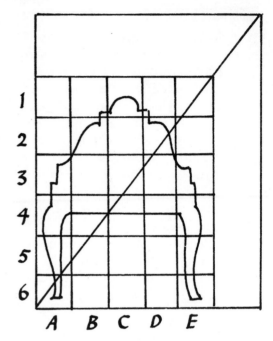

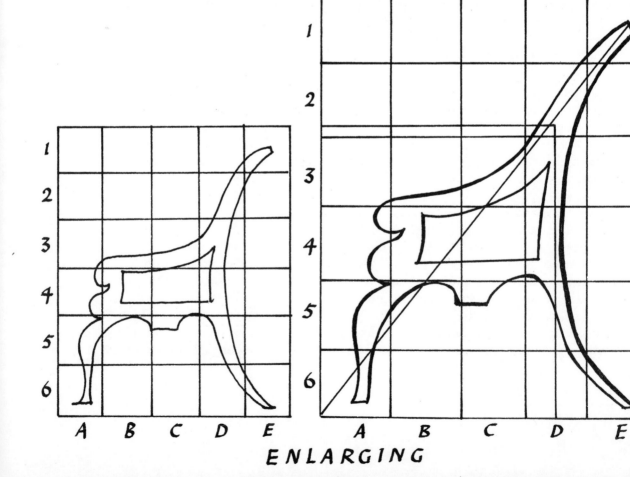

ENLARGING

plot the points of the pattern pieces. When joined, these will give the new smaller-sized pattern.

Enlarging a pattern is done in the same way, except that the left-hand vertical line is extended beyond the height of the original line until it gives the height of the larger pattern required.

PAINTING

The painting of a dolls' house is more important than is generally thought, judging by the surprisingly large number of well-made houses that have been overlaid all too liberally with thick and clumsy coats of unsuitable paint. There is a wide choice of paints and those used on a real house are not necessarily the best ones for the smaller version, for they remain as thick as ever.

Basically there are four kinds, those mixed with water and those with oil, those called tempera or emulsion paints that depend upon a suspension of oil and water, and those stains that are diluted with methylated spirits. Finally, varnish will change the appearance or even serve as a medium as is the case with enamels. I will describe each kind and what use it will best serve.

Watercolour Paints

These transparent colours that most of us have used since we were children are obviously most useful for fine work that is unlikely to be touched with water, such as actual pictures on the walls, the wall paper or little touching up jobs.

Their use can be extended by the addition of opaque colours that are similarly diluted with water, such as chinese white, to make what is known as gouache, or with poster colours. All these, of course, are not proof against water, but they are handy and perfectly adequate for 'inside jobs'.

Coloured inks, some of which are waterproof although occasionally fugitive, will often serve even better, particularly for fine lines on wallpaper or for staining something a brilliant shade.

Tempera and Emulsion Paints

These paints are similar in their handling to poster paints but when dry they are waterproof and will therefore serve even for 'outside' use. They can be bought in most art stores and those sold as 'Cryla colours', P.V.A. and so on are ideal for many jobs that in the past had to be done with oil paint. They are mixed with water, dry very quickly and can, if necessary, be varnished to provide a glossy finish.

Spirit Stains

Spirit stains were often used on the cheaper sets of dolls' furniture in Edwardian times. They are recognisably those pieces coloured brilliant acid green or carmine, often with a decorative paper edging. They are now enjoying a revival on very modern furniture and may be bought fairly readily in powder form and in a wide range of colours, including the wood stains, oak, walnut and mahogany. They are difficult to apply evenly over large areas, but this is rarely a problem in a dolls' house. The powders are dissolved in methylated spirit and applied with a soft brush or lint-free rag. It is often easier to use them on furniture before it is glued together. Once the stain is dry, a coat of white hard resin varnish will seal it in and protect the object against greasy stains and the marks of handling. I would use this stain on pieces of furniture, on floors and on doors and window frames that are intended to represent varnished or stained and polished wood.

Oil Colours

For the purposes of the tasks described in this book, I shall only deal with certain limited aspects of the complicated range of oil paints. Broadly speaking, they are the colours ground in oil and varnish and diluted, in the majority of cases, with turpentine substitute or white spirit. Unlike real life-size house painting, only a small quantity of any colour is likely to be needed and so the range of colours can be supplied by tubes of so-called 'Artists' oil colours bought at the art store. These are not suited for covering large areas with even coats of paint and for our purposes are best used as 'stainers' of white undercoat.

The house or piece of furniture to be painted should first have as smooth a surface as is to be had by sandpapering, then two coats of undercoat, thinned fairly liberally with white spirit and sanded between coats. The top coat can be of gloss paint (probably a white suitably coloured unless a dark colour is needed) which should be applied as thinly and evenly as possible. It is no use using it to obliterate imperfections for it is inevitably translucent. Alternatively, the final coat of paint can be of undercoat, suitably coloured, or as in the case of a roof, painted to imitate slates, which is then varnished to protect it against wear and tear.

Such a technique as this last is both easier to do and far more capable of a high degree of accuracy than the use of gloss paint or enamel. In certain cases a wax polish might prove better than varnish, particularly if you wish to achieve an effect of age and wear. The most important and usually neglected tool of the painter is his brush and only with the appropriate brush can the job be done well. A long thin soft 'liner' will make long thin straight lines and a broad flat brush an even coat but only if they are of good quality, correctly used and only if they are kept clean. They should be cleaned out first with white spirit and then washed with soap and lukewarm water.

I would limit my use of enamel or high gloss paint to small areas that imitate materials of a shiny ceramic-like nature such as fireplaces, tiles, stove enamel or polished metal, and in the latter case small tins of metal paint can be had.

Graining

This one time test of the painter and decorator's skill is now somewhat out of fashion. It is usually an attempt to make cheap wood look like oak or mahogany but occasionally the technique so took hold of its executants that it becomes a dashing end in itself, all whirls and blobs and unlikely patches of colour. On a small scale it is easy enough to do and very useful in a dolls' house where cardboard and paper may well have to imitate mahogany let alone deal. The undercoat should be fairly light, or high in tone, and pink or yellow ochre should be mixed into it—pink for mahogany, yellow ochre for oak and walnut. When dry a very thin coat indeed of diluted and darker colour is painted on and then scraped off in a variety of ways so that light and dark streaks appear in the manner of the grain of wood. A piece of cloth round a brush handle often serves very well and darker patches can be added with a brush to imitate the knots. The dry result can be varnished if a shiny surface is required.

Marbling

One can rarely use actual marble in a dolls' house and there was a surprising amount of it in real houses, on floors, table tops, washstands and of course almost always the fireplace. There are many varieties of marble and, with patience and practice, they can all be imitated in paint. Nevertheless, it is easier to choose the most typical, the long veined marble, for some of the less obviously patterned marbles do not lend themselves to a reduction in scale.

I imitate marble by giving the surface the customary layers of undercoat of whatever colour is appropriate and on to the dry undercoat I draw the irregular patterns of veins with a fine brush diagonally across the surface. I exaggerate the strength of these veins for when dry I cover them with a thin coat of translucent gloss enamel paint, brushed out so that the veins show through. This gives an effect of depth that cannot be achieved by painting the veins or pattern on to the topcoat.

Stencilling

This is a most useful and simple technique and enables you to manufacture wallpapers, floor-coverings, curtains, dados, friezes and all manner of repeated designs, copying old ones for restoration or making up your own new ones. I have a piece of white felt stencilled with brightly coloured roses that was made in the eighteen-forties and many of the floor papers made a few years later were stencilled.

The colouring materials vary with the surface for which they are intended so that on paper you would use poster or tempera colours, whilst on wood and metal you would use oil paint. Those sold as artists oil colours are of the right consistency and will only need the addition of a little fast-drying medium. For stencilling on textiles there are special colours, sold as 'textile stencilling colours' and they go on to the fabric remarkably easily and do not stain or run. Ordinary cartridge paper serves well enough for stencils that are to be used only moderately, although especially tough papers can be bought if the amount of use justifies it. It should hardly be necessary to describe a technique that most of us first used as children, but it should be remembered that it is often necessary to leave 'ties' where the stencil is likely to flap or tear away.

The design is usually traced on to the paper and then cut with a balsa knife, which is held vertically and still, whilst the paper itself is moved. If this is done on a sheet of glass, the paper moves very readily. After the design is cut, the paper should be rubbed with a little olive or linseed oil, or given a thin coat of varnish, to make it impervious to the paint. When not in use, the stencils should be kept flat under pressure. The brushes should have short bristles and an artist's old hog hair brush with the bristles cut with a razor blade to about half an inch is ideal. Mix the colours on a sheet of glass with a palette knife and spread the paint out thinly before dipping the brush into it, to avoid blobs. The brush should be held upright to get an even spread of colour and to avoid getting it under the edge of the stencil. This keeps the brush in good shape and a little practice will soon enable you to cover fairly large areas evenly. A variety of texture can be achieved by changing the movement of the brush and the thickness of the paint. An effect of shading can be achieved either by varying the thickness of paint or by applying a second colour over a part of the first. Sewing needles can be used to hold the stencil in place on paper or cloth for they will do less damage than drawing pins. Sellotape will do this job on wood or metal.

When making wallpaper or floor-paper for a dolls' house, use a fairly good quality but thin paper so that it will bend into position without tearing. A paper already patterned with a stripe, or self-coloured can, of course, serve as a start for a stencilled design. To save time, it is a good plan to draw the area of the walls or floor on to the paper, leaving a little spare at the edges, and so you will only have to paint exactly what is required. It is also necessary to mark in pencil the position of each motif so that the stencil can be accurately placed.

A stencil is needed for each colour and great care must be taken to place the stencil correctly against its pencilled register mark.

Fabrics should be stretched on a board above a few layers of newspaper and the colour should be well dabbed into the threads rather than allowed to coat the surface. For fine materials a thinner stencil and a brush with softer bristles will be needed.

PART THREE

FURNISHINGS

☆ FURNISHINGS ☆

Although this book is not intended to provide a history of dolls' houses, some account of the different periods and styles is inevitably involved and wherever an accurate date is possible it has been given. In the first chapter in this section I have made drawings of architectural features of dolls' houses from the 17th Century to the present day because it is so often necessary when renovating a house to begin by replacing missing glazing bars, doors or chimneys before actually starting on the furnishings. Some knowledge of the architectural features of the period can help to date a house more accurately than the decoration or furniture for the latter can have been added or changed at a later date.

In the second part of this chapter I have made drawings of typical decorative motifs fashionable at each period; I have deliberately chosen examples that are so typical as to be clichés, for the furnishing of dolls' houses is rarely subtle and the more boldly it advertises its period the more attractive it can be. The next five chapters deal with furnishings that are common to all rooms in the house—the wallpapers, floor-coverings, curtains, light fittings and the fireplaces, stoves and ovens.

I have made drawings and patterns for furniture for specific rooms; the drawing-room, the dining-room, the kitchen, the bedroom, the bathroom, the nursery and the hall, staircase and landing. These drawings show that dolls' house furniture not only follows the fashions of real furniture, though usually lagging behind for a decade or two, but offers a far greater range than could be found in the real house of the time. The most ordinary dolls' house might hold the most exotic dolls from France, Germany and Japan, who use furniture from Austria, Czechoslovakia, France, Germany, England or Russia. There is furniture that faithfully copies reality and there is dolls' furniture that only gives the genuine article a passing glance.

There are the fanciful European pieces (see plates 97 and 136) and the articles made from unusual materials such as beads, metals and feathers (plates 155, 183, 192, 193, 194). The time-lag in fashion makes dating very confusing, for articles which are said to be 1930 because they were bought at that date, could just as easily have been bought in the 'twenties, or even in the 'seventies, when we consider the mock Tudor Welsh dresser and four-poster.

31

The kitchen equipment on plate 123 is thought to be out of a late Victorian house, yet many of the pieces are identical to those in 18th Century kitchens, and the coffee roaster found in the same house is listed in a catalogue of some twenty or thirty years later.

The 17th Century baby houses aimed to be faithful reproductions of houses of their time, and they have the heavy furniture that is so typical. One can see immediately that they can seldom have been intended as playthings for children.

It is not until 1830 that dolls' houses take on the character that makes them look rather different from small scale models of real houses. At all times there have been dolls' houses which were craftsmen made and in the latest style and some of these still remain intact, such as the Rigg dolls' house and Queen Mary's dolls' house at Windsor. These are accurate copies of an adult way of life and are enormously interesting on many different levels. Nevertheless, the general run of dolls' houses were not built in the latest fashion but more often followed the tastes of the previous generation and were furnished with a collection of things of varying ages, even when they were bought at one time. Even furnishings made to order could turn out to be in the style of the craftsman's youth. Kitchen and bathroom furnishings are usually an exception to this state of affairs.

NUREMBURG DOLLS' HOUSE 1673

PLATE 2

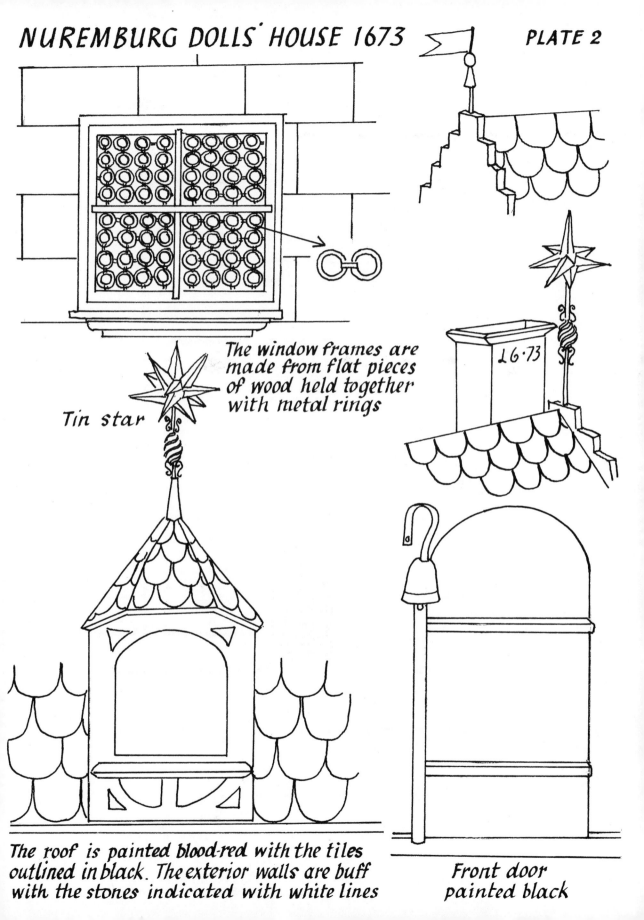

The window frames are made from flat pieces of wood held together with metal rings

Tin star

16·73

The roof is painted blood-red with the tiles outlined in black. The exterior walls are buff with the stones indicated with white lines

Front door painted black

The NORWICH DOLLS' HOUSE

The facade is painted to represent a brick house with stone long & short work, & the house was made during the first quarter of the eighteenth century.

MARY FOSTER'S DOLLS' HOUSE
C. 1810

PLATE 4

This house was made for Mary Foster of Liverpool. It is about 4' wide 4' high, & 20" deep. The walls are painted to represent ochre-coloured stone. The glazing bars are made from paper, & gilt paper is used for the fanlight. The decoration on the pediment is made from gesso.

Imposing dark red front door with brass fittings

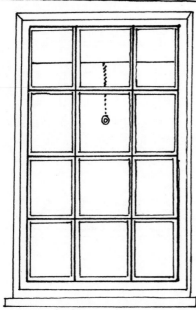

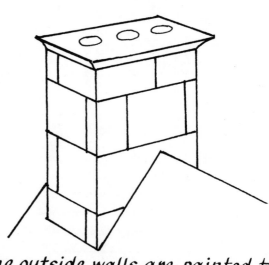

The outside walls are painted to represent golden stone. The door architecture is honey-brown. The window frames are white & the windows on the front of the house are false, but those on the sides are real. The roof is painted black.

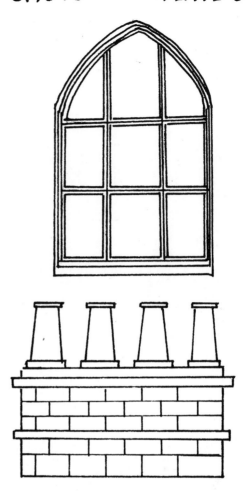

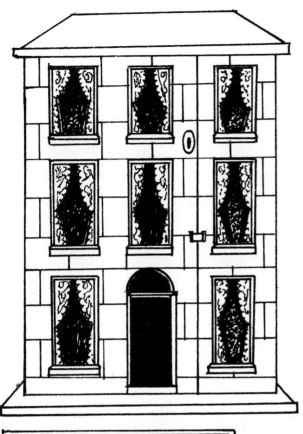

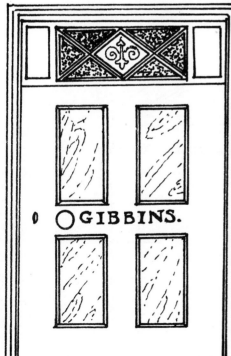

This Early Victorian Dolls' House is plain but well-proportioned. It is painted to represent putty-coloured stone & each stone is drawn on with white paint. The roof is painted shiny-black & it has a very low pitch. Unfortunately the window-frames, the front door & the chimneys are missing, & instead I have drawn details of other houses of the same date. Not many houses were made with the Gothic type of window like the one I have drawn.

PLATE 7

URSULA SOMERVELL'S DOLLS' HOUSE
1860

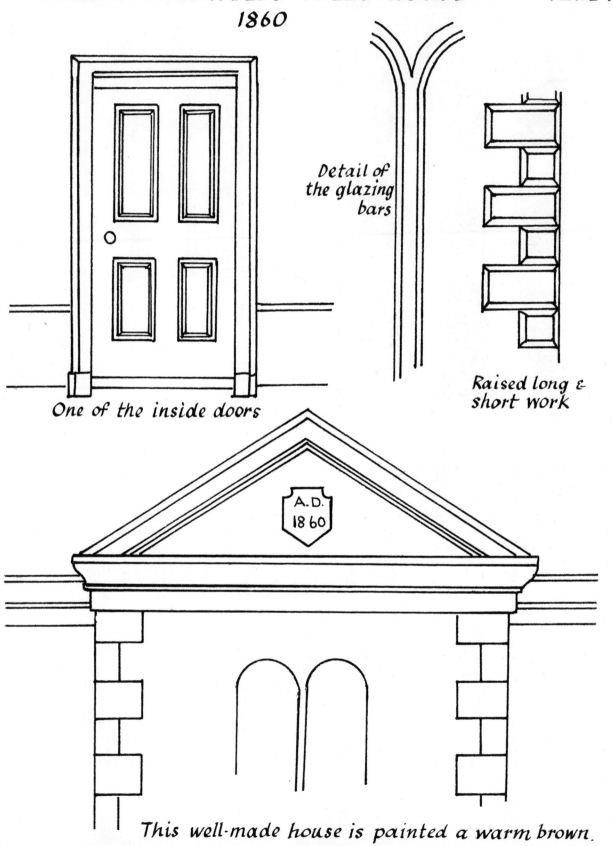

Detail of
the glazing
bars

Raised long &
short work

One of the inside doors

A.D.
18 60

This well-made house is painted a warm brown.

Details from Ursula Somervell's House
1860

PLATE 8

Upstairs windows

Front door

Downstairs windows

Chimneys

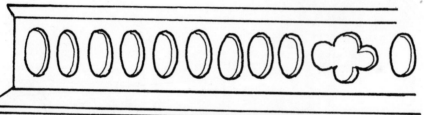

Barge
boarding.

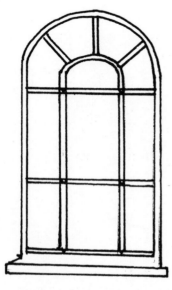

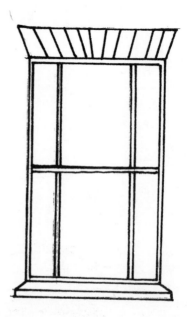

This dolls' house is made from natural polished wood with the half-timbering painted black. The shingle roof is made from overlapping pieces of wood. The chimneys are very tall & the doorway has glass panels. It is beautifully made but somewhat spoiled by the sanded path & felt lawn.

PLATE II

DOLLS' HOUSE
of 1900

This is not a very distinguished dolls' house & it is very badly painted with blood-red gloss paint with white gloss detailing, but it is unusual in having roof lighting for each upstairs room.

PLATE 12

EARLY EDWARDIAN DOLLS' HOUSE

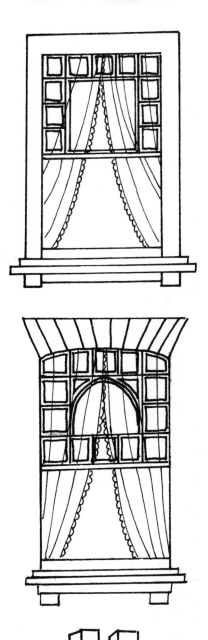

Very narrow front door crudely painted in two colours of green with white lines. Large hinges on the wrong side of the door.

Elaborate fretwork balconies.

The outside walls are covered with painted paper & the windows on the sides of the house are imitation but those on the front are real.

SMALL EDWARDIAN
DOLLS' HOUSE
C. 1910

PLATE
13

EDWARDIAN HOUSE
C. 1910

PLATE 14

15½" high, 9½" wide, 13" deep. Like real terrace houses this is fancy in front & plain behind. It is covered in red brick paper, with a slate paper roof & brown & green paint work. There are two poky rooms in front & three at the back.

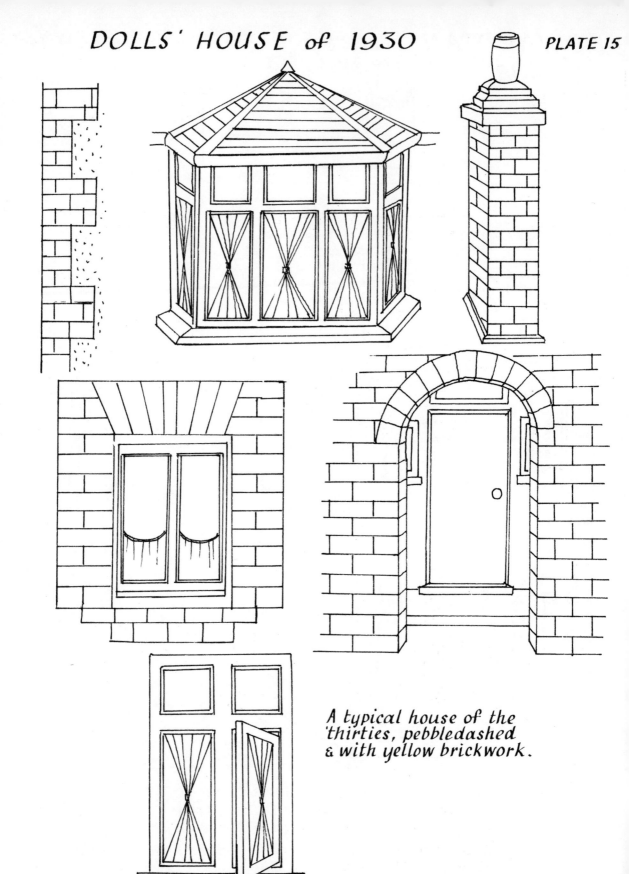

A typical house of the thirties, pebbledashed & with yellow brickwork.

1952

R.M.M
1952

3

A mid-twentieth century house designed in Regency style. The balcony, the decoration round the door and the colour scheme of white, grey, dark red, yellow ochre & navy blue all recall the Festival of Britain.

PLATE 17

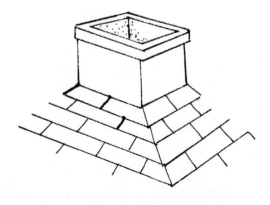

1970 DOLLS' HOUSE

The upper half of the dolls' house is in white weather-boarding. The lower half in yellow brick. There is a slate roof & a central chimney. The paintwork is all white.

DECORATIVE MOTIFS

PLATE 18

First half of 18th. Century

1759

1755

Second half of 18th. Century

1786

Second half of 18th. Century

DECORATIVE MOTIFS

PLATE 19

Early 19th. Century

1820

1845

1850

1860

DECORATIVE MOTIFS

PLATE 20

1860

1860

1870

1890

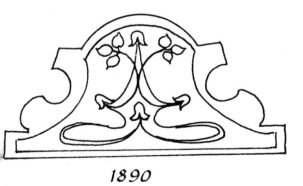

1890

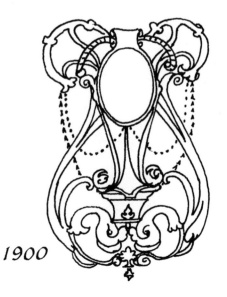

1900

DECORATIVE MOTIFS

PLATE 21

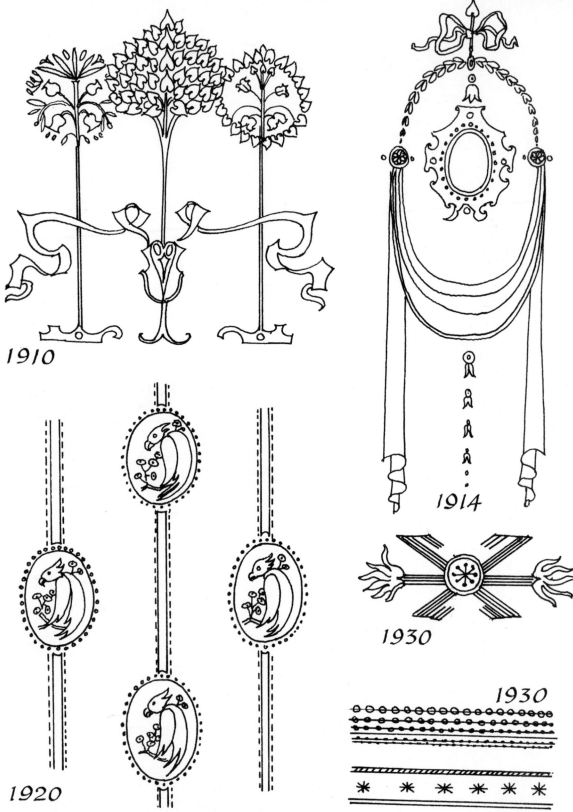

1910

1914

1920

1930

1930

DECORATIVE MOTIFS

1940

1940

1950

1960

1960

1960

1960-1970

1970

The early Dutch baby houses used a variety of wall-coverings; panelling rooms in painted or polished wood, and hanging them with paper, silk or some flowered cloth. The Nuremberg dolls' house of 1639 has some inside walls that are painted to imitate stone, a fashion that was to be repeated in the mid-19th Century. With the importation of mahogany in the early 18th Century, panelling became lighter in weight. Panelling was sometimes painted in plain colours, white, or with panels of decorative scenes in grisaille. Less important rooms were, of course, not panelled, but merely colour-washed, or in the case of actual dolls' houses, coloured paper was used. The Blackett baby house of 1740 has a bright blue wallpaper hand-painted with flowers. The 18th Century house usually had dadoes in the principal rooms. Chinese wallpapers were imported in the early 18th Century and are to be seen still in use on a dolls' house of 1810.

By 1820, bright coloured wallpapers were in common use. Some examples have a harsh dolly blue background, others have small simple patterns of dots or wavy lines. Queen Victoria's dolls' house has a pink wallpaper in the upper room edged with a border of roses and leaves. I have seen several houses of this era decorated in a similar manner.

A popular choice of colours in Regency times was terracotta and maroon and bright acid colours patterned with gold motifs such as stars, lyres and wreaths and this fashion continued in use in dolls' houses until the middle of the century.

The Early Victorian style of wall decoration, in real houses, was elaborately patterned designs with stripes and flowers and gold. In dolls' houses we find pale brown wallpaper with gold leaves and white wallpaper with gold fern fronds and pale lilac walls with gold and grey decoration. On the landing and hall of an 1840 dolls' house I have seen marbled paper used.

The mid-Victorians liked heavy cornices and they were particularly fond of damask wall-coverings, plenty of gilt and lots of marble. Dining-rooms were traditionally red, with a pattern either in a darker red or in gold, and this fashion continued for all of half a century. Flowered and trellised wallpapers were often used for bedrooms. One very pleasant dolls' house of the eighteen-sixties has in the hall and landing walls of dull sage green with brown stained woodwork, and one of the rooms has a pale green wallpaper overpainted with deeper green naturalistic flowers. The majority of Victorian dolls' houses have dadoes in the main reception rooms. Broadly speaking the use of pattern increases as the century goes on and a partiality for flowers reaches its climax in the elaborate conservatories of the end of the century.

The frieze becomes a fashionable motif in the latter part of the 19th Century.

One room in a dolls' house of the seventies has a shallow frieze decorated with a landscape painting of a distant view of trees, windmills and winding river, repeated all round the room. Heversham House, of 1855, has a broad frieze in one room of a blue and white Dutch landscape. In a house of the 'nineties, one room has nursery rhyme figures and another a frieze of birds.

Art Nouveau, so typical of the end of the century, is slow to influence the conservative decoration of dolls' houses although a debased version of the famous water-lily design sometimes appears on a frieze. A broad frieze was fashionable during the nineteen-twenties, above a picture rail or even a pot rail, together with plain wallpapers. With the fashion for hanging only one picture or a mirror in the 'thirties the picture rail goes and with it the frieze, and wallpapers are little more than faint ambiguous textures. Unlike real houses the majority of dolls' houses had a dado rather than a frieze although I cannot see why this should come about.

Painted panelling in a house of 1740.

Georgian wooden panelling of 1775

The major problem with papering a dolls' house is getting into the small rooms with our large hands. The ceiling should be done first and a small dolls' house can be turned upside down, but a larger one obliges you to turn yourself upside down. Instead of measuring each wall it is simpler to make a template from a piece of brown paper. Cut this slightly larger than the wall. Press it on to the wall and with a sharp point score along the edges. Mark doors and windows by rubbing with the finger. Trim all this to shape and use it as a pattern. The plastic wallpaper pastes sold today are the best to use for they do not mark the face of the paper. Use this paste fairly stiff and lavishly and press the paper firmly on to the walls, using a soft cloth. Start pressing in the middle of each wall and smooth the paper outwards in all directions, making sure that there are no wrinkles or bubbles. If you are unused to wallpapering do not be discouraged by the result at this stage. The paper will be dark and discoloured by the wet paste and a few bubbles may now appear, but if you did not leave any when smoothing the paper, these will disappear as the paper dries, as they are caused by the paper swelling.

I have often found that fabric will serve better than actual wallpaper, presumably because it is really of the right period, or it is a reprint of an old design or because the pattern is itself more refined than can be effected on real wallpaper. I had thought this to be my own idea, but I have since read of sprigged muslin being used in a dolls' house of 1800. If you are using a rather stiff material, such as linen or glazed chintz, then it can be applied in exactly the same manner as wallpaper. Unfortunately silk, or fine cotton, assumes a tripe-like consistency when pasted and it is almost impossible to manage and so it is better to mount it on another firmer material such as 'iron-on' stiffening used in dressmaking. The lightest weight is quite stiff enough for this purpose. Using the brown paper template, cut out the pieces of stiffening and iron these on to the fabric. Then cut the fabric to exactly the size of the stiffening. Apply the paste to the stiffening and stick the whole on to the walls in the same manner as a paper.

Most wallpapers made for real houses have patterns too large for dolls' houses, but some designs do have stripes of tiny flowers or other minor motifs that can be extracted from the full width and used on their own. Self-coloured wallpapers, fine stripes or stippled effects can look well, but they should be tried in position to see if they achieve the right atmosphere. If it looks too new or jars in some way, then do not use it even if it is of the correct scale and period. Special dolls' house wallpapers can be bought in sheets measuring 22" × 30" from craft shops or direct from a Liverpool firm called Lucas's (Hobbies) Ltd., 7 Tarleton Street, Liverpool 1. Unfortunately most of these papers are appropriate only for a lush dwelling of the 'forties or 'fifties and do not look right in an old house, or, for that matter, in a modern one. The same firm sells the traditional patterned papers that imitate bricks, slates, tiles and parquet floorings. These have changed so little in the last sixty years that they can often be used on an older house without the fact being too evident. End papers printed for books are often very well designed and of an appropriate scale for a dolls' house. They are sold by Kettle of 127 High Holborn, London. There is also a shop called 'Paperchase' in Tottenham Court Road, London, that has such a wonderful collection of papers of every kind, including dolls' house wallpaper, that one is spoilt for choice.

The addition of a frieze or dado, or even a decorative border, can enrich a room and I have often added a cut-out frieze in white cartridge paper to contrast with a rich dark paper. This is a simple operation. Measure the combined lengths of the walls of the room and cut a piece of rather thick white paper to this length and about $2\frac{1}{2}$ inches deep. Fold this paper in a concertina fashion, making each fold the width you would like your finished pattern to be. About $2\frac{1}{2}$ inches to 3 inches is a good width (see plate 32). On the top fold of this paper draw the design and cut it out through all the thicknesses. You will then have a complete frieze for the whole room. When this is pasted on to the walls, the creases you have made will disappear. This frieze can be as simple or elaborate as you wish and it can be pierced with holes or painted in *trompe l'oeil*.

I have made panelled dadoes from card rather than wood, which is both easier and neater (see plate 32). For this I have used fairly thick mounting card in two layers. Each card should be cut to fit each wall and it usually needs to be about 4 inches deep, depending on the scale of the house. The first layer of card is glued to the wall and the second card has holes cut out of it about 2 inches by $2\frac{1}{2}$ inches wide. These are cut with a bevelled edge and this is glued on top of the first card. Obviously the proportion of the panels will have to fit into the length of the wall. If you wish to add a skirting board a strip of card about $\frac{1}{2}$ inch high and cut on a bevel can be glued to the base of the panelling. This card can be painted with any water-based paints such as poster or tempera colours or emulsion paint.

The fashion for putting a border round the ceiling, down the edges of the walls and along the top of the dado or skirting is not only decorative but useful for concealing untidy joins and minor imperfections. I have edged paper and fabric wall-coverings with various materials, ribbons, gimp, and decorative paper borders, but best of all has been the embossed metallic edging used on Christmas cake frills. Early Victorian houses often have a very similar embossed gold edging.

1820

1840

A strange Early-Victorian wallpaper with deep blue pattern on a white ground.

A similar design of 1970 with white on orange.

White background with lavender pattern. 1820.

Dining room paper in an 1820 dolls' house. Dark red on red.

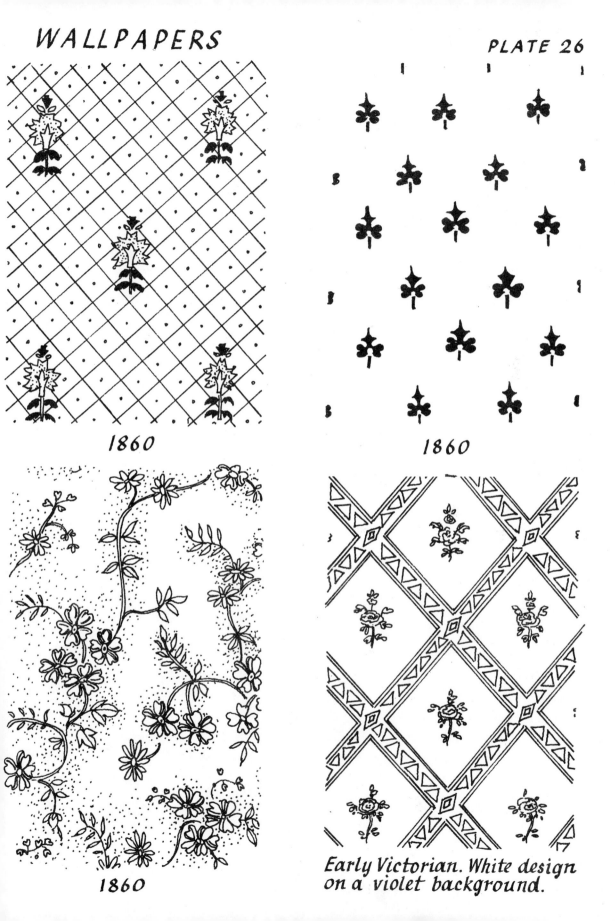

1860

1860

1860

Early Victorian. White design on a violet background.

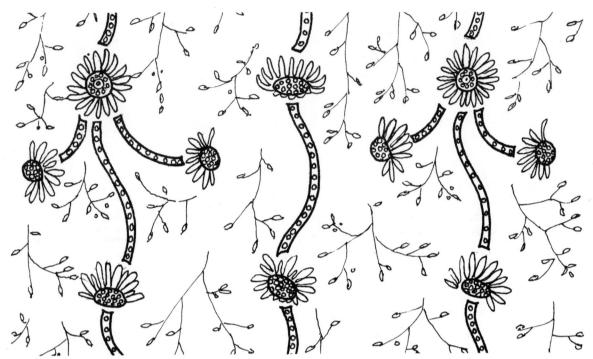

1860 Wallpaper, rather large in scale but pleasant because of its pale colours: pale green back ground with darker green line drawing. White petals on the daisies & yellow centres. Easy to copy for a dolls' house if you skip the spidery grasses.

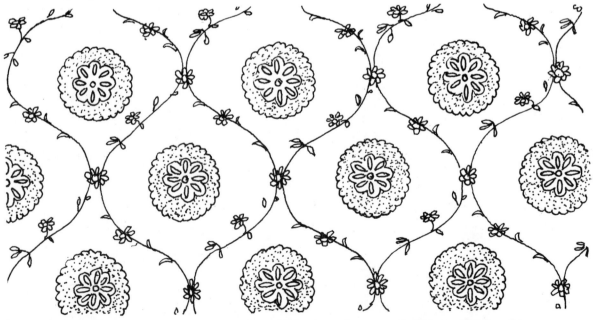

Wallpaper from an early Victorian dolls' drawing room. The background is acid green. The dotted areas gold & the lines & petals are royal blue.

A Victorian wallpaper, with a pale green & pink design on a cream ground

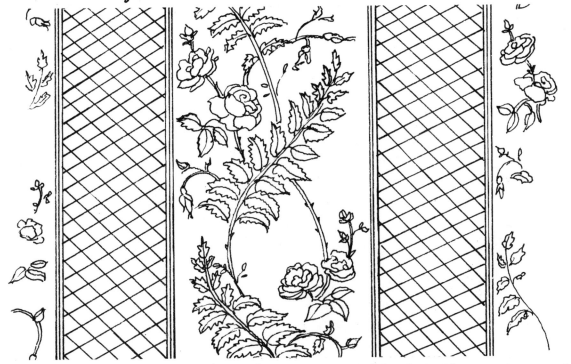

Victorian wallpaper with silver on white trellis, red roses & green leaves.

A 1900 wallpaper which could be reproduced by sticking strips of crimson shiny ribbed paper to a plain ground & stencilling the design between the stripes.

An early 20th. Century wallpaper from the same dolls' house. Actual size. Pale blue ribbons on a cream ground.

1920. Green, red & blue designs on fawn grounds

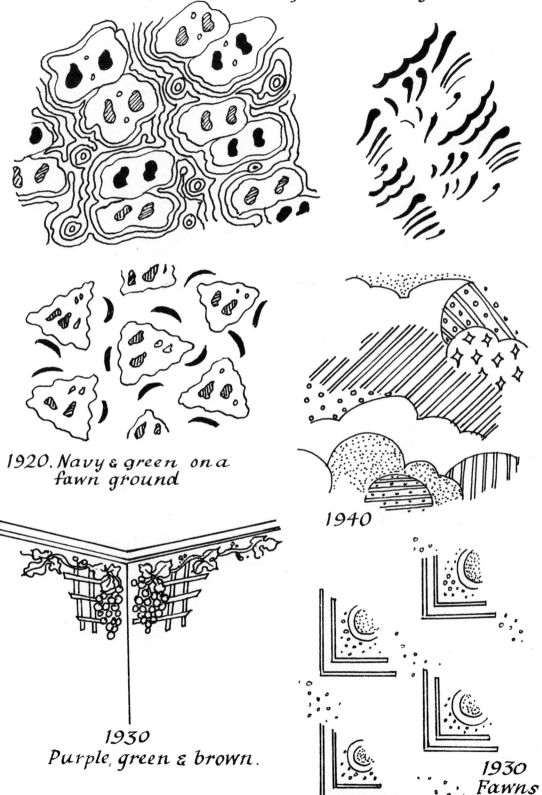

1920. Navy & green on a
fawn ground

1940

1930
Purple, green & brown.

1930
Fawns

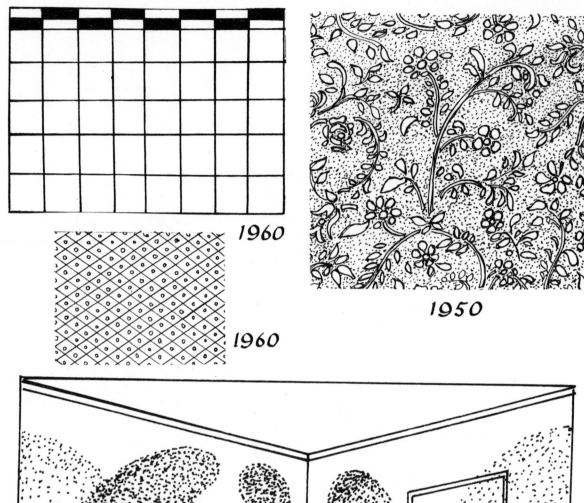

1960

1950

1960

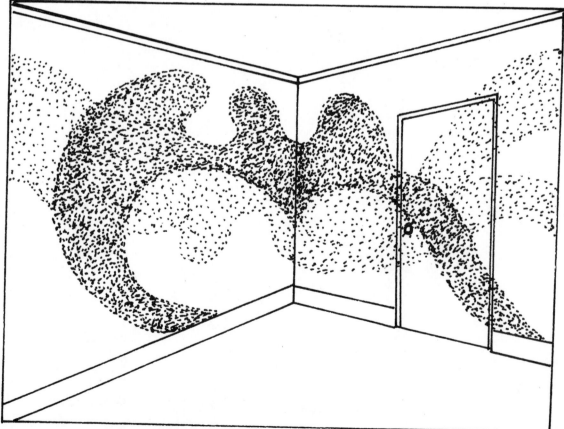

1970 . Stencilled shapes in red & orange

PLATE 32

Folded card.
Cut away shaded areas.

A cut paper frieze.

A dado of card.

In the 18th Century, most baby houses had uncarpeted floors as had the real houses of the period. These were usually of polished or painted wood, sometimes of oak, or in the case of very grand houses, inlaid marquetry. Not all floors were bare and in the Westbrook baby house of 1705, there is a gros-point carpet in deep reds, blues and greens, and Anne Sharpe's baby house has petit-point rugs and there are references to carpets in houses of the 1730 to 1740 period. The kitchen floors were usually painted to imitate tiles, black and white, grey or light red.

Sometimes carpets have been added to baby houses at a later time. The carpet in the Blacket baby house is an example of this and I have drawn the design of this carpet (see plate 40) because it is such a basic needlework pattern. Rugs were used sparingly in 18th Century rooms as may be seen from the paintings of the time, such as those conversation pieces by Devis and Zoffany, but as soon as we get to the 19th Century there are carpets in all but the poor houses and dolls' houses rarely, if ever, seek to depict the houses of the poor.

Most dolls' house carpets are worked in tapestry which is that kind of needlework that is worked on counted threads that entirely cover the canvas. There are many types of stitches to choose from but the most popular are: cross stitch, tent stitch, straight Gobelin stitch and oblique Gobelin stitch (see plates 33, 34). There are two kinds of canvas available, single and double thread, and tapestry needles are long and blunt and have a big eye.

The drawings of the more common stitches are, I think, self-explanatory, but there are three other stitches which are very suitable for making carpets and they require some explanation. They are chain stitch and knitting stitch and they are both worked on a double thread canvas, and they are used to make imitation oriental carpets.

Chain Stitch Tapestry (Plate 34)

This is best worked in a wide variety of colours as the nature of the stitch helps the colours to blend into each other. The stitches are worked in rows and each row must be begun at the same side of the canvas and each row completed as you go along. Because the first stitch is always completed by the next stitch, the thread has to be changed as the row progresses when a colour change is necessary.

Knitting Stitch Tapestry (Plate 34)

Knitting Stitch is worked in two rounds. The stitches in the first two are set diagonally over two double vertical threads and half a double diagonal thread. The stitches in the second row are worked in the opposite direction so that the two rows complete the stitch.

For both the chain stitch and the knitting stitch you should have a needle threaded with each colour needed for the design.

Single Knotted Stitch (Plate 34)

For the real enthusiast, there is the single knotted stitch which was originally designed to imitate oriental carpets.

Each stitch is composed of meshes of thread which are fastened on to the canvas by a backstitch. I am not sure of the official way of doing this stitch but I have worked it out in the manner that I describe and this does give the same results.

The stitch is worked on a single thread canvas and the loop which will form the pile of the carpet is made over a piece of wire which should be about $\frac{1}{16}$ inch thick. The first step is to place the wire along one of the horizontal threads at the top of the canvas and bring the stitch under the wire and one strand of the canvas. Then bring the stitch up and over the wire, threading it through to the back of the canvas, two threads along and to the right of the starting point. Now bring the stitch up again through the original starting point and down again through the hole two threads along to the right. This has formed the backstitch. The stitch is now brought to the front of the canvas through the hole one thread below and this completes the stitch which is worked on a basis of two threads along and one thread down. As the stitch goes over the wire, it makes the loops which, when cut, form the pile of the carpet and so it is possible to regulate the depth of the pile by the thickness of the wire. When a row of stitches is completed, run a razor blade along the centre of these loops and lift the wire away. The design for the carpet will have to be drawn first on squared paper, indicating the colours, and the colours will have to be changed as you progress along the counted threads.

Sometime in the first half of the 19th Century, a new kind of floor-covering appeared in dolls' houses. It is a printed paper that represents carpet or linoleum. The patterns are almost always geometrical, rarely floral, and if flowers are used they are stylised. They were usually brown, fawns or greens, but the tapestry carpets of the same period were of a richer colouring. About the turn of the century these papers became smaller and smaller in design until quite elaborate designs were drawn on a 1 inch square grid. They have almost disappeared today and the only remaining design is that of a parquet floor of an unpleasantly raw yellow ochre colour.

During the latter part of the 19th Century, Persian carpet designs were painted on paper for rugs and stair carpets and these were particularly suitable for the very small rooms of the time. Not infrequently you will find thick unsuitable carpeting glued or nailed to the floor of old dolls' houses and sometimes the removal of this will reveal the original paper floor-covering.

Two kinds of mats are shown in plate 45. Although different in period and style, they can be made by the same technique and so I have kept them together. The top drawing represents rush matting, so popular during the nineteen-sixties, and the lower drawing represents an American Shaker rug of the nineteenth century. Both are made by sticking string, wool, silk or cotton to an adhesive first-aid dressing. To make these rugs, pin the first-aid dressing sticky side upwards on to a board and, with a sharp pencil, roughly indicate with dots the outline of the pattern. Cover half the dressing with a thin sheet of plastic to prevent the material or your hands sticking to it as you work. The squares of rush matting should be worked one at a time with string. Choose a string of the right scale and of a colour appropriate to rushes. If the string is too white, dye it to a golden colour before you start, with ink or culinary dyes. Start by laying the end of the string on the outside edge of the top left-hand square and work inwards towards the centre, keeping the corners as square as possible. It is a help to use a pin to push the string into position. As each square is completed, press it firmly between the fingers and thumb to make it flat and the warmth of the hands gives better adherence.

The Shaker rug can be made with either wool, silk or cotton but choose that with a twisted thread or there will be loose strands on the top. This rug should be done in rich colours; deep blues, golds and reds. This technique should allow you to make a variety of surfaces, such as chair seats, stool tops, etc.

Some Unusual Carpets and Rugs

In a mid-19th Century dolls' house, there is a carpet made from ivory coloured velvet, delicately embroidered, and I have seen felt stencilled to represent carpet. There are flock wallpapers used very successfully as carpets in old houses. Rugs were often made from pieces of fur but it must be fur with the shortest possible hair such as mole or mouse. Years ago my son made for me a moleskin rug for a birthday present. Its feet looked very pathetic stretched out on a serrated edge of the pale blue felt backing. I have heard of mouse skin rugs although I cannot remember seeing one. The heads of 'Trophy' rugs should be lightly padded and beads used for the eyes. The claws can be depicted with stitches. A piece of fur felt from an old hat merely cut to size is rather uninteresting, but it does make a convincing rug.

Hand-woven rugs can also be made at home by stretching the warp of cotton strands over the top of a box and weaving the weft of different coloured threads backwards and forwards over and under these strands until the rug is complete.

Tumbletwist rugs for modern houses can be made from white embroidery cotton, using the single knotted tapestry stitch, but the loop should be made over a slightly thicker wire to increase the size of the loops, which in this case should be left uncut.

There are rugs that children traditionally make for their dolls' houses. These are the crochet rugs and the knitted rugs and those pieces of material edged with crochet and ones made from cork work in rainbow wool, laboriously produced with a bobbin and pins. The most unusual rug I have read about is that described by Julian Huxley in his autobiography. As a surprise for his young sister, he skinned a Poplar Hawk caterpillar and varnished the skin to make a rug for her dolls' house, and he remarks that he thought it would have done well for Titania's palace.

PLATE 3.

PLAIN CROSS STITCH

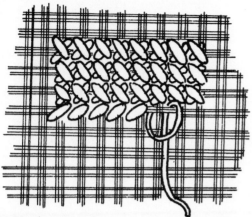

TENT STITCH

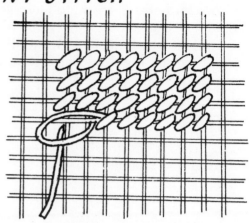

Worked on double canvas. It is worked in two rows, one sloping towards the left & the returning one sloping towards the right. In the first row the thread is carried diagonally across a square of threads, two horizontal & two vertical. The thread is then taken downwards & underneath the two horizontal threads on the second row. The stitches are worked from the lower right-hand corner of the square to the upper left-hand corner.

Worked on single canvas from right to left, & to make sure that the stitches are kept even the thread should be carried forward under two vertical threads of the canvas. This stitch is often used in conjunction with other stitches, but it is good to use on its own for a dolls' house carpet as the result is not too thick.

STRAIGHT GOBELIN STITCH

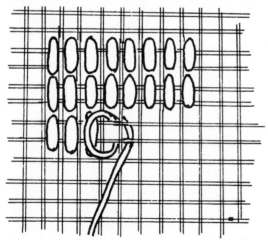

OBLIQUE GOBELIN STITCH

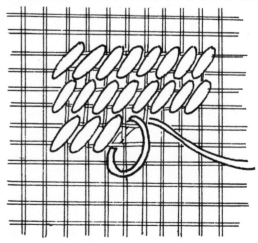

Worked on single canvas in horizontal rows. The thread is carried vertically over two threads of canvas, leaving one thread of canvas between each stitch

Worked on single canvas. The stitch is made over one vertical & two horizontal threads.

PLATE 34

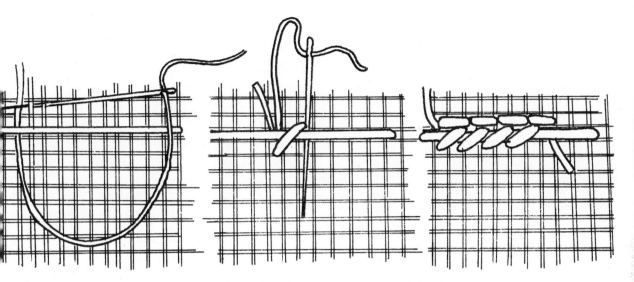

The single knotted stitch.

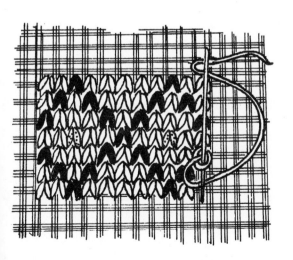

Chain stitch on double canvas.

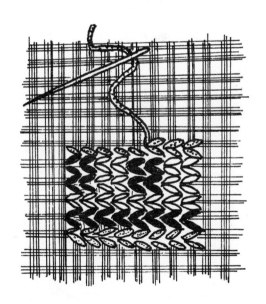

Knitting stitch on double canvas.

PLATE 35

Paper floor-covering from a house c. 1820, but probably added later. Drawn actual size. The paper is brown paper with a stencilled design in white with small chocolate-brown flowers.

PLATE 36

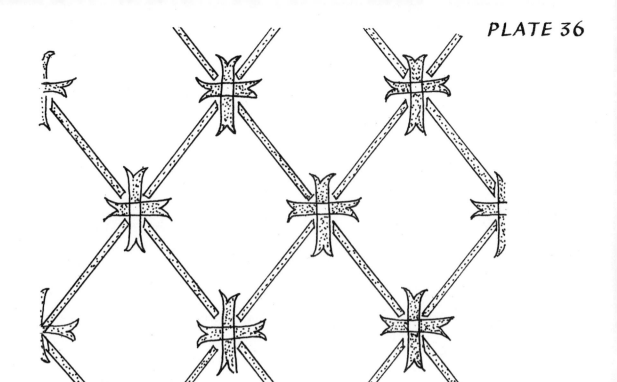

Early Victorian paper floor-covering. Dark green background with gold decoration & a black outline.

Early Victorian paper floor-covering. Pale green background with fawn motif & dark green outlines.

PLATE 37

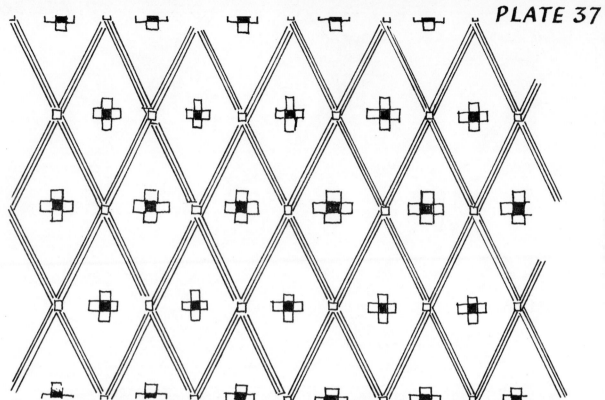

Carpet from the dining room of Maude Mary Landsdowne's dolls' house of 1860. Alternating yellow ochre & powder-blue background with a black design.

Carpet from the drawing room of the same house. Faded green petit-point worked with fawn & brown motif in a half-drop pattern.

PLATE 38

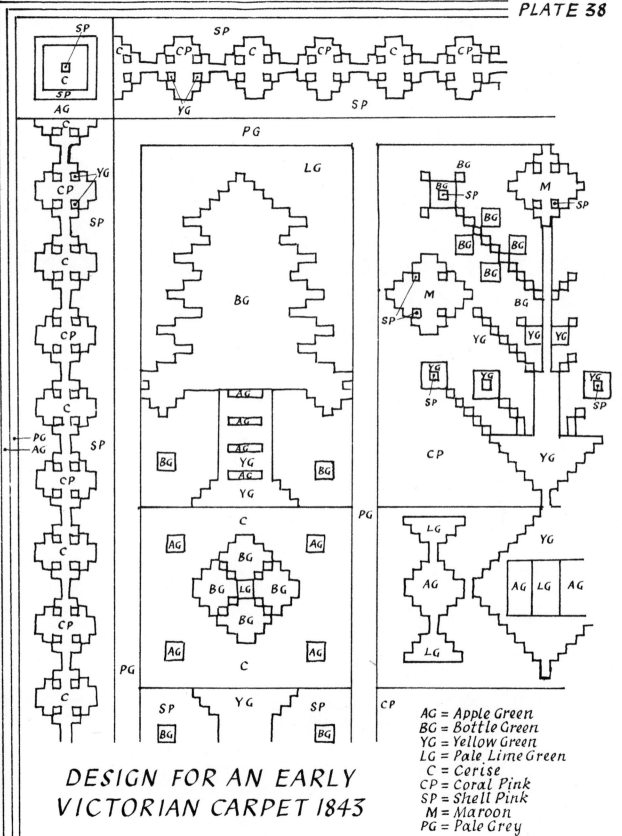

DESIGN FOR AN EARLY
VICTORIAN CARPET 1843

AG = Apple Green
BG = Bottle Green
YG = Yellow Green
LG = Pale Lime Green
C = Cerise
CP = Coral Pink
SP = Shell Pink
M = Maroon
PG = Pale Grey

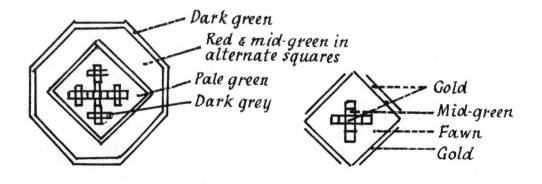

Dark green

Red & mid-green in
alternate squares

Pale green

Dark grey

Gold

Mid-green

Fawn

Gold

PLATE 40

Very dark green ☐ Very pale green ▨ Mid green ▨ Dark red

This is the carpet from the Blackett Baby House, although it is not as old as the house.

■ Red ▨ Pink ☐ Pale green ▨ Dark green

Victorian petit-point carpet, about 1865. White background.

PLATE 4

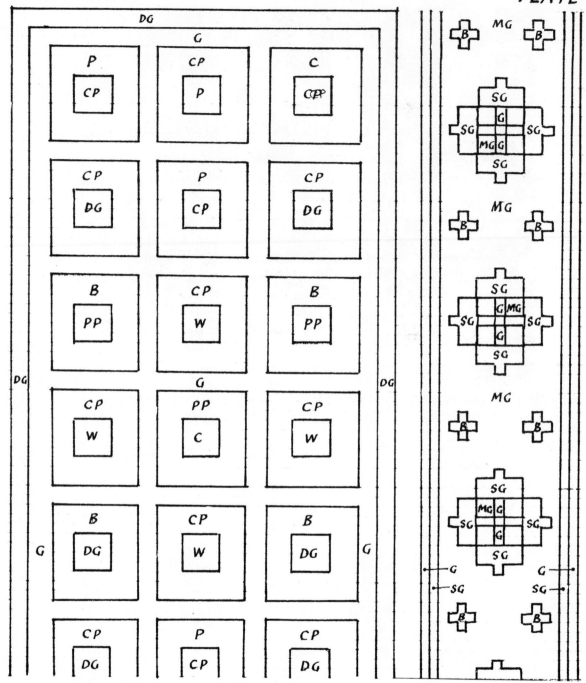

Victorian Runner. 1880's

C.P. = Coral pink   D.G. = Very dark green
  P. = Dark purple   B. = Dark brown
P.P. = Pale pink   G. = Pale grey
  W. = White   C. = Cerise

Victorian Stair Carpet. 1870's.

M.G. = Mid grey
P.G. = Pale green
  G. = Gold
  B. = Light brown
S.G. = Sap green

PLATE 42

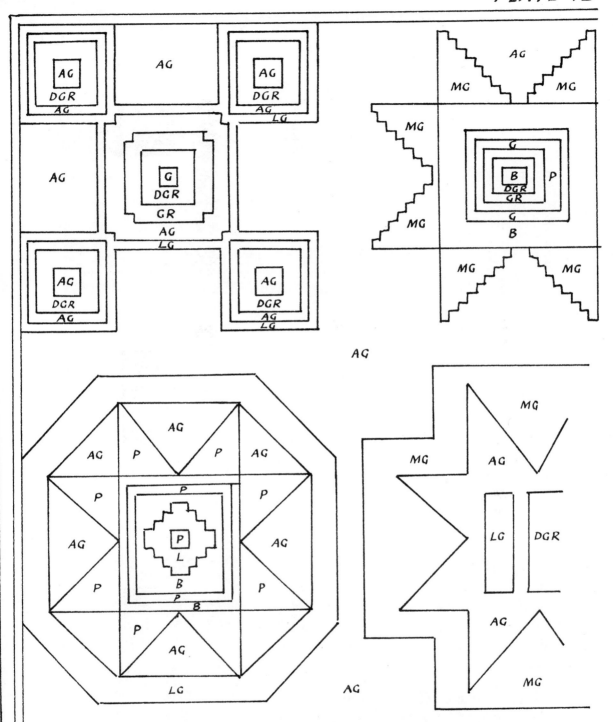

Late Victorian design for a carpet
12" x 12"

AG = Apple green (very pale) DGR = Dark grey B = Dark brown
LG = Leaf green G = Gold P = Rich plum-purple
GR = Grey MG = Moss green L = Lilac

PLATE 43

A Wilton-type carpet from Queen Mary's Dolls' House
C.1920

Printed Rug
1920

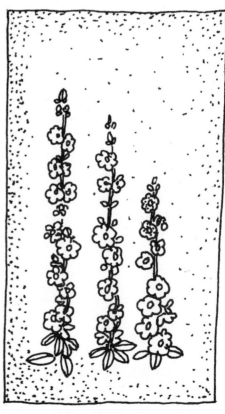

Wool Rug
1930

PLATE 44

Modern 'Persian' rug. Actual size.
In Indian red, blue, gold, black & green.

Modern Scandinavian-type rug. 1970.

PLATE 45

Rush matting, 1960.

American shaker rug.

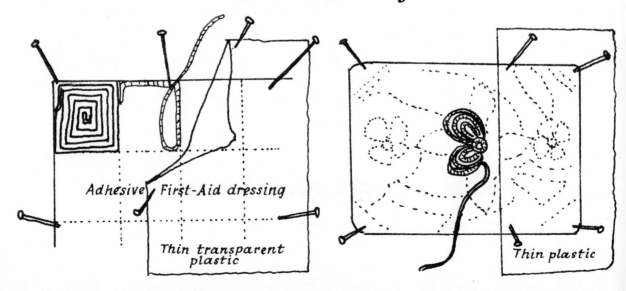

Adhesive First-Aid dressing

Thin transparent plastic

Thin plastic

The curtains found in dolls' houses are almost always disappointing. This seems strange when there is so much scope and when, in real life, window furnishings have been so decorative. I can imagine that in many cases the first curtains are lost to us because they were quickly soiled and replaced, perhaps by children, with either curtains of a later period or simpler bits of cloth, whatever came to hand. They are, of course, far more difficult to make than one would imagine and always difficult to hang in a convincing manner. Inevitably, in desperation, they are looped back to the wall, whatever the fashion of the time. In fact, had we only the historical evidence of the dolls' house furnishings, we might well believe that this fashion for tied back curtains has persisted from 1700 until today.

I have drawn examples of dolls' house curtains from the mid-18th Century, together with examples of full size curtains. I have not drawn in this section the designs for the materials because they are so similar to the patterns of wallpapers that have already been drawn (see plates 24 to 31). These drawings give the general style of design to look for during the different periods and they are drawn to dolls' house scale so that they can be traced or copied, perhaps for embroidery or for stencilling on to a fabric.

The choice of material for curtains is vitally important if it is to give the right period atmosphere, hang well, and enhance the other furnishings in the room. Not surprisingly, thin materials are essential but they should be, for their thickness, of a heavy weight. The new crease resisting fabrics are quite unsuitable.

There are many ways of hanging curtains apart from the ubiquitous method of tying them back. They may hang straight down as they usually do today, or be crossed over as they were in Regency times, a fashion kept up in the world of boudoirs and chi-chi hairdressers, or they can be hung in separate tiers as is the fashion in America. This last style is obviously a practical one for it gives privacy and light, but it does not seem to have caught on elsewhere. This is rather surprising when you think of the obvious advantages of such a system when compared to half net curtains or muranised glass.

Before the 20th Century development of metal and plastic runners with little wheels, the majority of curtains were hung from rods. Sometimes these rods were themselves made into a decorative feature but they were more frequently hidden by a pelmet of wood or cloth. From 1750 onwards, pelmets of draped festoons were fashionable and remained so until the beginning of the 19th Century. In the mid-19th Century, the rods were often exposed and decorated to match the room. During the first half of the 20th Century frills made from the same material as the curtains were used instead of pelmets, to give the fashionable country cottage effect, and at the same time the box-like wood or three-ply pelmet came into fashion, in a do-it-yourself kind of way. These were stained or painted, usually in the jazzy or the Egyptian Cinema style (see plate 53).

In the 'sixties, runners became so discreet that it became superfluous to cover them with frills or pelmets.

Happily the curtains in dolls' houses do not require to be drawn for warmth or privacy. They can be pinned or glued to the wall, or hung on string or wire or elastic, or stuck to double faced Sellotape, or threaded on to wire rods or runners. In a small dolls' house it is usually better to have simple curtains, such as a straight piece of lace without gathers. The most common problem is the control of gathered curtains and to avoid extra bulk one can turn under only one thickness of material or, if it does not fray, dispense with all turnings. A decorative border, such as a narrow ribbon or a length of tape decorated in an appropriate style, will enhance a thin plain cloth and ease the problem of turnings.

After sewing the curtains, I find it easier to mould them to shape by pinning them on a flat surface until they take a convincing form. They can then be sprayed with hair lacquer and will retain their shape after the pins have been taken away (plate 53). Stronger fabrics that resist the control of hair spray can be dipped into a solution of Polycell. This will not harm the majority of fabrics but should not be used on materials with a thick pile or on ones where the dye is not fast. The strength of the Polycell will determine the rigidity of the curtains so do not overdo it and make them look like corrugated iron. Rustless pins hidden in the folds of the curtains and along the edges of the floor will hold curtains in position and after a year or so they can be removed, for the curtains will by then have abandoned the struggle. Thin pliable wire can be threaded through the hems and bent to form folds but it must be wire that will not oxidise or the curtains will soon be ruined.

I have used curtain rods in several mid-Victorian houses. They are easy to make and appropriate for the era. By far the most successful were made of dowelling covered with gold metallic paper, so much shinier than gold paint, and with knobs at the ends made from fancy gold beads (plate 53). Heversham House, of the eighteen-eighties, has very lovely bone curtain rods made by its present owner. For runners I have used small brass rings, or loops of ribbon to match the curtains and I have found the latter method the best (plate 53). The rod will need the support of two brackets. A small rod can be held with two gold-headed pins, but for a heavier curtain something more noticeable might be required and for this I have used elaborate gold sequins pierced by pins, the metal holders from Christmas tree candles and attractive Victorian buttons (plate 50).

If the curtains are to be looped back, decorative holders will be needed to imitate the brass and ormolu fittings found in actual houses. The curtains can be held back by a cord or by a piece of appropriate cloth attached to the holder. There is a make of Turkish Delight that supplies in each box a pair of gilt tin tongs and these make ideal curtain holders (plate 50).

Fabric pelmets are easier to make if the material is ironed on to one of the stiffening materials used for dressmaking. The shape can be drawn on to the stiffening and the fabric cut away afterwards without fear of fraying. Decoration can be added to this and the whole glued to the wall above the curtains, or on to a piece of wood that will allow it to project from the wall (plate 52).

A very attractive pelmet for small curtains can be made from the decorative brass edgings sold by the American shops mentioned in the section on lighting fittings (page 97). I include a drawing of a similar metal pelmet in a dolls' house of 1840 (plate 47).

The mouldings sold for picture frames are often very adaptable for pelmets and it is simple to cut them to size and glue them to the wall.

Curtains are not exclusive to windows for they are needed on the four-poster and half-tester beds, where no limit was put on the decorative conceit of their hanging and their pelmets. There were carved and gilded pelmets, plumes, pleated silks, tassels, fringes, ribbons and bows.

Alcoves and doorways and some Victorian fireplaces were, of course, also curtained or draped with cloth.

Bathrooms and kitchens often had translucent paper glued on to the windows, for privacy, and this can be imitated with greaseproof paper, but to look real it will require to have drawn on to it designs appropriate to the period of the house. These can be drawn in waterproof Indian ink or in a variety of colours. A suitable pattern is that for carpets (plate 39), suitably reduced. You have to decide which side will be seen, or even do the design on both sides. The paper can be made more transparent by rubbing with a little oil. It can be glued to the window with one of the plastic wallpaper pastes such as Polycell.

Blinds

This form of window covering has been used at most times and they are occasionally found in dolls' houses. The Blackett dolls' house of 1740 has ruched paper silk blinds that serve instead of curtains (plate 52). Ruched blinds of thin material were used from the middle of the 18th Century to Regency times, when they went out of fashion. They returned to fashion in early Victorian days and they are still considerably used in rather elaborate interiors today and they are called a Marquise blind.

The simpler and more utilitarian blinds of the 19th Century were made of glazed cotton or linen in a limited range of colours, white, cream, dark green and navy blue, and they could look all too often very depressing indeed (plate

50). For some reason, Scotland has remained loyal to these blinds when no one else used them, although they have recently shown signs of returning to fashion in bright colours and pretty floral designs.

I have seen several dolls' houses with Venetian blinds, mainly French houses of about 1900. The blinds have been made of wood or card slats, painted pale blue or green and glued to strips of narrow ribbon and fixed to the windows with wire (plate 52). I have not yet seen any of the now excessively fashionable plastic Venetian blinds in dolls' houses, but they very probably exist.

To protect their basements and ground floor kitchens, the Victorians used iron bars, and their combination with dark green blinds and heavy curtains must have been very dispiriting for the inmates. Nevertheless, it is intriguing to find all this in a dolls' house. Bars can be made from thin metal rods jammed into the window frames. Another piece of window furniture that I have seen painted on to an 1840 dolls' house is a framed mesh, placed across the lower part of the window so that it could be opened to let in the air whilst the flies were kept out.

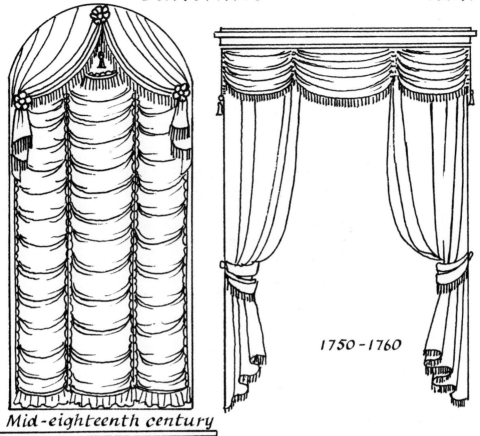

Mid-eighteenth century

1750-1760

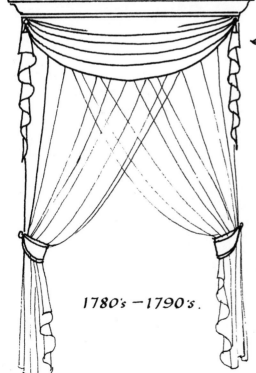

1780's — 1790's.

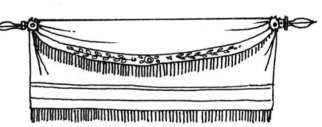

Regency pelmet.

Regency pelmet.

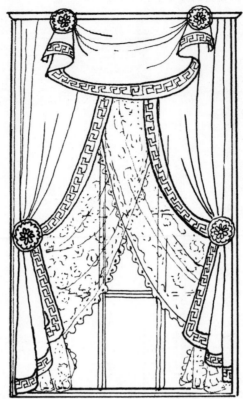

1810

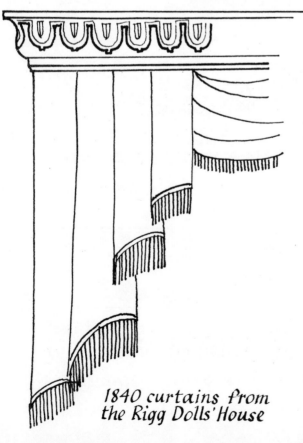

*1840 curtains from
the Rigg Dolls' House*

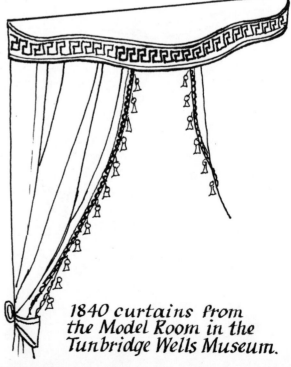

*1840 curtains from
the Model Room in the
Tunbridge Wells Museum.*

PLATE 48

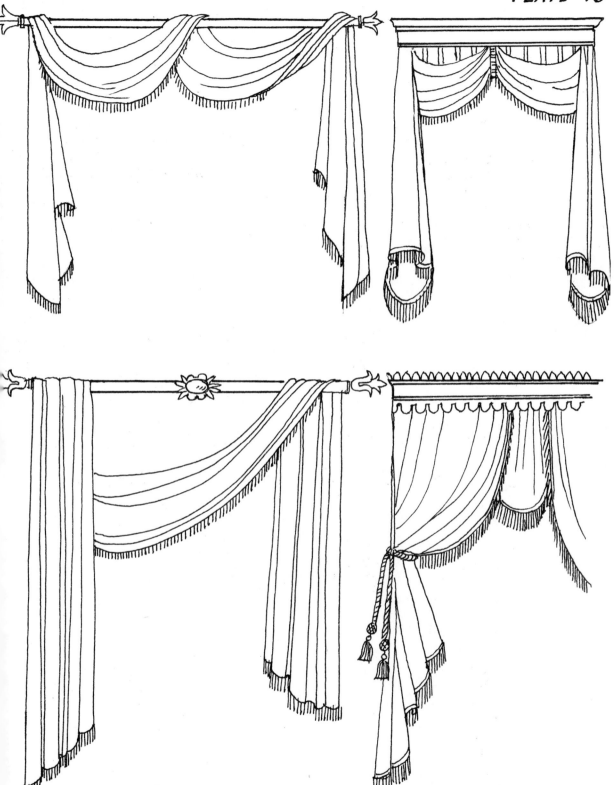

Draperies of the eighteen-fifties.

CURTAINS

PLATE 49

Curtains from Sunnyside House, 1890.

PLATE 50

Metal sweet tongs
make excellent curtain
holders.

Metal buttons for
curtain holders.

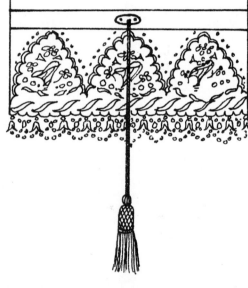

Cream linen blind.
Very pretty hem,
worked on net. 1900.

Late 19th. Century curtained
fireplace

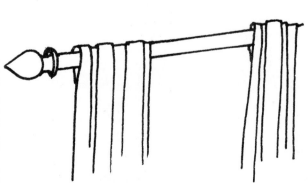

Fine muslin curtains on
a brass rod. 1860.

Cream linen blind on a
wooden roller. Wooden
slat in the lower hem. 1860.

PLATE 51

GERMAN CURTAINS 1900

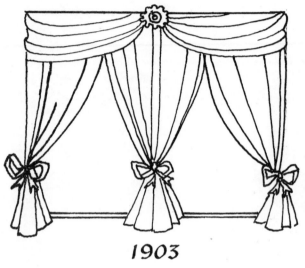

1903

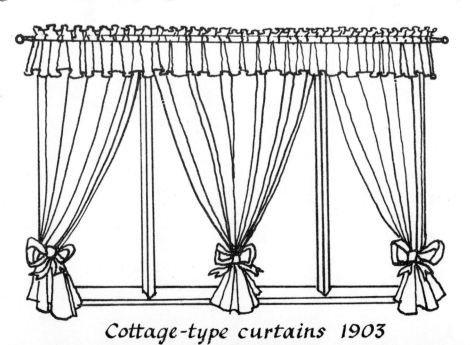

Cottage-type curtains 1903

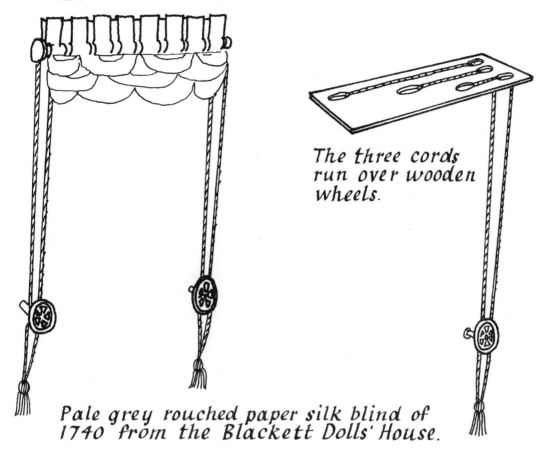

The three cords
run over wooden
wheels.

Pale grey rouched paper silk blind of
1740 from the Blackett Dolls' House.

1880 window.
Venetian blind.

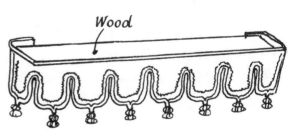

Wood

Pelmet.
Glued onto wood.
See page 27

PLATE 53

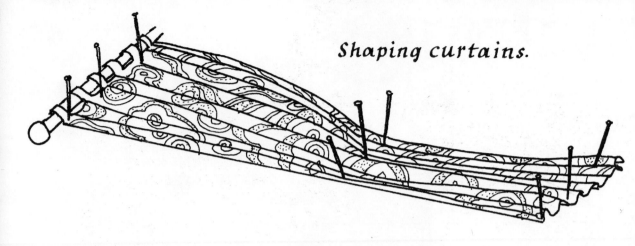

Shaping curtains.

Curtains with decorative edging.
See page 26.

Wooden pelmet.

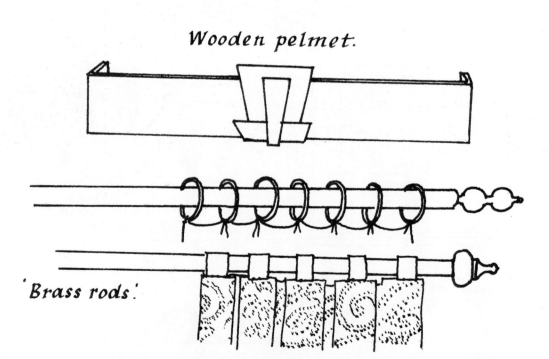

'Brass rods.'

I The Garnett Dolls' House. *c.* 1860. This dolls' house is 52″ high, 52″ wide and 21″ deep. It is painted to represent brick, and the window and door frames are painted to imitate marble.

II The Hall and Staircase in the Garnett Dolls' House. The construction of the hall and staircase is described on page 231. The cloakroom at the back boasts a tin w.c. and a washbasin. Note the telephone on the hall table—a later addition.

III The Dining Room of the Garnett Dolls' House. The cut-out paper frieze, the tapestry carpet and much of the furniture in this room are described in the text.

IV The Drawing Room of the Garnett Dolls' House. The recently applied wallpaper is made from small-scale parts cut from ordinary life-sized wallpaper.

V The Bedroom of the Garnett Dolls' House.

VI A Dolls' House in a Cupboard. The addition of two upright divisions was all that was needed to allow this cupboard to be used as a dolls' house.

VII The Nursery in the Cupboard. The floor covering is a modern printed paper, but the walls are papered with a genuine Victorian print.

VIII The Drawing Room in the Cupboard. The walls are covered with dark green Victorian silk. The Chinese wall-hanging and the silk embroidered Persian mat are both 19th-century.

IX The Kitchen in the Cupboard. An accumulation of genuine 19th-century kitchen equipment and mysterious odds and ends.

X The Bedroom in the Cupboard. The wallpaper is a Victorian cotton print with a frieze of upholstery gimp of the time. The floor covering is a reprint on cotton of a Regency wallpaper from the Brighton Pavilion. The bed and the chair are made from straw (see pages 259–60) and the leather trunk holds a set of Victorian clothes.

XI The Rigg Dolls' House. This house is in the Tunbridge Wells Museum. It was made in 1840, and it is 6′ high, 5′ wide and 2′ 6″ deep. A white-painted house remarkable not only for its quality, but also for the unity of its contents. Perhaps only here can you peep into a real house of 1840 and see its contents as they were at the time.

XII The Interior of the Rigg Dolls' House. A house made and furnished by craftsmen of the day to adult requirements. The carpets were especially made in Brussels.

XIII A group of tables, two of them of brass. The construction of the expanding table and the gate-legged table are described on page 159.

XIV A matching set of Regency style furniture, probably made a little later in the century (see page 141).

XV A set of dolls' house chairs of wood, raffia, straw and cast metal.

XVI 19th-century bathroom furniture of painted tin and porcelain. Note the pair of porcelain slippers.

XVII Nursery furniture: an early telephone, a vacuum flask, a radio and a gramophone record that plays 'God save the King'.

XVIII Kitchen. The construction of the dresser is shown on Plates 115 & 116. Old equipment for kitchens like this can still be bought piecemeal, for a great quantity was manufactured.

XIX Fretwork furniture. This unusual and large set of furniture was made in the early 1920s by Alfred Bowness, a craftsman of Messrs. Waring & Gillow. It is in the style of the 1890s and it is all made from tea chests and cigar boxes. The wood is left unstained but it is beautifully constructed and finished.

Candlelight was the only means of lighting until about 1800 when oil was used for lighting the main rooms. In about 1840 gas came into general use although it had been invented some forty years earlier. Dolls' houses have gas fittings from about 1850 onwards, but they continue to be furnished with candlesticks, chandeliers and oil lamps, as indeed did real houses.

The first practical electric lamp was made in 1810 but had to be operated by wet cell batteries. They were used from 1846 in the theatre, and in parts of France they were used as street-lighting from 1855. London did not have electric street-lighting until 1879. Until 1920 each bulb had to be blown and thousands of glassblowers did nothing else, but after this they were machine made and electric lighting became almost universal.

Equally slowly neon tube lighting developed from its invention in 1910 to its widespread use at the beginning of the Second World War.

Beautiful lighting fittings have been made especially for dolls' houses, silver candlesticks for the old baby houses and well turned brass ones for the more modest houses. In Victorian times, a great many imaginative lamps, chandeliers and candelabras were in soft metal, gilt or silvered, although now faded to pewter. The oil lamps had glass chimneys and were in many cases working models. Some were made of turned wood, the old ones often quite beautiful, but later ones rather crude.

Wall lights have appeared for several centuries and still do in the nineteen-seventies. We can now buy matching sets of wall lights and chandelier made in transparent plastic to represent crystal drops.

Older dolls' houses have occasionally been electrified, usually to their disadvantage, for the earlier fittings were gigantic. The switch by the door would be as big as the dining-room table. Today, complete electric fittings of the correct scale can be bought and they are ideal for a modern house.

I have described in the chapter on glass how to adapt a wine-makers air lock for use as an oil lamp and how to make a glass chandelier from beads.

Twentieth-Century Lampshades (Plate 57)

I have seen several of these lamps and there is one in the Russell dolls' house made from black wire and beads, a typically over-complicated way of making such a piece of furniture. The shade is excellent and is made from parchment with a design of grapes drawn on in coloured inks, in dirty lemons and brownish purples. I have drawn a pattern for the lampshade which can be modified, if necessary, for a shade of a different era. If you wish it to be narrower, cut a piece from each end; if you want it broader, add a piece to each end. It can be made from ordinary drawing paper and the design can be drawn with

97

waterproof ink. Rub the back of the paper with oil to achieve a parchment effect. On such a small scale cloth shades require the fabric to be mounted on a stiffener such as paper or iron-on dress stiffening material. It is essential that the fabric be very thin for even a fine velvet would look like a heavy carpet at such a scale.

I have drawn two bell shaped plastic lampshades that I found recently being sold as Christmas tree decorations. They are the same shape as the old electric light shades that have hung in our corridors for forty years or more and when inverted and mounted on a brass button and a candle placed inside, they make a good copy of some of the early Victorian candleshades used on dining tables.

On the same page of drawings I have shown two Art Nouveau lamps with Tiffany glass shades, articles now in great demand in real houses. The effect, when lit, is of stained glass in muted colours of orange, brown, purple and green and the design follows the familiar swirls of Art Nouveau grapes, wild roses and lilies. To imitate such a shade, I bought a small plastic baby's rattle that had one half of the ball of clear plastic. I separated this half and drew on it the design in plastic acrylic paint, outlining the shapes with black and filling in the colours with transparent paint.

Reading lamps and lampshades have for so long been a field for the amateur craftsman that they are found to be made of the most varied, even unlikely, materials. A multitude of small objects lend themselves to adaptation and I show several on the appropriate page (plate 58).

In the 'twenties and 'thirties, geometrical shapes were fashionable and lamps were made of slabs of wood glued together in a zig-zag fashion faintly reminiscent of Egyptian forms. These were stained or painted with enamel colours in the favourite black and orange colours of the time. Urn-shaped wooden lamp bases were decorated with pokerwork and had parchment shades with hanging wooden beads. When old title deeds had no longer to be kept, there was a fashion for wrought-iron lamps with square shaped shades made from these deeds.

War-time brought a rash of pitiful improvisations and bottles and jars of every kind were used as lamp bases. This passion for bottles lasted for a long time.

In the 'fifties, there was a fashion for dark opaque shades and only small circles of light were thrown down on to the desk or table. The more cottage-like interiors kept to their ginghams and handwoven cloth.

All sorts of miniature objects can be adapted to imitate these varied fancies; scent bottles, the vaccine bottles from the vet or doctor, painted on the inside; and the plain grey plastic column of the new cotton bobbins. This last will make a suitable stand for a modern lamp and it has the added advantage of a hole through the centre to take the electric wiring (plate 58).

PLATE 54.

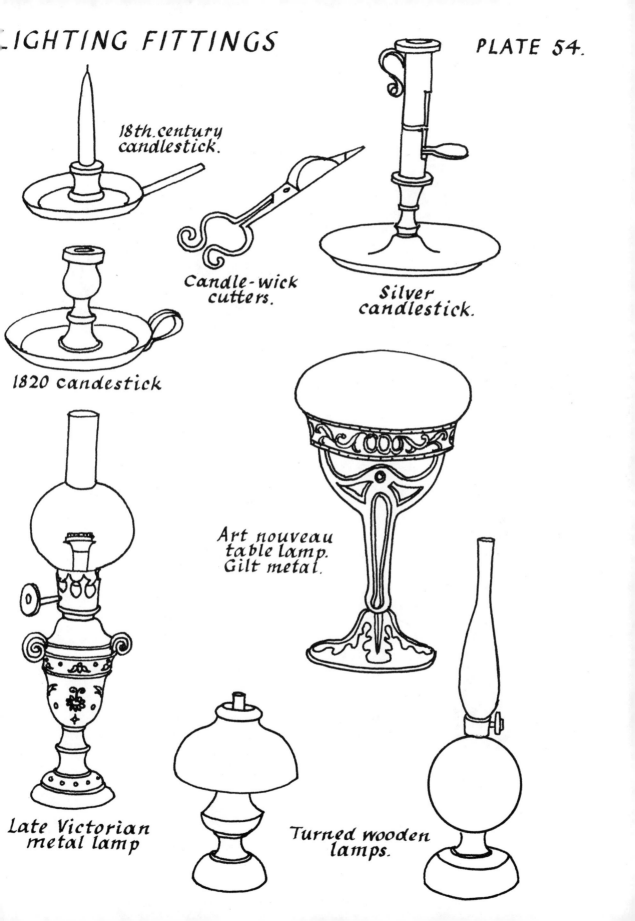

18th century candlestick.

Candle-wick cutters.

Silver candlestick.

1820 candestick

Art nouveau table lamp. Gilt metal.

Late Victorian metal lamp

Turned wooden lamps.

Eighteenth century
chandelier.

Metal chandeliers, candelabra
& wall light. All about actual
size. Victorian.

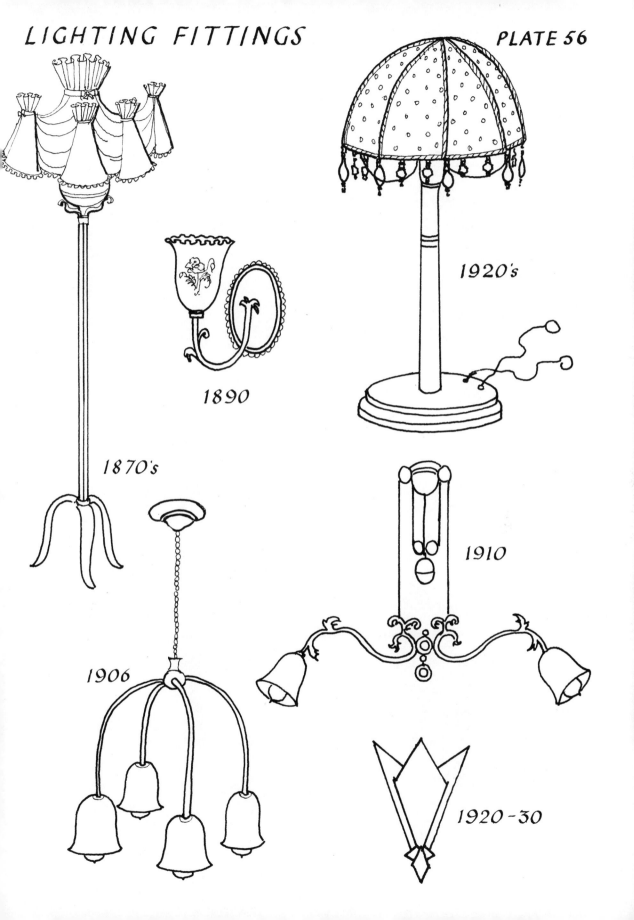

PLATE 56

1920's

1890

1870's

1910

1906

1920-30

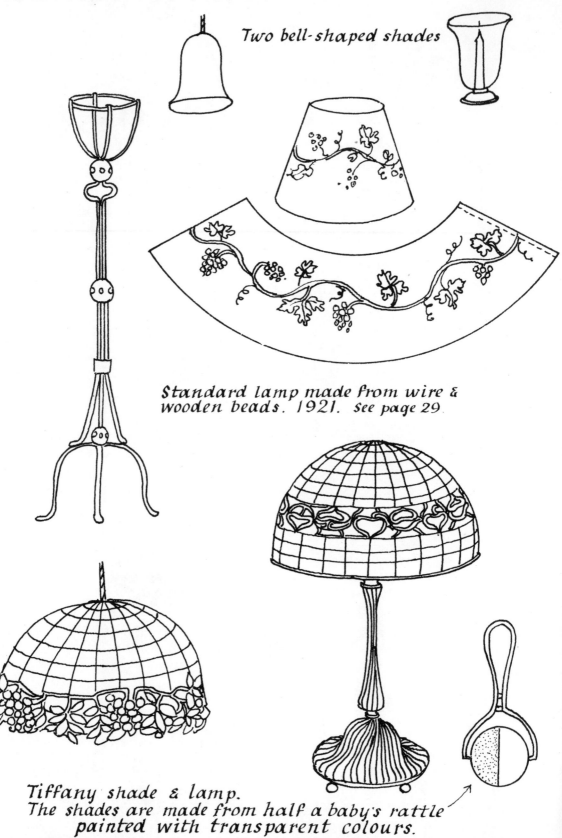

Two bell-shaped shades

Standard lamp made from wire &
wooden beads. 1921. see page 29.

Tiffany shade & lamp.
The shades are made from half a baby's rattle
painted with transparent colours.

CANDLESTICKS & MODERN TABLE LAMPS

PLATE 58

Victorian. Gilt

Brass. Victorian

Brass. 1900

Brass. Early 20th. century.

Turned wood. Early 20th. century.

Brass. Early 20th. century.

Brass. 1960 Actual size.

Victorian gilt. Actual size.

1960-70

Modern reading lamp. Made from plastic cotton spool.

1950-60 lamp. Made from brass candlestick.

1970. Modern lamp. Grey plastic tube for the base & white bead for the globe.

Loop of wire shaped to hold the lamp shade.

The early Dutch baby houses had the best of everything and their pictures were painted, in miniature, by professional artists of the day. A similar standard has been achieved for a few later dolls' houses that were intended for adult display, but apart from these notable exceptions, the standard of the pictures in dolls' houses has never been very high. The few good ones are exceptional and will be noticed at once. The delight of finding something small enough would appear to have smothered any question of whether or not it was appropriate. Miniature prints of old masters are easy enough to come by, but when they hang in the house they look wrong and I feel that it is far better to search for something contemporary with the house and, if possible, typical of the more obvious tastes of the period. Prints from old books are the most obvious and the richest source, and after about 1850 the daguerrotypes and photographs of the time are very suitable. Those printed on glass and held in narrow metal frames are particularly suitable (plate 59). There is a wide range of subject amongst the Baxter prints made after 1835 (printed oil colours on paper) although these are now sought after by collectors and are therefore expensive (plate 59). Small pieces of petit-point embroidery make excellent pictures so long as you are careful to choose designs appropriate to the time.

One would expect the pictures in a Georgian house to be portraits or classical landscapes, hung rather high on the walls and perhaps above the doors of a panelled room. Miniature copies of oils in watercolour would perhaps be suitable for such a home but probably outside the scope of most people. There are some alternatives that might be more practical such as the shell pictures behind bevelled glass, in a round or hexagonal frame. The glass and rim of an old watch might serve for the frame and the shells be made of grains of rice, tapioca, sago and so on, suitably coloured (plate 59).

There are cut-out paper pictures, silhouettes of black on white and vice versa, and those pictures made by piercing holes in a light paper to expose a darker one beneath (plate 59). Such 18th Century do-it-yourself pictures were still fashionable in Regency times as were the glass pictures. These were usually of biblical scenes, or of popular heroes like Nelson, and were made either by painting scenes on to the back of the glass or, more cheaply, by sticking a coloured engraving to the back of the glass, peeling off almost all the layers of paper and applying a varnish. If you attempt such a painting, remember that all is in reverse, foreground and details first, then the background and the sky. They have a fine rich stained glass sort of effect.

Memento mori and similar scenes of death and despair were much in vogue during the Regency period and painted memorial cards of the time may sometimes be found.

Samplers, usually worked by children, were much in fashion throughout the last century, and they can either be worked by hand on a fine linen or, if this is too difficult, they can be imitated with rather dry watercolour on cloth.

Pictures made up of grasses and seaweed were much in vogue during the earlier half of the 19th Century (plate 59).

There is, of course, the rich field of 'Scraps', like those used by the Victorians to make screens, and these will come from old collections or from the richly coloured old-fashioned labels found on cigar boxes, spaghetti packets, etc. Kate Greenaway's illustrations have recently been reprinted, and in the present century the Mabel Lucy Attwell children and the Bonzo dogs are typical dolls' house pictures.

Cigarette cards are a good source of pictures and have been in existence since 1880. Some were printed on silk and there was a set brought out by Spinet, the super Virginia Cigarette, which reproduced the old masters on fine linen. They depicted popular favourites of the time—The Laughing Cavalier, Dante and Beatrice, The Infant Samuel, and were as small as $2\frac{3}{4}'' \times 2\frac{1}{2}''$ and as large as $4\frac{1}{4}'' \times 2\frac{3}{4}''$. They seem most at home in the houses of the early 20th Century and a set of, say, cricketers would look very well framed in passe-partout for the study or the hall.

Pictures went out of fashion in the 'twenties and the walls of the Russell dolls' house of 1921 look strangely empty. The only pictures are a set of prints in a back corridor. Pictures of this era are more likely to be in the nursery and the attics, although framed photographs stood about everywhere, on the piano, the dressing table, and on the chimneypiece in profusion. Pictures didn't really return to fashion until after the Second World War and those most characteristic of the time would be Picassos or formal abstracts.

Picture Frames have their fashions too, although the standard gilt frame changes only in a very minor way over several centuries. The early baby houses have richly carved and gilt baroque frames and deep ebony Dutch frames. Those of the 18th Century are lighter and more elegant to match their furniture. In Victorian times, the frames become rather heavy and ornate and are usually gilt, occasionally with a velvet or plush mount. Towards the end of the century, a frame of black, with a gilt slip, is very typical and those of oak, where the ends project (plate 60) were everywhere used for prints, texts and photographs.

The early 20th Century was obsessed with oak and frames of every thickness were made from this rather unsuitable wood. Small prints, such as etchings, were framed with narrow black mountings and large cream mounts.

Mid-20th Century frames were thicker and lighter in colour, rarely gilded, and occasionally painted white, and they continue in use today, although large abstract paintings are usually framed with a very narrow band of metal, gilt or wood, which is of course fairly easy to fabricate on a small scale for a dolls' house.

A few years ago, it was possible to buy miniature gilt frames very well modelled in the ubiquitous plastic (plate 60) and I found lately a gift shop that sold miniature gilt plastic altars (plate 60) in the centre of which were small frames about $1\frac{1}{2}$ inches high holding religious prints.

This was a remarkably good buy, for the frame made an excellent photograph frame and the rest of the altar, with the top sawn off, made a good fireplace for a very small dolls' house.

The 'do-it-yourself' shops have plastic strip moulding which is ideal for modern picture frames. They are easily cut with a razor blade and can be glued together with plastic glue and painted. Brooches with the pin removed make excellent frames, of a style contemporary to the brooch.

Pictures are generally hung on string or from a ring hooked over a nail, but I notice in Ursula Somervell's dolls' house that the string was caught together near to the picture and this made a pleasant change. Modern pictures are usually hung in such a way that the cord or wire does not show and it is probably a good idea to glue them to the wall.

Shell picture.
Georgian.

Prick picture.

Mid-Victorian photograph
in gilt frame.

1850. Seaweed picture.

INDIAN SETTLEMENT
PRINTED
BY
G BAXTER
INVENTOR PATENTEE

LICENSE GRANTED TO WORK
THE PROCESS

Baxter print.

Small Victorian brass
frame. 1870.

Gold plastic frame. 1960.

This frame is made from stems of rushes split longitudinally. The plan of the frame is drawn onto a piece of stiff paper & then the eight pieces of rush that are needed to make the frame are cut & glued into position on the paper. When the glue is dry the paper is cut away from the outer edges of the frame with a sharp balsa knife.

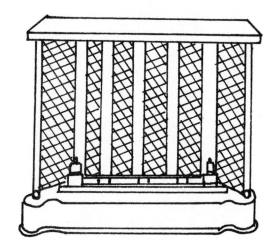

Gold plastic altar adapted to make a small fireplace & a picture frame.

I always like to see mirrors in dolls' houses for they help to lighten the dark interiors, multiply many of the objects and enable us to see the back of objects that are sometimes too delicate to handle. Mrs. Fuller Maitland's dolls' house has a mirror covering almost the whole of one side wall and when the house is adjusted to reflect a light, the whole room is flooded with a dramatic unreal glow.

The Bryant dolls' house has large mirrors that represent windows in the drawing-room. They are, like everything in the house, beautifully made, with marble consoles beneath them and gilt pelmets above. The addition of glazing bars would have probably made them more like real windows. I have used this idea for a dolls' house that I am making in a cupboard that cannot have holes cut into it for windows.

On plate 62 I have drawn four mirrors that are very easy to make. The top left-hand one is drawn from a mirror in a Gothic style house of 1840 and it has the bright glitter that one associates with this age. The whole is made from mirror but only the centre rectangle remains as a reflecting surface. The panels on each side are white glass and this effect can be achieved by scratching the backing from these areas with a razor blade and then repainting with white paint. The smaller top rectangle is gold paper, as are the corners and the edgings, and the applied decorations are red and blue glass beads. The mirror at the top right is a very successful 'instant' Venetian mirror. It is a handbag mirror edged with silver paper trimming. This silver edging is both embossed and cut away to leave the mirror exposed between the roses and the leaves, and this gives a very satisfactory result. These edgings are from cake frills, which make the most useful trimmings throughout a dolls' house. I have used them not only for picture and mirror frames, but for wallpaper borders and for decorating furniture. They have a notably Victorian look. The third mirror on this page is made in the same way, using only the centre portion of the gold edging; thin strips and rosettes are cut from the same paper.

Sequins, especially the hexagonal ones, can be used for decorating frames, and lengths of string can be glued to the edges of mirrors and painted white or gold (plate 62). Bright insets of coloured foil look very well. If the mirror is large, it is probably wisest to glue it firmly to the wall, but a small one can be hung from a cord which is held to the mirror back with sticky tape (plate 62).

109

PLATE 61

Regency overmantel mirror.

Turned
brass
swing
mirror.

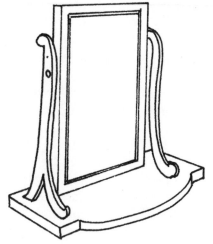

Victorian painted metal
swing mirror

Early Victorian
gilt mirror.

Early Victorian gilt swing mirror
with two matching vases.

Victorian gilt metal
mirror with candle.

1840 Dolls' House mirror.

Dolls' House Venetian mirror.

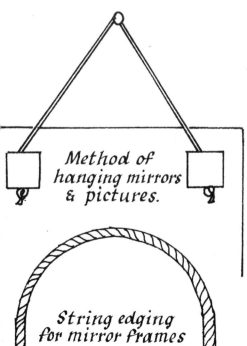

Method of hanging mirrors & pictures.

String edging for mirror frames

Gilt paper mirror frame.

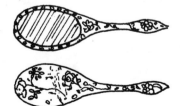

Victorian hand mirrors. Actual size. Covered with floral printed paper.

Regency type mantel clock

Cut 1
in wood
$\frac{1}{2}$" thick.

Columns.
cut 4

Cut 1 in wood.
$\frac{1}{2}$" thick

Cut pediment in
wood. $\frac{4}{10}$" thick.

Wall clock.
1890

Fireplaces, Stoves and Ovens (*Plates 64–75*)

You may well feel that the blank wall of a dolls' house would be enhanced by a fireplace, although it would be unwise to add a chimney breast to a wall that has its original wallpaper, unless you can copy it exactly. A chimney breast certainly gives more variety of shape to a room and allows for a more interesting disposal of the furniture. It is important that it should be of the right proportions and these are not necessarily those of the correctly reduced scale for sometimes accuracy of measurement will produce an air of sterility. The best way to decide this is to take a piece of stiff paper the height of the room and fold it into shape and hold it against the wall. Try several widths and depths until you feel that you have the proportions to your liking.

I describe how to make a kitchen oven in some detail, and I give plans for other fireplaces where the method of making them is much the same. The width of the chimney breast in my example may seem rather excessive but the room that it is intended for is very deep, and I want ample space to hang a set of metal meat covers and a clock, thus making the whole display the focal point for the room.

If the room is very small, then the chimney breast can be cut from a solid piece of wood but for anything big a lightweight structure is better and this should be glued to the wall for nails might project to the outside. The wallpaper which will cover the chimney breast will ensure that the whole is secure. To fix a fireplace without a chimney breast, I would use an edging of gummed paper with only $\frac{1}{8}$ inch overlapping the fireplace. The wall paper will hide the gummed paper and there will be no unsightly gaps round the edges. If the room has its original wallpaper it may be possible, by wetting it, to peel back the paper behind the fireplace so that it can be reglued over the gummed edging.

Dutch oven
from baby
house of 1697

18th. century
salt box.

South German stove.
18th. century.

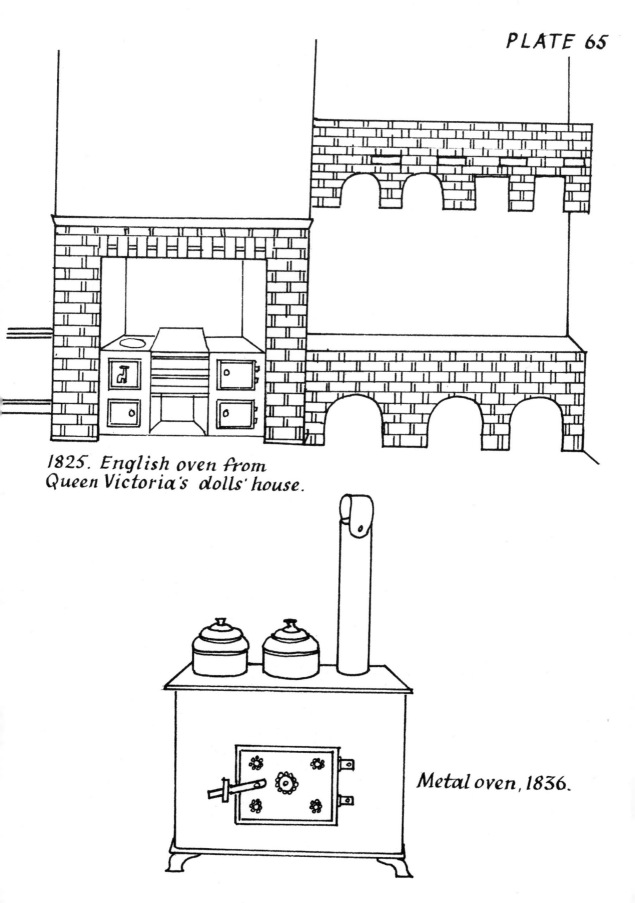

PLATE 65

1825. English oven from
Queen Victoria's dolls' house.

Metal oven, 1836.

PLATE 66

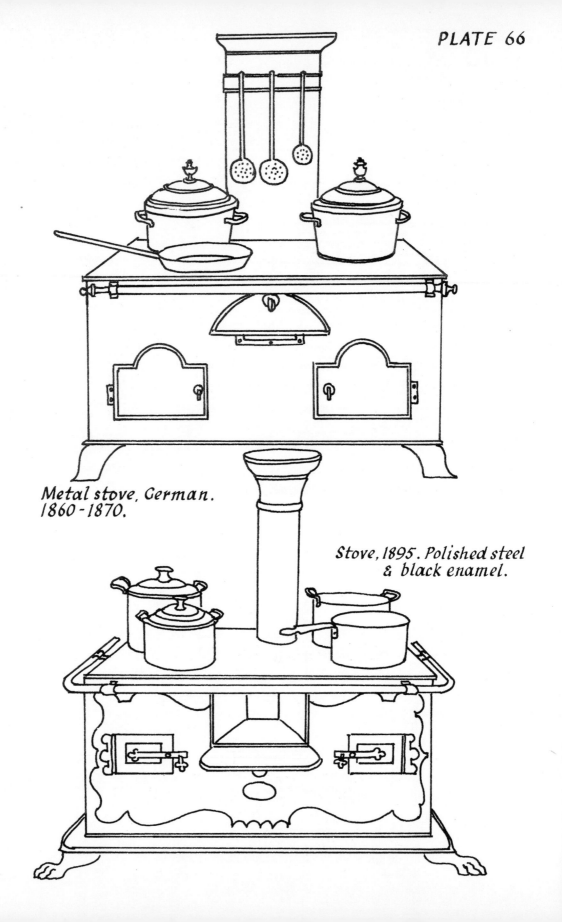

Metal stove, German.
1860 - 1870.

Stove, 1895. Polished steel
& black enamel.

PLATE 67

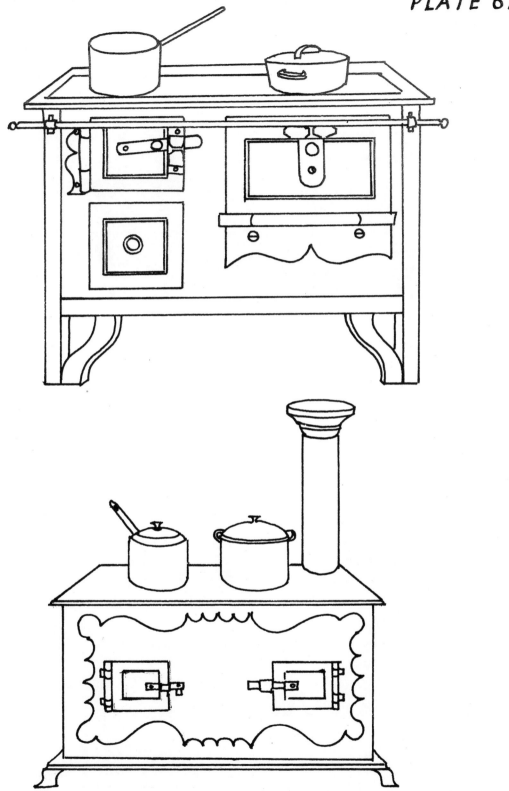

Two metal stoves. Late 19th. or early 20th. century.

OVENS

Iron & aluminium pans. 1920's
Given as advertisements.

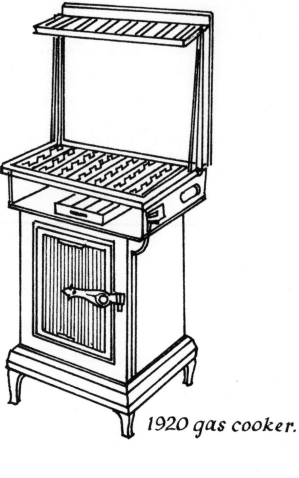

1920 gas cooker.

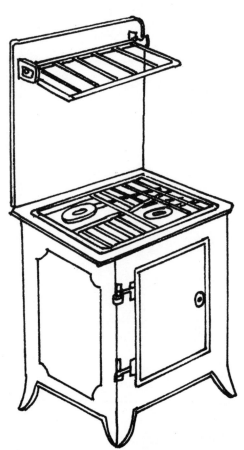

1950 oven. Painted metal,
with plastic door & rack.

1920 stove

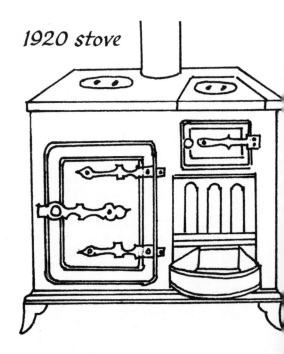

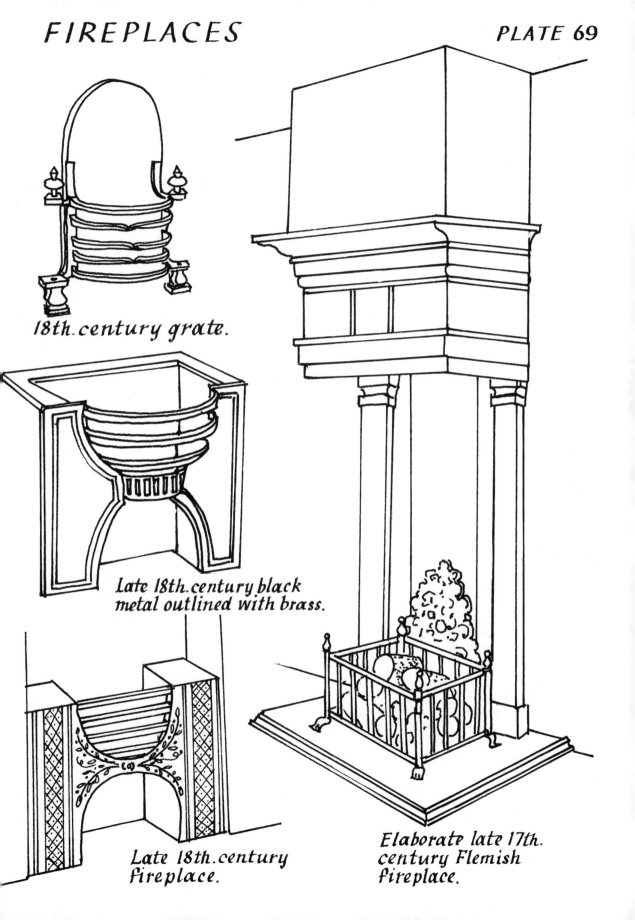

18th. century grate.

Late 18th. century black
metal outlined with brass.

Late 18th. century
fireplace.

Elaborate late 17th.
century Flemish
fireplace.

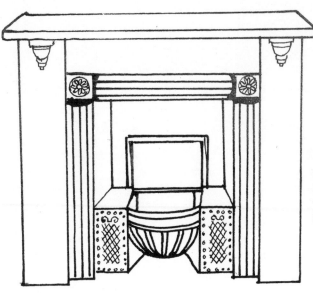

Fireplace of 1835. White painted surround. Black grate with brass basket.

Early 19th. century fireplace.

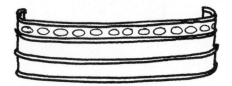

Victorian brass fender.

Victorian iron fireplace with pierced brass fender.

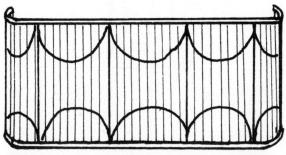

Wire & brass fireguard. 1840.

1840 fireplace. Marbled surround, black metal grate & a brass ash-guard. The fire is ready laid.

A nice set of brass fireplace furniture.

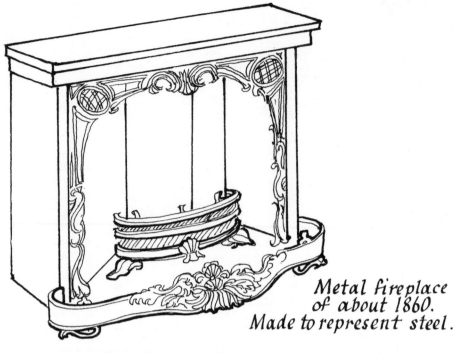

Metal fireplace
of about 1860.
Made to represent steel.

Brass fittings.

French fireplace. Third quarter of the
19th. century. Black & brass

Tin fireplace of 1880.

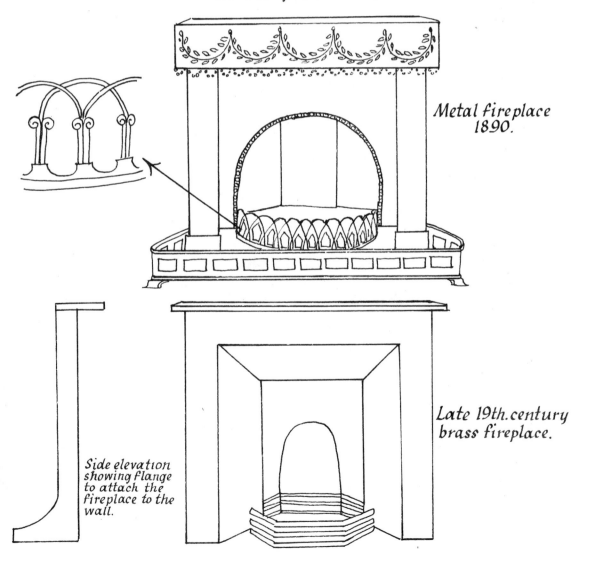

Metal fireplace
1890.

Late 19th century
brass fireplace.

Side elevation
showing flange
to attach the
fireplace to the
wall.

Painted tin
fireplace. 1920.

Edwardian
wooden fireplace.

PLATE 75

Valor-Perfection stove.
1920-1930.

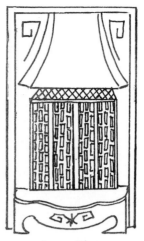

Gas fire.
1930 to present day.

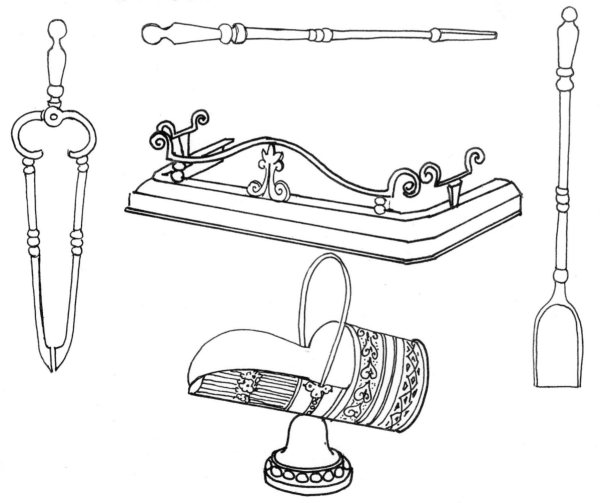

Late Victorian brass fireplace furniture.

A Mid-Victorian Oven (Plates 76–78)

The kitchen for which I am designing the oven is 17 inches wide, 18 inches deep and $16\frac{1}{2}$ inches high and to suit this proportion I decided to make a chimney breast 7 inches wide and $1\frac{1}{2}$ inches deep.

To make the structure I used lengths of balsa wood $1\frac{1}{2}$ inches wide and $\frac{1}{8}$ inch thick. I cut two lengths the height of the room for the uprights and five pieces $6\frac{3}{4}'' \times 1\frac{1}{2}''$ for the cross struts. These I glued into place, one at the top, one at the bottom and one $5\frac{1}{4}$ inches above the base and the other two I spaced evenly between this one and the top one (plate 77).

I then glued a piece of thin card $11\frac{1}{4}'' \times 7''$ on to the front and another piece $16\frac{1}{2}'' \times 7''$ on to the back (plate 77). Into the space which is to take the oven, I glued two uprights $\frac{1}{4}$ inch from the outside edges (plate 77). These form a support for the fireplace surrounds. The oven hobs are made from two pieces of wood, one $3'' \times 1\frac{1}{4}'' \times \frac{1}{2}''$ and the other $3'' \times 1\frac{1}{4}'' \times 1\frac{1}{4}''$. The smaller one fits on to the left-hand side. The larger piece has five oval joiners' nails through it, two for the horizontal bars and three for the vertical bars of the grate. These are hammered into the smaller piece of wood leaving a gap of $1\frac{3}{4}$ inches for the fire (plate 77). This structure is glued into the opening. To make a neat job of the oven, use a thin card. Plate 78 gives the shapes and sizes of the pieces needed. I used metal tags that are sold as plant labels, made of aluminium with raised edges, and they are ideal for use as parts of ovens and fireplaces. I used one of them, cut to 2 inches, to decorate the back of the chimney and I glued one to the left-hand hob. Another I bent to form an ash-pan and a brass split pin made a centre knob for this and the oven door handle. The hinges are cut from the metal tags and fixed with brass pins. I cut off the raised edges of the tags and used them to edge the oven door. For the final trimmings I used a small brass tap from a modern bathroom set and on the top of the stove I used a metal washer for a boiling ring.

When assembled it was painted with several coats of black enamel, leaving the shiny edges of the metal labels and the bars of the fire unpainted.

The overmantel is made from two uprights of wood $5\frac{1}{4}'' \times \frac{1}{2}''$ and a horizontal $7'' \times 1''$, topped by a shelf $7'' \times 1''$. This should be painted to imitate stone and a bobble-edged fringe can be added to the shelf.

I include a pattern for the hearth, of squared tiles, that can be painted on card or American cloth and glued to the floor. Brass and steel fenders and fire-irons are usually easy to buy and the fenders still only cost about 75p and they do give an authentic finish to a fireplace. I think they were made as small gifts in the past and not specifically for dolls' houses.

PLATE 76

A mid-Victorian oven.

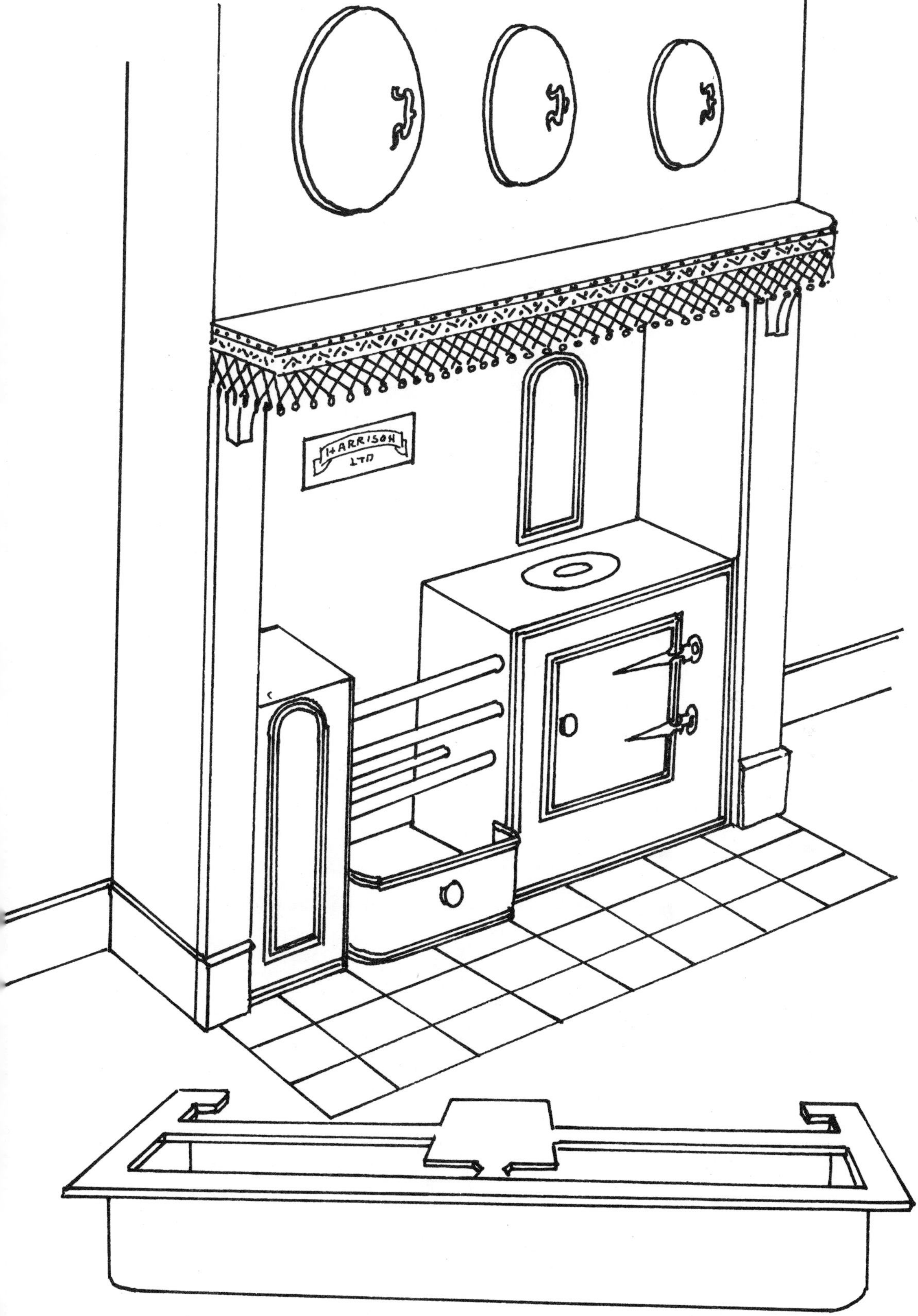

HARRISON
LTD

PLATE 77

Construction of the mid-Victorian oven.

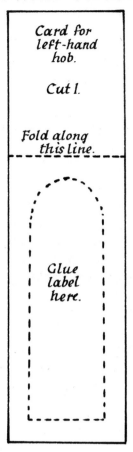

Card for
left-hand
hob.

Cut 1.

Fold along
this line.

Glue
label
here.

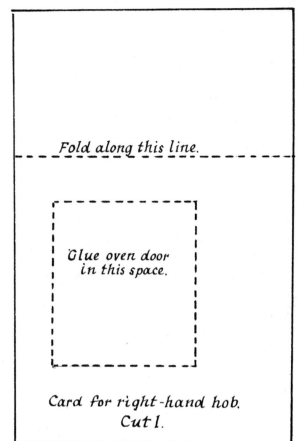

Fold along this line.

Glue oven door
in this space.

Card for right-hand hob.
Cut 1.

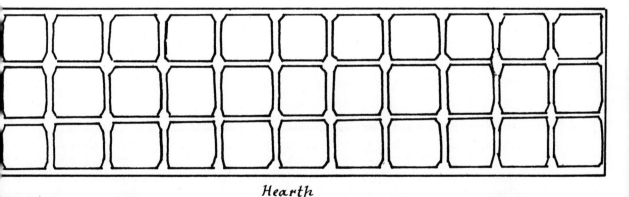

Hearth

Oven
door.

Hinge. Cut 2.

HARRISON
LTD

Name plate. Cut 1.

Angle bracket to
hold mantelshelf.
Cut 2.

An Early Victorian Corner Fireplace (Plates 79 & 80)

This fireplace is designed to fit across the corner of the room. It will be easier to see, and admire, than one affixed to a side wall. There are three corner fireplaces in the Scadbury Manor baby house of 1730–40. Perhaps they were more common in Georgian houses than in those of a later date. This fireplace can be made of card and painted black but it would look even better made from thin flexible metal with the decoration painted on to it. If metal is used it should be fixed to side hobs of solid balsa wood with small pins.

(1) A Mid-Victorian Fireplace (Plates 81–82)

This fireplace is typical of the period, with a marble surround and a curved back to the grate. I built it of balsa wood strips and card. Two pieces of flexible metal served for bars. The decorative edging is of string glued to the fireplace. This string will need extra coats of paint because of its absorbency but when it eventually dries shiny it looks like an elegant twisted cast-iron edging. The decorative finial is a piece from a jet necklace shaped like a rose.

(2) A Mid-Victorian Fireplace (Plate 83)

This is one without a chimney breast and to compensate for this lack I made it rather deep, which gave it a French air, particularly when it was painted to imitate a dark grey marble. The fireplace itself is black, edged with gold Russia braid.

A Late Victorian Over Mantel (Plate 84)

This old over-mantel was given to me and although it was rather crudely made it had a strong period flavour to it. I therefore thought plans for its simple reconstruction worth including. The factors that make for the period atmosphere seem to be the crude yellow ochre graining and the solid black line decoration.

An Edwardian Over-Mantel (Plate 85)

This complicated piece of furniture looks better and more authentic when made up than might appear from my drawing. It is made of two thicknesses of wood. A, C, D, E, F, G, H, J and K are of wood $\frac{1}{8}$ inch thick. I painted it yellowish-greyish white to give the effect of age and I glued with Polycell thin mirror-like foil to the shaded areas.

This piece of furniture, without the mirror, would double for a kitchen cabinet with a set of drawers below.

White or green paint, or graining, would be correct for this period.

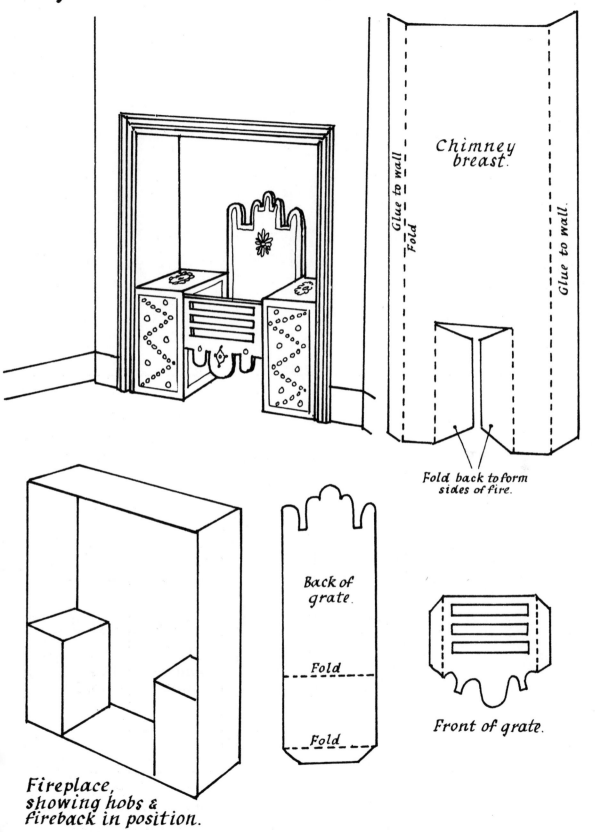

Chimney breast.

Glue to wall

Fold

Glue to wall.

Fold back to form sides of fire.

Back of grate.

Fold

Fold

Front of grate.

Fireplace, showing hobs & fireback in position.

PLATE
80

Cut across this line.

Glue to wall

Fold on dotted line.

Fold back at right angles to form the sides of the Fireplace.

Cut along this line.

Fold back at right angles to form the sides of the fireplace.

Fold on dotted line.

Glue to wall.

Fold forward to form the top of the fireplace.

Back of fireplace.
(Cut 1)

Plans for an early Victorian corner fireplace.

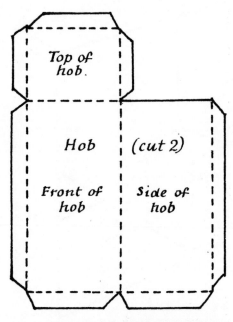

Top of hob.

Hob   (cut 2)

Front of hob   Side of hob

Fold on dotted lines to make hobs.

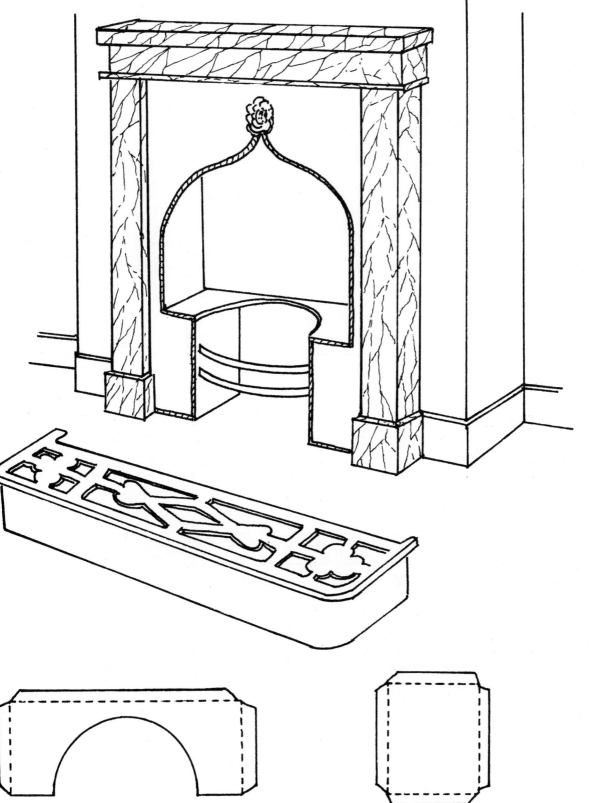

Cut out of thick card & fold on dotted lines.

Make a box 3″ wide by 3½″ high & 1″deep. Glue the shaped piece of card to the front of this box. Set this into the chimney-breast leaving it protruding by ¼″.

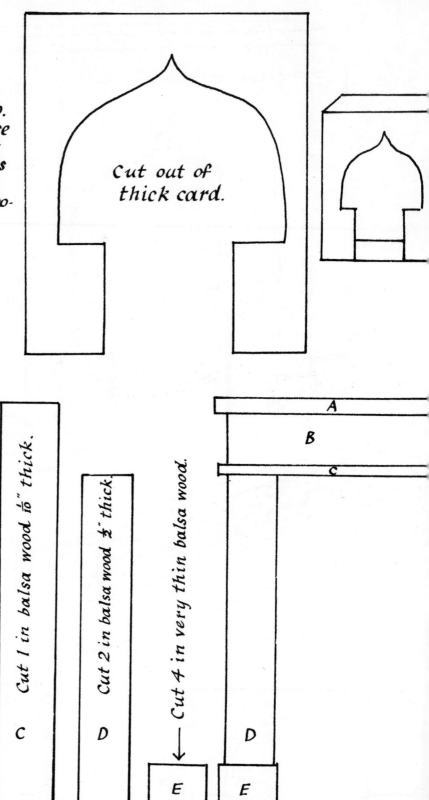

Cut out of thick card.

Cut 1 in balsa wood ⅛″ thick.

A

Cut 1 in balsa wood ½″ thick.

B

Cut 1 in balsa wood 1/16″ thick.

C

Cut 2 in balsa wood ½″ thick.

D

Cut 4 in very thin balsa wood.

E

A

B

C

D

E

A MID-VICTORIAN FIREPLACE (2)

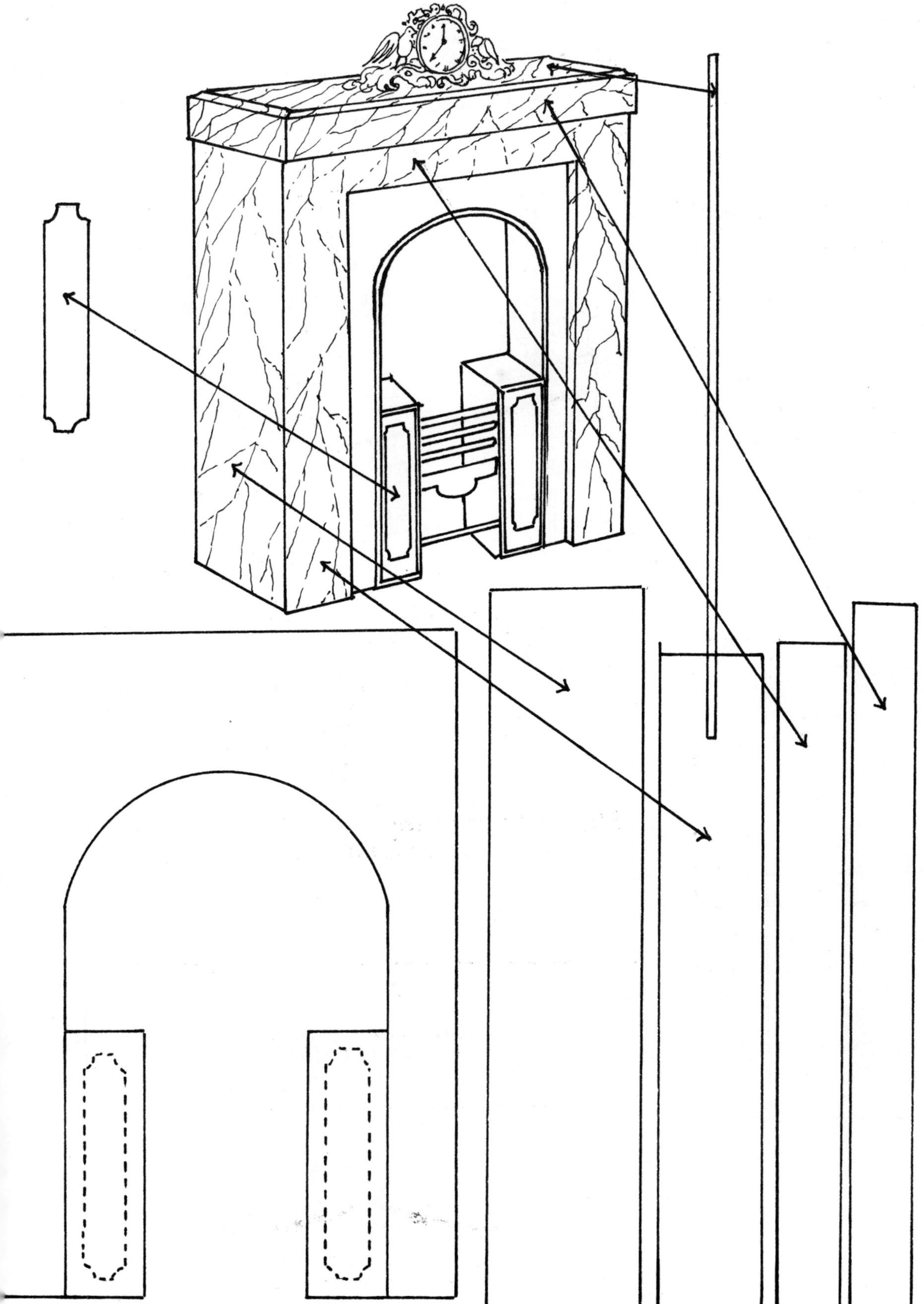

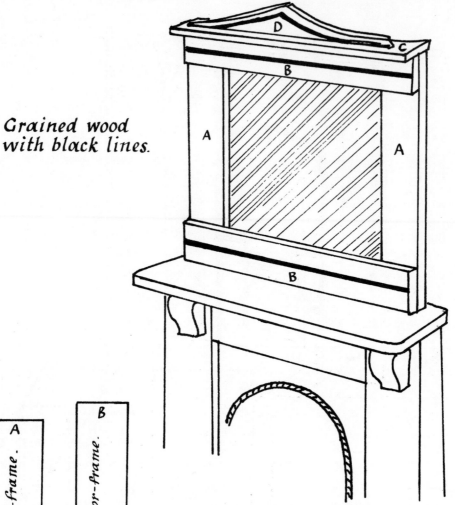

Grained wood
with black lines.

Vertical pieces of mirror-frame.
Cut 2 in wood ⅛" thick.   **A**

Horizontal pieces of mirror-frame.
Cut 2 in wood ⅛" thick.   **B**

Mirror to be glued on the back, & paper
pasted across to hold it in place.

C

Top shelf. Cut 1
in wood ⅛" thick.

D

Top decoration.
Cut 1 in wood ⅛" thick.

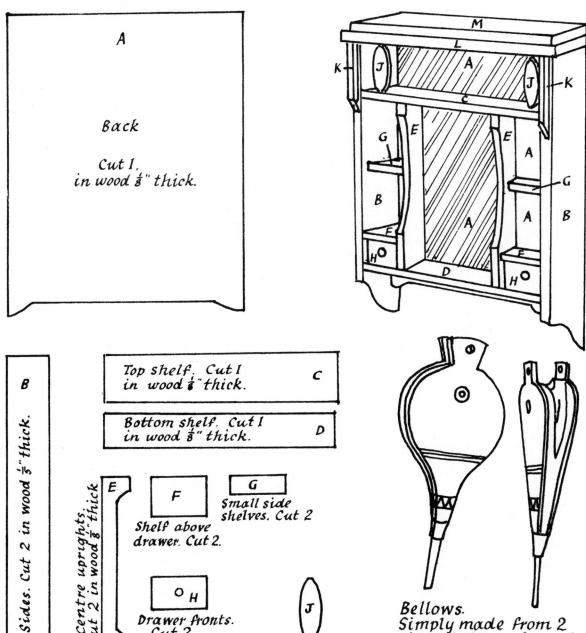

A

Back

Cut 1,
in wood ⅛" thick.

Top shelf. Cut 1
in wood ⅛" thick.   C

Bottom shelf. Cut 1
in wood ⅛" thick.   D

B

Sides. Cut 2 in wood ⅛" thick.

Centre uprights.
Cut 2 in wood ⅛" thick.

E

F

Shelf above
drawer. Cut 2.

G

Small side
shelves. Cut 2

H

Drawer fronts.
Cut 2.

J

All the small pieces cut in wood ⅛" thick.

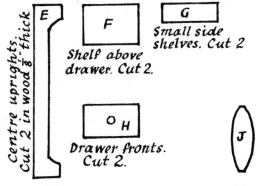

Bellows.
Simply made from 2
shaped pieces of wood
held together with a
thin leather gusset &
bound with thin metal.

K

Cut 2.

L

Lower piece of cornice.
Cut 1 in wood ⅛" thick.

Upper piece of
cornice. Cut 1
in wood ⅛" thick.   M

An Edwardian Fireplace (*Plate 86*)

The tall, narrow tiles are typical of Art Nouveau and can be painted on card with enamel colours and the joins can be drawn afterwards with ink. The surrounds can be made from picture moulding and the over-mantel with its decorative frame is an extra to the main structure. The ash-pan and fender can be cut from thin metal and the heart design painted.

A Fireplace of 1930 to 1940 (*Plate 87*)

The more modern the fireplace, the easier it is to make, for simplicity of construction and cheapness of material grow ever more paramount, as does a more bizarre vulgarity, for I have seen a pink tiled fireplace of this era made in the shape of a fox terrier dog with the fire between its legs.

My example of a tiled fireplace is simple and typical and easily made by cutting it from a solid piece of wood $3\frac{1}{2}$ inch long by $2\frac{1}{2}$ inches high by $\frac{1}{2}$ inch deep. The hearth is another piece of wood $4\frac{1}{2}$ inches long by $1\frac{1}{2}$ inches wide and $\frac{1}{2}$ inch deep. If this is painted in poster paint to a shade of oatmeal and then stippled with a sponge, the whole can be varnished to give the effect of glazed tiles. The hearth has an electric fire with imitation coal, which you can imitate with tiny pieces of real coal! A clock, some brass ornaments, an oval frameless mirror and a bronze companion set complete the picture.

A Modern Electric Fire (*Plate 87*)

The last pathetic, although efficient, remains of a fireplace is the electric two-bar radiator set into the now superfluous chimney breast. This can be made from card covered with silver foil. The unit ADFC is the curved recess for the bars and can be glued into place. The bars are made from the long spools from an old-fashioned sewing machine (plate 87). These can still be bought cheaply from the sewing machine shops. They are covered with red metal foil and bound round with fuse wire. A switch can be made from wood or card or a small button.

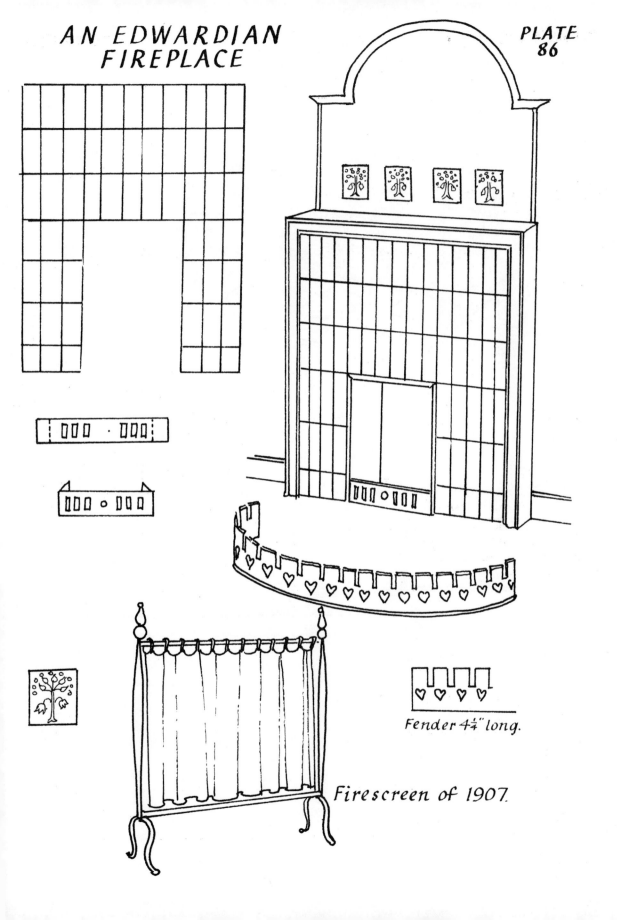

AN EDWARDIAN
FIREPLACE

PLATE
86

Fender 4¼″ long.

Firescreen of 1907.

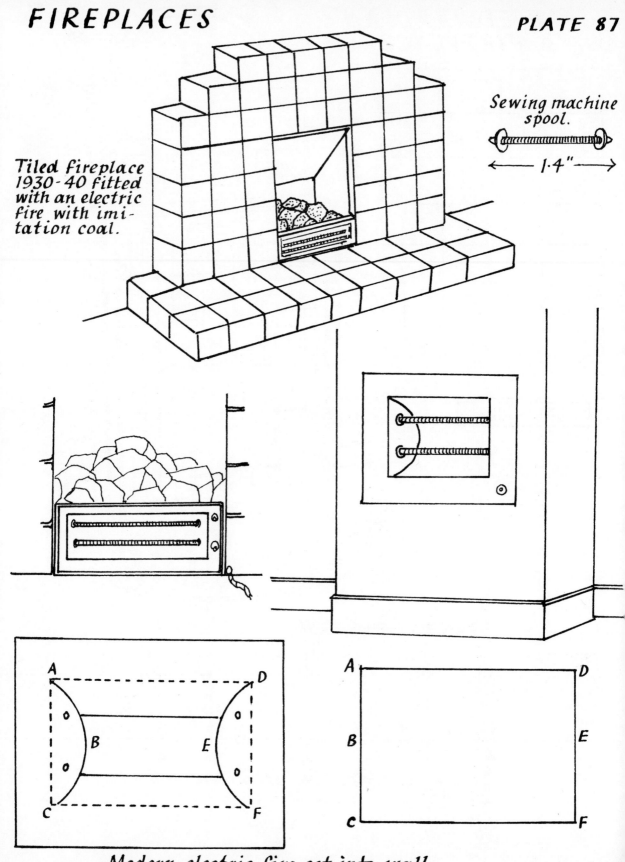

Tiled fireplace 1930-40 fitted with an electric fire with imitation coal.

Sewing machine spool.

← 1·4" →

Modern electric fire set into wall.

Throughout the 18th and 19th Centuries there was little basic change in the nature of these rooms. Their names and the details of decoration changed, but they retained their function until the First World War. Since then, the lack of servants and the rapid development of labour-saving devices run by electricity has made fundamental changes that are familiar to us all.

The rooms of dolls' houses slowly follow the fashions of the day and in the older houses there are large kitchens for servants, and dining-rooms were used exclusively for meals, but some rooms in real houses are rarely copied. These are the breakfast or morning rooms, larders, sculleries and servants' halls.

The pattern of living that followed, until fairly recently, and that reflected in dolls' houses, was for a small, cheerless, utilitarian kitchen, a dining-room that was really a living-room and a 'front' room, lounge or parlour that was reserved for display. The dolls' houses now rarely reflect the older pattern of living experienced only by the very rich, and have begun to copy the way of life developing in the 'sixties which is for a large, comfortable kitchen and one general purpose living-room with the dining table in either, or even both of them.

Regency Drawing-room Suite (Plates 89, 90, 91)

This is a small set of well proportioned furniture. The chairs are under 3 inches high and are $1\frac{3}{4}$ inches wide. The sofa is about the same height and $5\frac{3}{4}$ inches long. The table has an oval marble top $3\frac{3}{4}'' \times 2\frac{3}{4}'' \times 2\frac{1}{2}''$ high. The top rail of the chair and the arms of the sofa are chamfered to make the shape more interesting and the arms are set at a slight angle. The upholstery and padding is difficult to assemble because it needs to be very precise and well shaped. Wadding is laid on card, for which I have given patterns. It should be firm and thicker in the middle. The upholstery material is stretched over this and glued to the back of the card. Any excess is trimmed away. These pads are glued to the wooden structure and trimmed with thin gold edging.

Drawing-room Furniture, 1875–80 (Plate 94)

My drawings show a beautifully coloured set of furniture where the wood is painted black with designs printed on paper that is glued on top of the painted wood. These designs of pink roses and pale blue ribbons on a black ground are most elegant.

The furniture is upholstered in dull green velvet, edged with gold paper held into place by tiny gilt pins.

The odd chair is about the same date and is made of varnished wood with a woven basket-work seat and back.

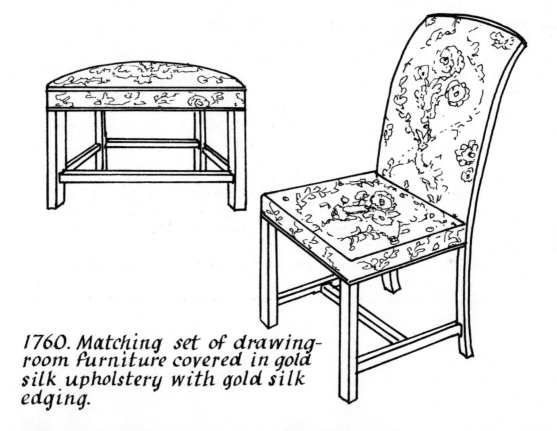

1760. Matching set of drawing-
room furniture covered in gold
silk upholstery with gold silk
edging.

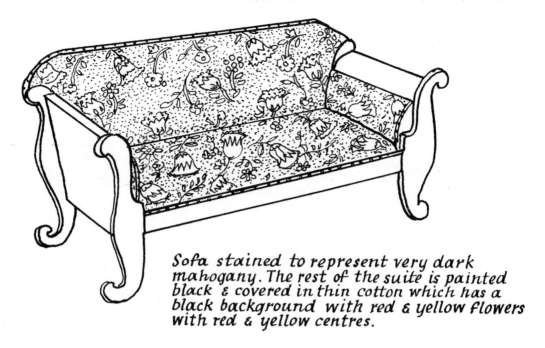

Sofa stained to represent very dark mahogany. The rest of the suite is painted black & covered in thin cotton which has a black background with red & yellow flowers with red & yellow centres.

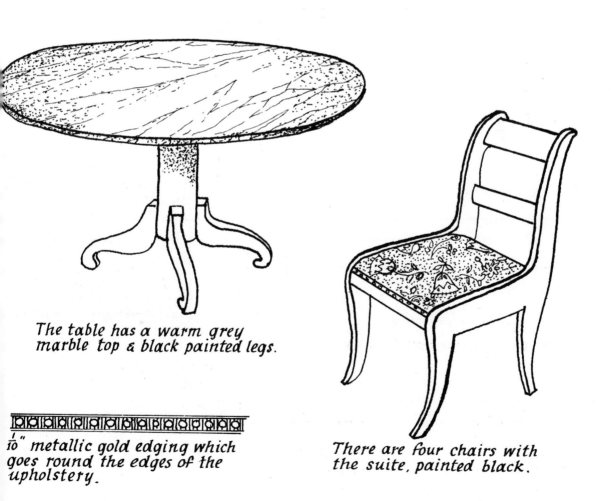

The table has a warm grey marble top & black painted legs.

$\frac{1}{10}$" metallic gold edging which goes round the edges of the upholstery.

There are four chairs with the suite, painted black.

REGENCY CHAIR.

PLATE 90

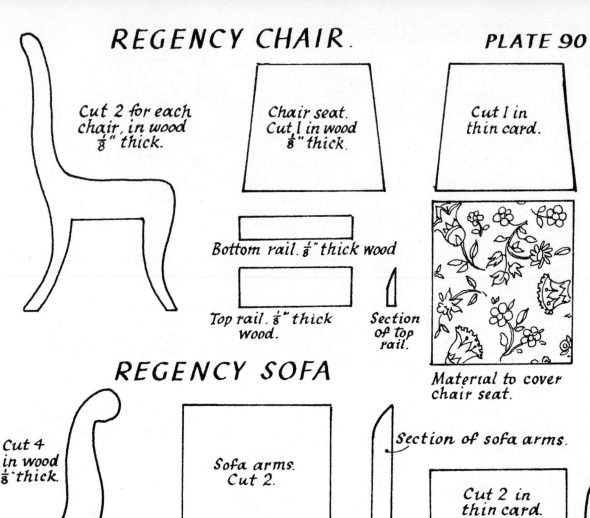

Cut 2 for each chair, in wood ⅛" thick.

Chair seat. Cut 1 in wood ⅛" thick.

Cut 1 in thin card.

Bottom rail. ⅛" thick wood

Top rail. ⅛" thick wood.

Section of top rail.

Material to cover chair seat.

REGENCY SOFA

Cut 4 in wood ⅛" thick.

Sofa arms. Cut 2.

Section of sofa arms.

Cut 2 in thin card.

Section of padding on arm

Material to cover padde arms

Also cut material to cover sofa seat ½" larger all round

Base of sofa. Cut 1 in wood ⅛" thick.

Front facing for sofa ⅛" thick wood

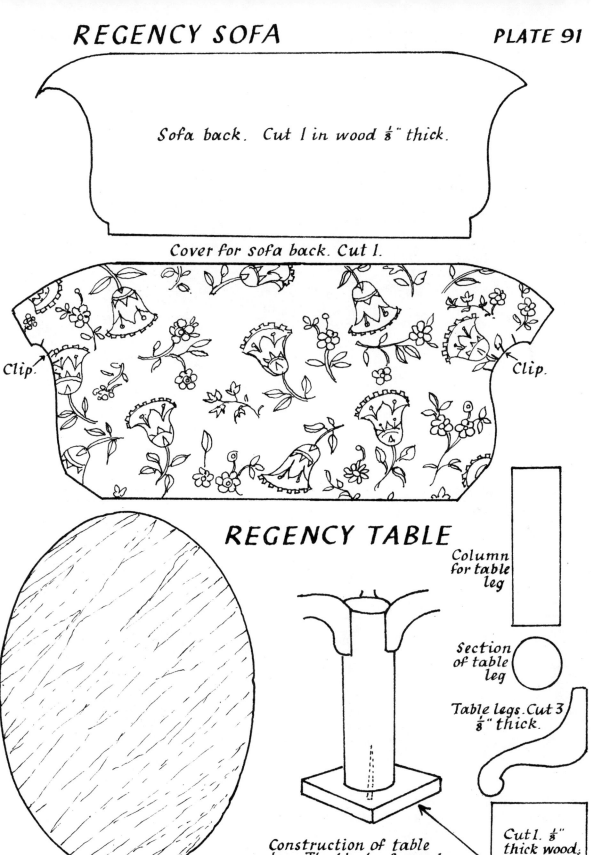

Sofa back. Cut 1 in wood ⅛" thick.

Cover for sofa back. Cut 1.

Clip.

Clip.

REGENCY TABLE

Column for table leg

Section of table leg

Table legs. Cut 3 ⅛" thick.

Construction of table leg. The block of wood gives a larger surface area to glue to the marble.

Cut 1. ⅛" thick wood.

Marbled top. 2⁄10" thick.

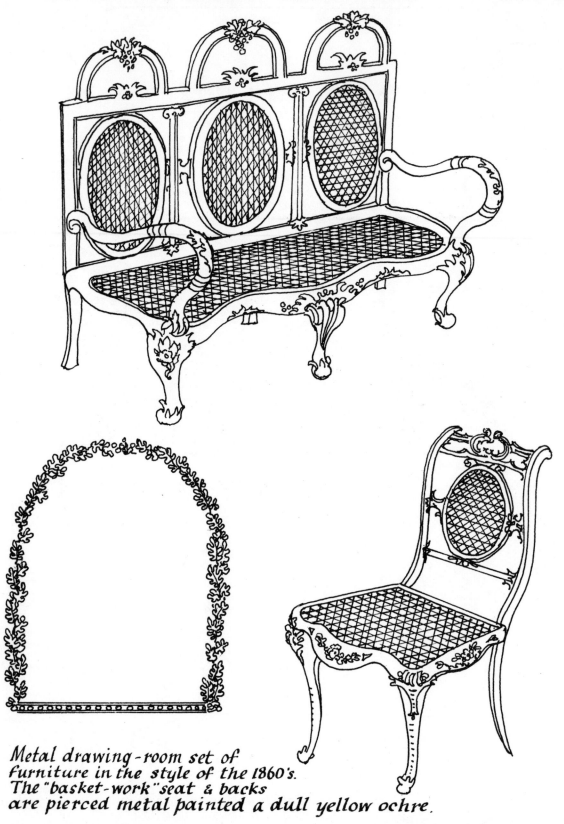

Metal drawing-room set of
furniture in the style of the 1860's.
The "basket-work" seat & backs
are pierced metal painted a dull yellow ochre.

PLATE 93

CHIFFONIER.

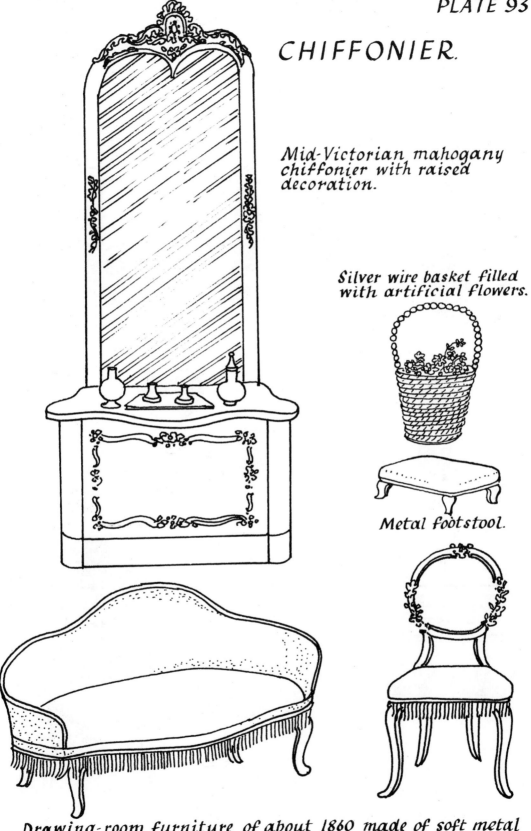

Mid-Victorian mahogany chiffonier with raised decoration.

Silver wire basket filled with artificial flowers.

Metal footstool.

Drawing-room furniture of about 1860 made of soft metal bronzed & upholstered in faded orange velvet with a deep crimson fringe.

PLATE 9

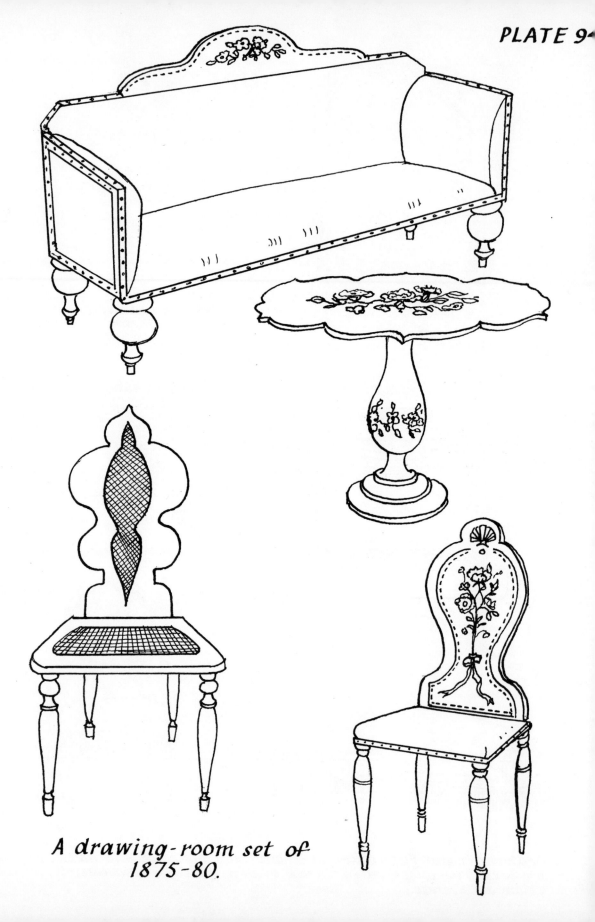

A drawing-room set of 1875-80.

Drawing-room Furniture of 1880 (Plate 95)

This set of furniture from the Salford Museum is in an oval box and each piece is numbered. It is made to represent a pale yellow smooth wood like satinwood and is extremely fragile, well proportioned and delicately put together. There is also a sofa that matches the chairs which are covered in red velvet. The inside of the desk is lined with paper that has a white background covered with minute pink designs. The knobs are of beautifully turned wood.

A Victorian Piano (Plates 99, 100)

This piano is stained and polished as blond mahogany. The base, A, the three side pieces, C, D and E, are all made from wood $\frac{2}{10}$ inch thick and all the other pieces are $\frac{1}{8}$ inch thick. The three legs are turned to a good proportion. The flap is hinged with a piece of material glued to the inside surface. There are only three keys and three black notes and these are hung from the fascia board L by wires.

A Mid-Twentieth Century Armchair (Plates 102, 103)

This chair is made from stiff cardboard, thin card, wood, foam plastic stuffing and cloth. As it is quite small, 3 inches high, $2\frac{1}{4}$ inches wide and 2 inches deep, it needs thin material for the covering and because it is the type of chair suitable for a comfortable lounge, I have used light brown satin.

First cover the seat E in the cloth, glueing the edges to the underside, then glue to the stiff cards A and F, a layer of foam plastic $\frac{1}{4}$ inch thick. The foam plastic on piece A requires to be trimmed until it is only $\frac{1}{10}$ inch thick at the edges. These two pieces are now covered with cloth and the piece F should be finished off by glueing a piece of non-fraying material across the underside. Piece A should be buttoned to give a dimpled look and beads or French knots can be used for this effect. Cover the thin cards, A, B and D with cloth, stretched tight, and with small neat turnings. The covered pieces B are now glued over the shaped wooden arms, C, and these arms are glued to the chair seat, E. The padded back, A, is glued to the arms and seat and a few dressmakers' pins hold this firmly in position. The thin card, A, is now glued to the back of the chair and the piece, G, is covered by a piece of non-fraying material and glued to the bottom of the chair. Four feet are set well back from the edges to raise it without showing themselves. The cushion, F, is best held with a dab of glue.

Obviously a settee can be made to match if the sizes of the seat and back are doubled.

*From a box of dolls'
furniture of 1880.*

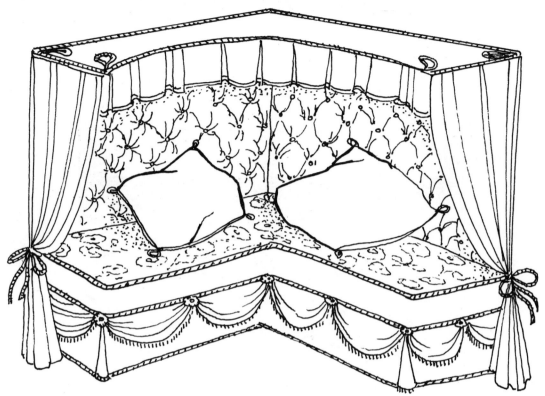

"Cozy corner" of 1890. Gold silk padding & gold braid.

French velvet chair of 1860-70.

A modern English equivalent chair of 1960-70 covered in cream wool.

PLATE 97

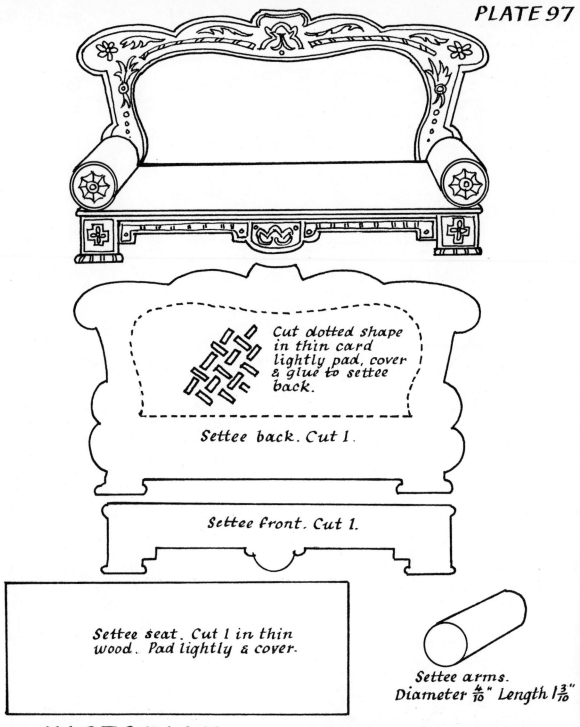

Cut dotted shape
in thin card
lightly pad, cover
& glue to settee
back.

Settee back. Cut 1.

Settee front. Cut 1.

Settee seat. Cut 1 in thin
wood. Pad lightly & cover.

Settee arms.
Diameter $\frac{4}{10}$" Length $1\frac{3}{10}$"

VICTORIAN SOFA

Cheap Victorian sofa of simple construction. The back & front & the front of the arms are covered with ivory-coloured paper, engraved with elaborate black designs. The upholstered seat & back are covered in thin cotton print with a red & black basket-work pattern. The arms are $\frac{4}{10}$" wood dowelling & the rest is of $\frac{1}{8}$" thick wood, all glued together. Such paper-covered furniture was sold in sets of chairs, sofas, cabinets & sideboards.

PLATE 98

Upright piano. 1830-40. 7" high. A solid block of wood covered in black leather with a pretty pleated red silk panel edged with gold.

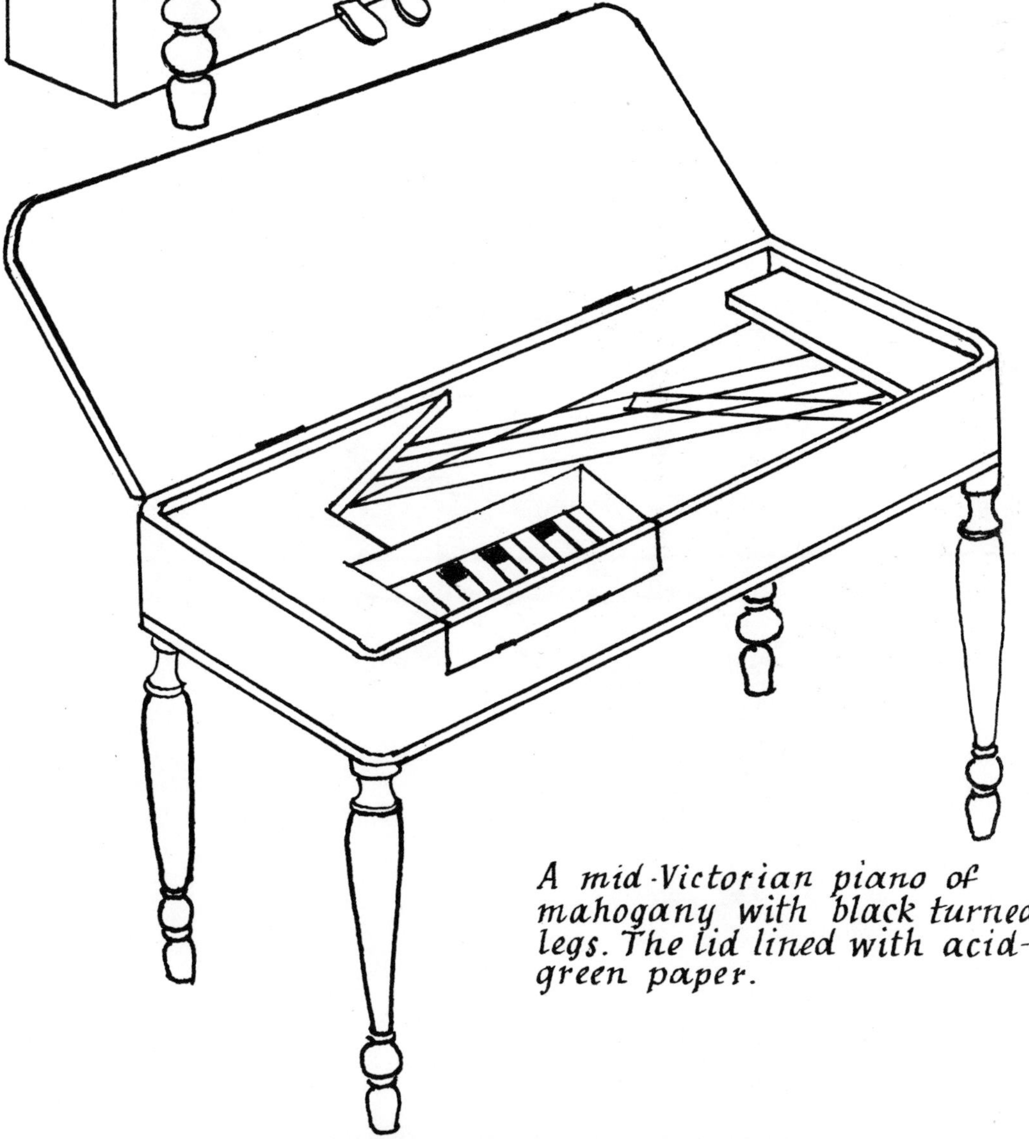

A mid-Victorian piano of mahogany with black turned legs. The lid lined with acid-green paper.

VICTORIAN PIANO

PLATE 99

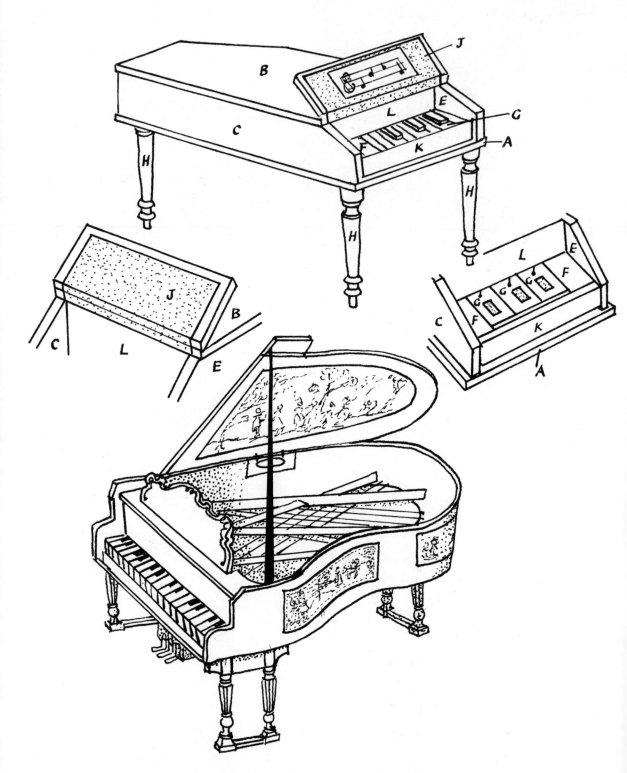

Modern piano made in Japan (plastic)

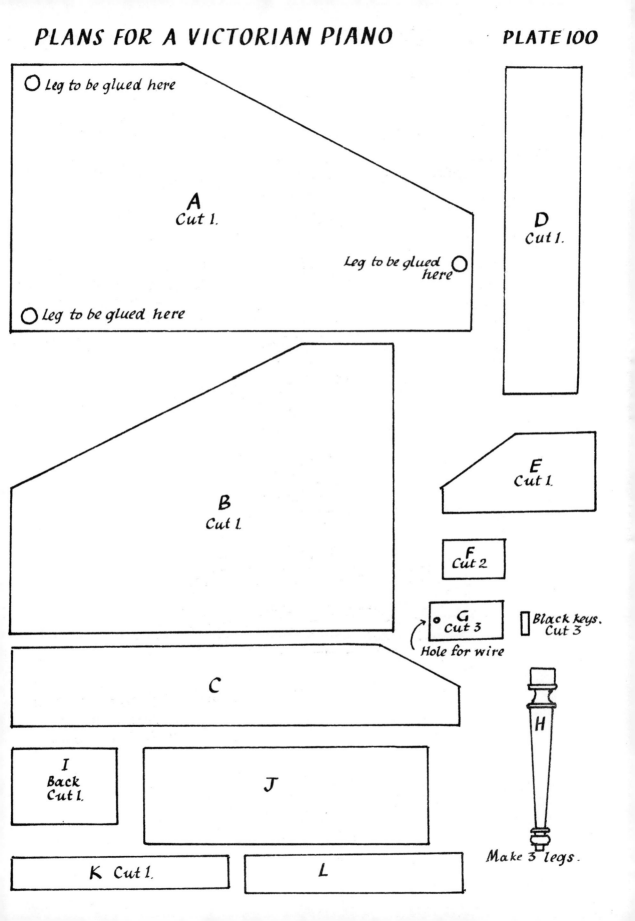

PLANS FOR A VICTORIAN PIANO

PLATE 100

A Cut 1.

Leg to be glued here

Leg to be glued here

Leg to be glued here

D Cut 1.

B Cut 1.

E Cut 1.

F Cut 2

G Cut 3

Hole for wire

Black keys. Cut 3

C

H

I Back Cut 1.

J

Make 3 legs.

K Cut 1.

L

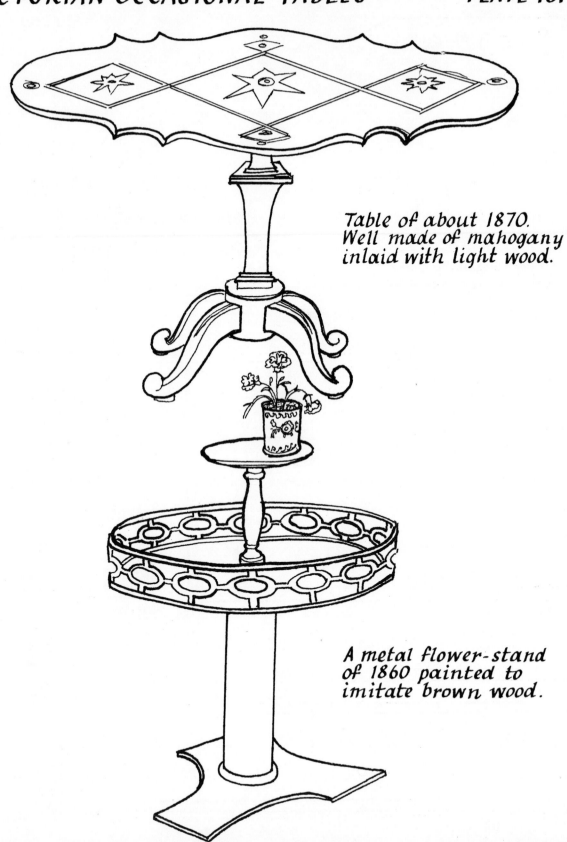

Table of about 1870. Well made of mahogany inlaid with light wood.

A metal flower-stand of 1860 painted to imitate brown wood.

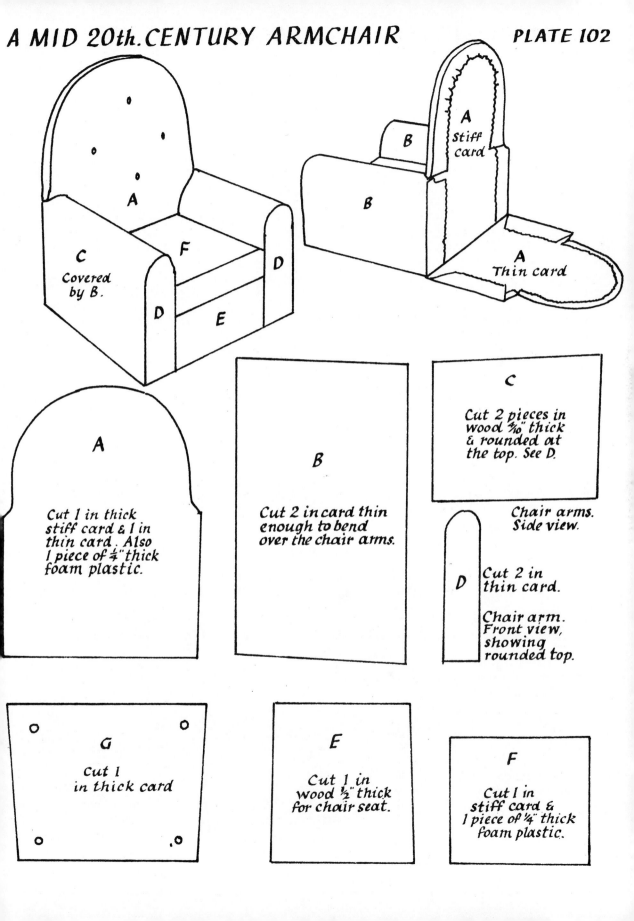

A
Stiff
card

B

A
Thin card

B

A
Covered
by B.

C

F

D

D

E

A

Cut 1 in thick
stiff card & 1 in
thin card. Also
1 piece of ¼" thick
foam plastic.

B

Cut 2 in card thin
enough to bend
over the chair arms.

C

Cut 2 pieces in
wood ³⁄₁₀" thick
& rounded at
the top. See D.

Chair arms.
Side view.

D

Cut 2 in
thin card.

Chair arm.
Front view,
showing
rounded top.

G

Cut 1
in thick card

E

Cut 1 in
wood ½" thick
for chair seat.

F

Cut 1 in
stiff card &
1 piece of ¼" thick
foam plastic.

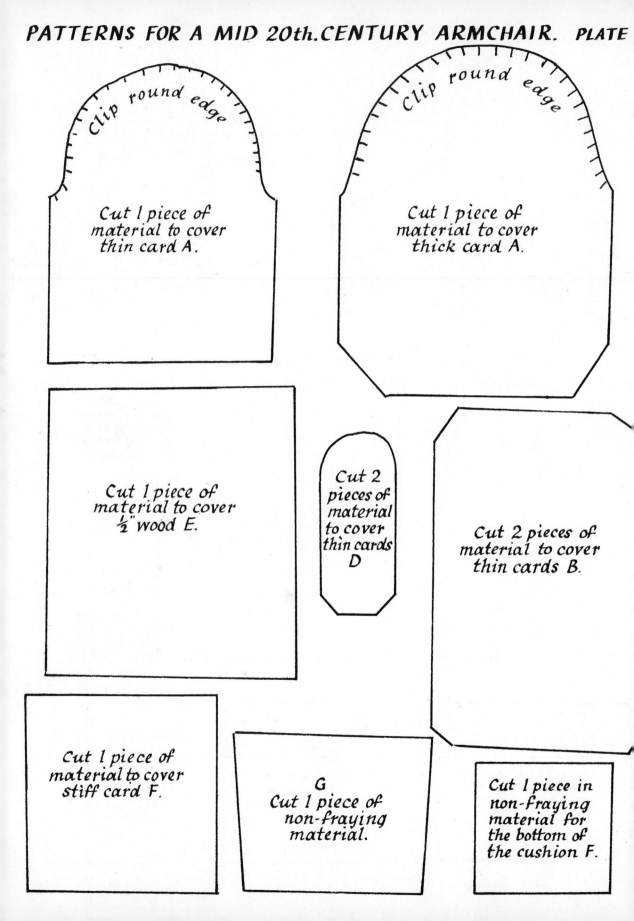

Clip round edge

Cut 1 piece of material to cover thin card A.

Clip round edge

Cut 1 piece of material to cover thick card A.

Cut 1 piece of material to cover ½" wood E.

Cut 2 pieces of material to cover thin cards D

Cut 2 pieces of material to cover thin cards B.

Cut 1 piece of material to cover stiff card F.

G
Cut 1 piece of non-fraying material.

Cut 1 piece in non-fraying material for the bottom of the cushion F.

A Telescopic Table (Plate 104)

This is a very well made Victorian expanding dining table. It is complicated to reproduce. It is $4\frac{1}{10}$ inches long by $3\frac{1}{10}$ inches wide by $2\frac{4}{10}$ inches high and it expands to $5\frac{6}{10}$ inches when the leaf is inserted. It is stained and polished to a light golden mahogany. My drawing shows the top upside down without the legs, so that you see the four runners, G, in position. The two outer runners are glued to one half of the table with the broad side of the runner facing downwards. The other runners are slotted into these with the broad edge facing upwards and they are glued to the other half of the table. The two pieces E and F are glued across the runners, one at each end, and their purpose is to stop the table coming into two halves when it is opened to take the extra leaf, which is $1\frac{1}{2}$ inches wide. The four square corner pieces, D, are glued into position $\frac{2}{10}$ inches from the outer edge and the side pieces, B and C are fitted between them and they have to be adjusted to make a good fit. Lastly the four turned legs are glued into place.

In the process of making this table, it is a good idea to keep assembling it with and without the extra leaf to ensure that everything is being glued into its correct place.

A Gate-Legged Table (Plates 105, 106)

This table was made of $\frac{1}{4}$ inch thick mahogany. It is simplest to stain and polish before assembly. The table is made by first laying the piece marked B and the two pieces marked A in position on a flat surface wrong side up. A piece of adhesive tape $4'' \times 3''$, with the corners cut away, is pressed on to these pieces and it will serve instead of metal hinges. Piece C is glued to the centre of piece B and the legs, D, are glued to each corner of this piece. The swinging legs are made by glueing the spindles E to the legs, D, as indicated in plate 106. Through the free ends of the pieces E, put the rigid wires which also go through the two pieces of wood marked C. The second piece of wood marked C is glued to the table legs $\frac{7}{10}$ inch from the bottom.

Living-room and Dining-room Suite, 1970 (Plates 111, 112, 113)

The recently developed pattern of living that centres round a large kitchen and a living room with a dining area calls for a new arrangement of furniture.

The set I have drawn is for a 1970 dolls' house and I have included not only the table and stand chairs, but patterns for a matching settee and easy chairs. These would, in real life, be of laminated wood, lacquered in black, white or strong clear colours. To dolls' house size it can be made in ply or in laminated card. A smooth finish is essential for this type of furniture.

The cushions should be made from lightweight plastic less than $\frac{1}{2}$ inch thick. They should be covered in a modern print or a moygashel fabric with a slightly rough weave.

The table I have drawn has alternative patterns for the top so that it can be made either as a dining table or a coffee table. I have drawn it with a transparent top which could be of Perspex. This would be safer than glass. It should be glued to the table top with Araldite.

A Victorian Slopstone (Plate 120)

Very few old dolls' houses have a sink in them, although they are crammed with stoves and cooking utensils. Presumably this is because the sink was usually in the scullery and water was carried everywhere. Not many real houses retain their old slopstone, so I include a drawing and patterns for one. I tried to make individual bricks, for the piers, of Plastone, but they shrank and warped. I therefore made solid wooden blocks which I painted with poster colour to imitate bricks, varying the shades of individual bricks and making the joins with a heavy pencil line that dented the soft wood slightly. The sink itself is made from five pieces of soft wood glued together and the edges are sandpapered to simulate wear. The slopstone in reality would be of stone, or yellow or brown saltglaze pottery. It would be excellent to make one of actual fired clay but the painted wood can serve very well. In older houses there would have been a pump rather than a tap. The slopstones are shallow so that there is room for tubs and buckets. Wastepipes and stand pipes can be made of soft wire, or metal rods.

The top of the draining board can be painted, to represent sandstone, in poster colour, thickly applied and stippled with a stencil brush. While I was making the slopstone, I noticed in the garden a piece of old stone that was flaking into layers about $\frac{1}{16}$ inch thick. With care I was able to cut this with a fretsaw so that it could be glued to a piece of wood, to hold it together, and used for the draining slab. It pays to have a good look round before embarking on anything for there is a surprising amount of adaptable material to hand about the house. Wooden butter pats, with their finely grooved faces, make the most realistic draining boards.

TELESCOPIC TABLE

PLATE 104

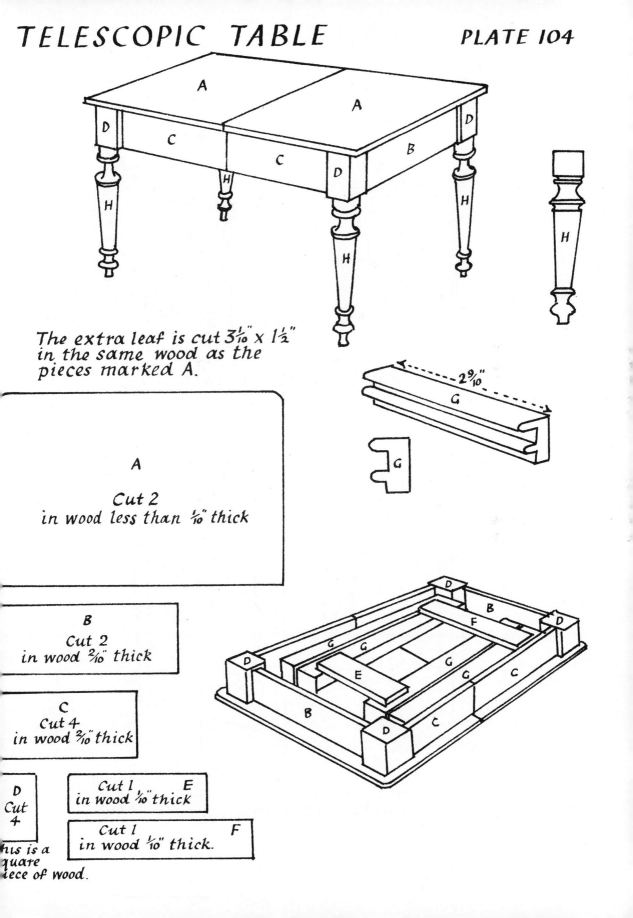

The extra leaf is cut $3\frac{1}{10}"$ x $1\frac{1}{2}"$ in the same wood as the pieces marked A.

$2\frac{9}{10}"$

A

Cut 2
in wood less than $\frac{1}{10}"$ thick

B
Cut 2
in wood $\frac{2}{10}"$ thick

C
Cut 4
in wood $\frac{2}{10}"$ thick

D
Cut 4

This is a square piece of wood.

Cut 1   **E**
in wood $\frac{1}{10}"$ thick

Cut 1   **F**
in wood $\frac{1}{10}"$ thick.

Edwardian refectory table in light oak.

Victorian mahogany gate-legged table.

A GATE-LEGGED TABLE

PLATE 106

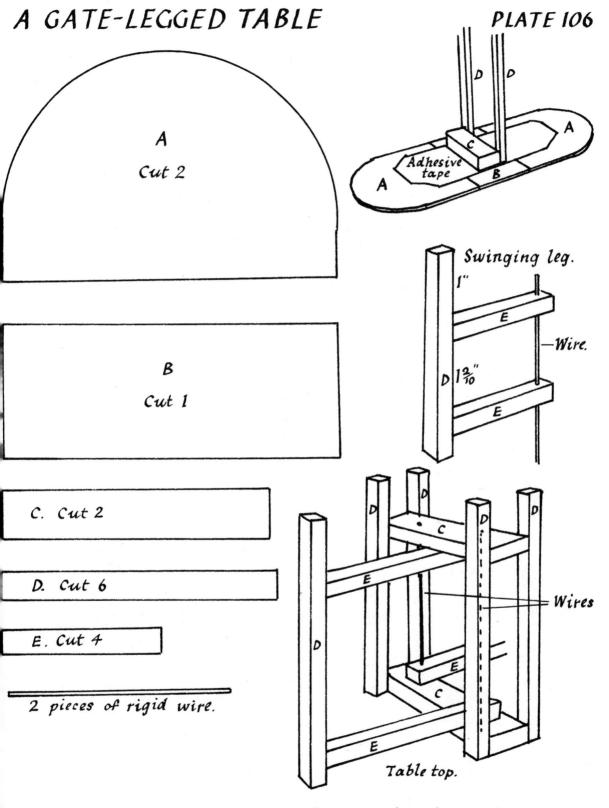

A
Cut 2

B
Cut 1

C. Cut 2

D. Cut 6

E. Cut 4

2 pieces of rigid wire.

Adhesive tape

Swinging leg.

1"

D $1\frac{2}{10}$"

Wire.

Wires

Table top.

Construction of table legs.
(The table is turned wrong
side up.)

Dining-chair, covered
in grey silk. 1740.

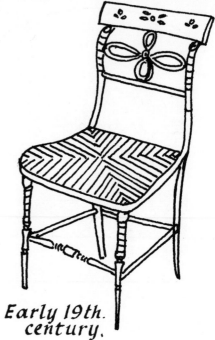

Early 19th.
century.

Late 19th. century chair.

Chair, c. 1880.

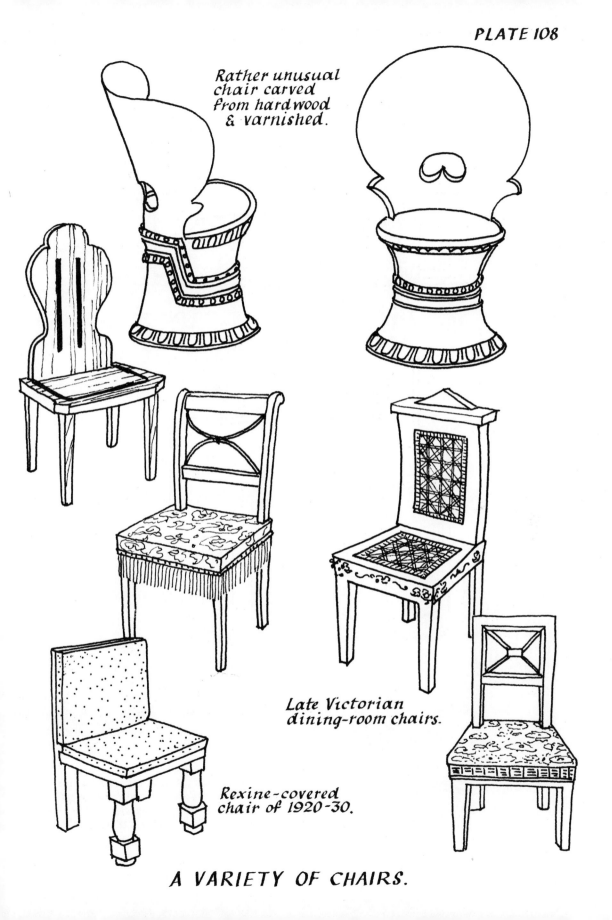

PLATE 108

Rather unusual
chair carved
from hardwood
& varnished.

Late Victorian
dining-room chairs.

Rexine-covered
chair of 1920-30.

A VARIETY OF CHAIRS.

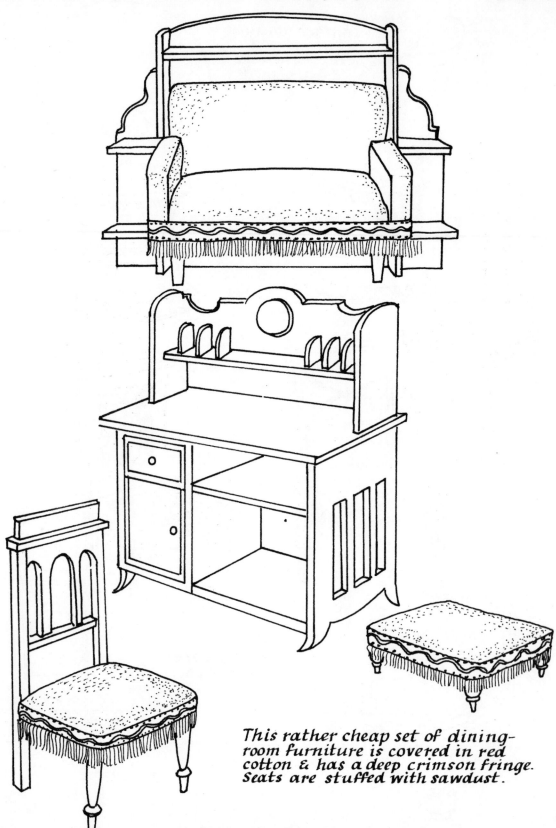

This rather cheap set of dining-
room furniture is covered in red
cotton & has a deep crimson fringe.
Seats are stuffed with sawdust.

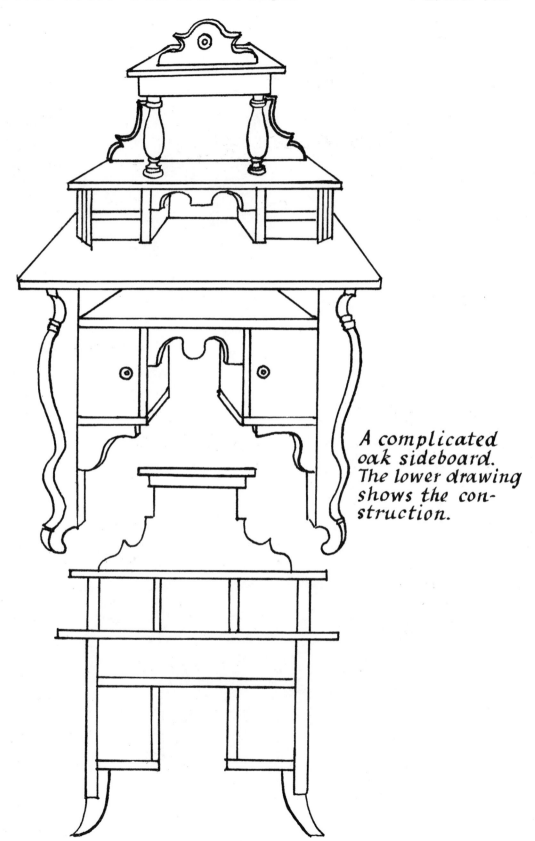

A complicated oak sideboard. The lower drawing shows the construction.

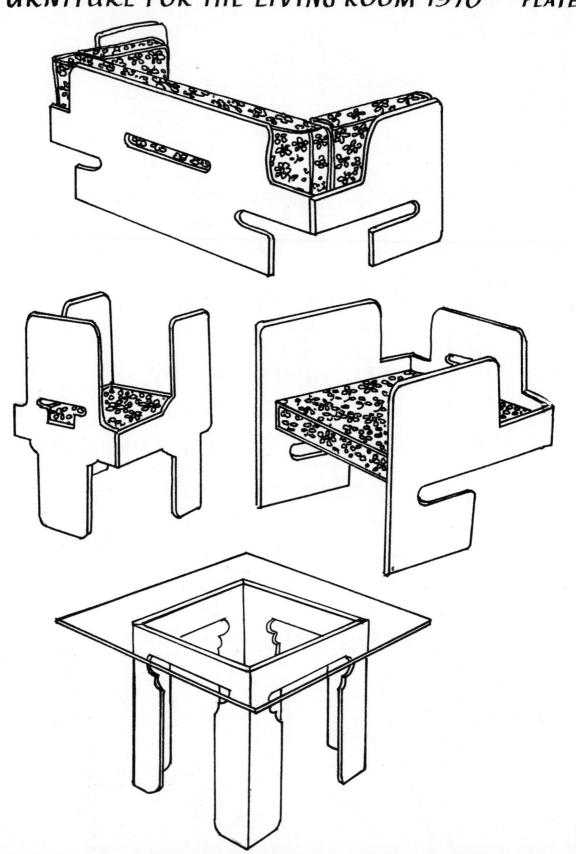

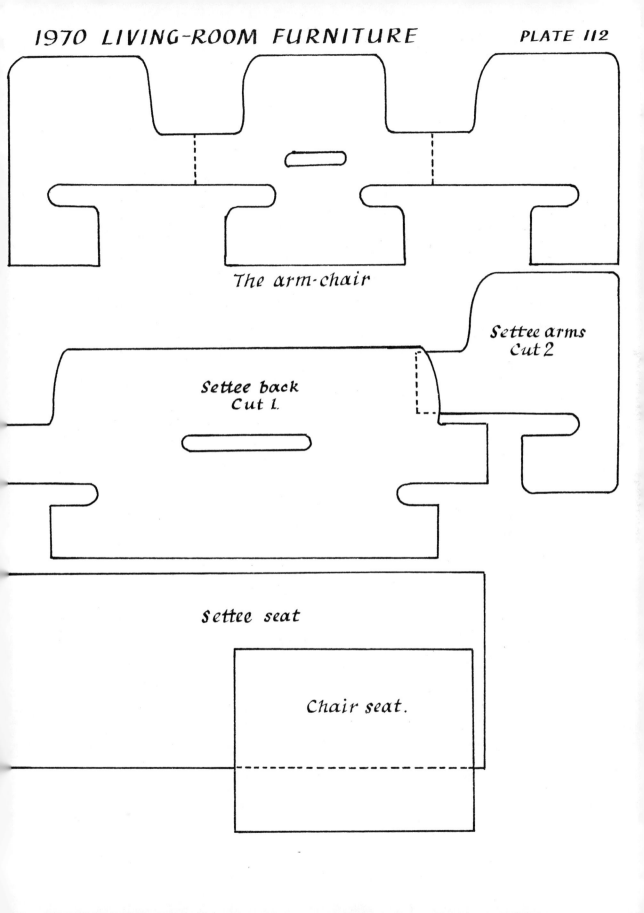

The arm-chair

Settee arms
Cut 2

Settee back
Cut 1.

Settee seat

Chair seat.

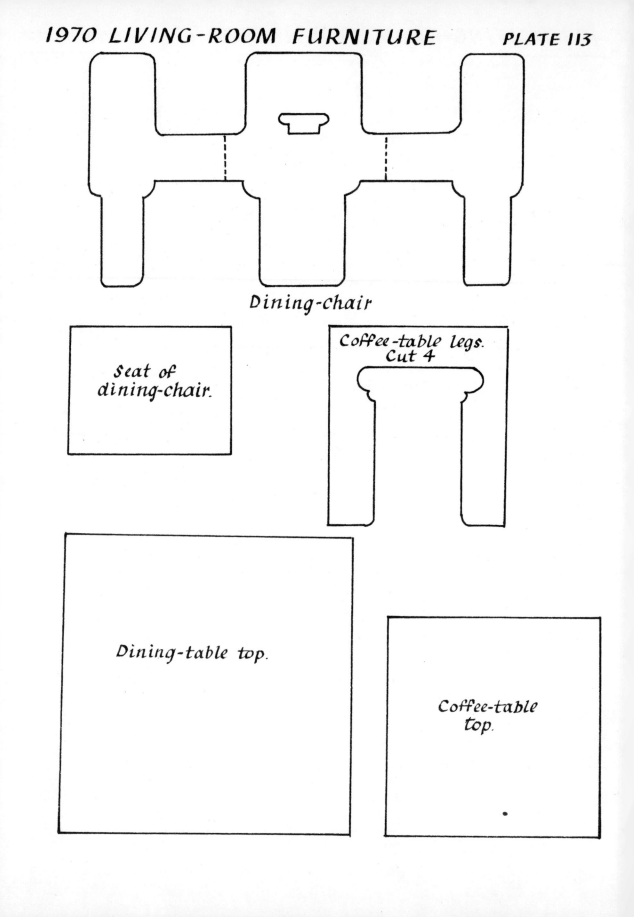

Dining-chair

Seat of
dining-chair.

Coffee-table legs.
Cut 4

Dining-table top.

Coffee-table
top.

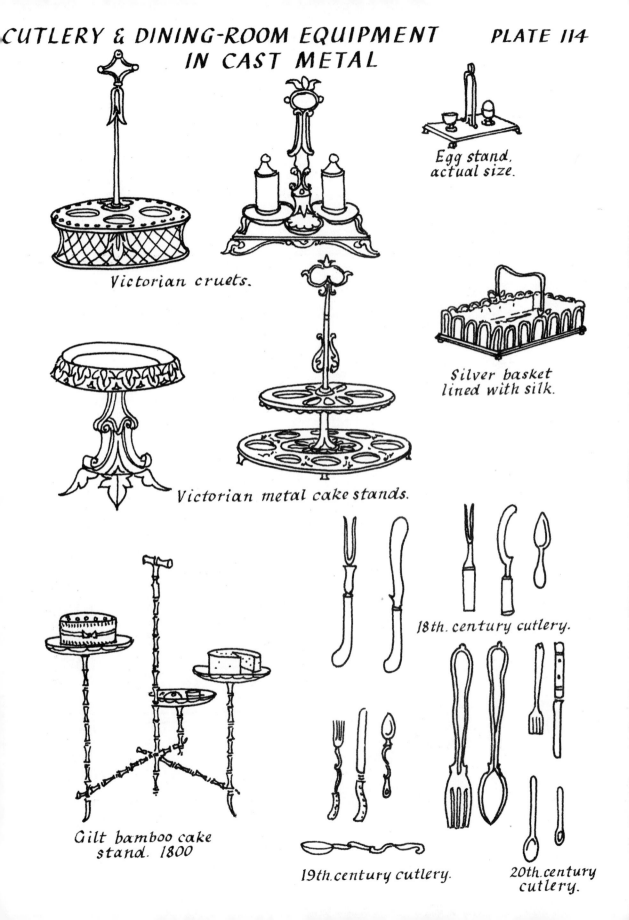

Egg stand,
actual size.

Victorian cruets.

Silver basket
lined with silk.

Victorian metal cake stands.

18th. century cutlery.

Gilt bamboo cake
stand. 1800

19th. century cutlery.

20th. century
cutlery.

A Victorian knife-box.

A modern knife-box

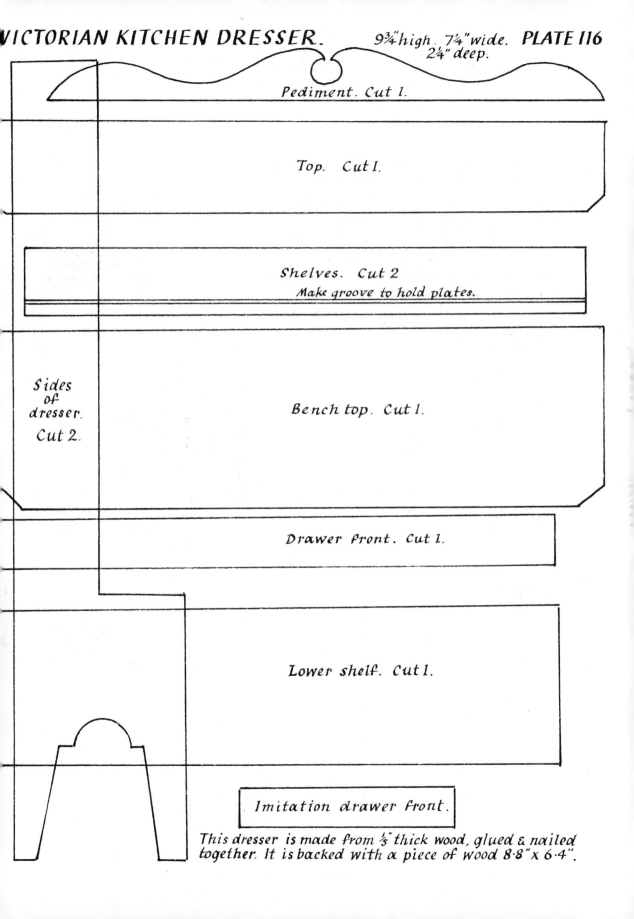

Pediment. Cut 1.

Top.   Cut 1.

Shelves. Cut 2
Make groove to hold plates.

Sides
of
dresser.

Cut 2.

Bench top. Cut 1.

Drawer front. Cut 1.

Lower shelf. Cut 1.

Imitation drawer front.

This dresser is made from ⅛" thick wood, glued & nailed together. It is backed with a piece of wood 8·8" x 6·4".

1910-20 KITCHEN CHAIR & SETTLE.

This is furniture made in the early part of the 20th. century. It is made from wood which is stained to represent dark oak, & is fitted with cushions. Linen, with a Jacobean pattern, or ging-ham would make suitable covers for the cushions.

Part G, which is the piece of wood that holds the chair seat, is set at an angle.

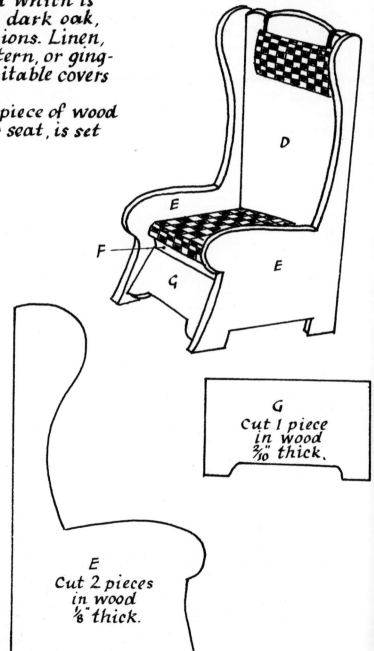

F
Cut 1 piece in wood. 2/10" thick.

D
Cut 1 piece in wood 2/10" thick.

G
Cut 1 piece in wood 2/10" thick.

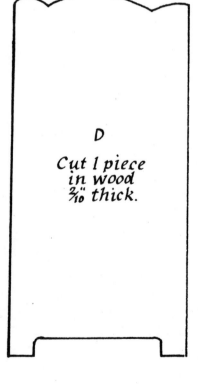

D
Cut 1 piece in wood 2/10" thick.

E
Cut 2 pieces in wood 1/8" thick.

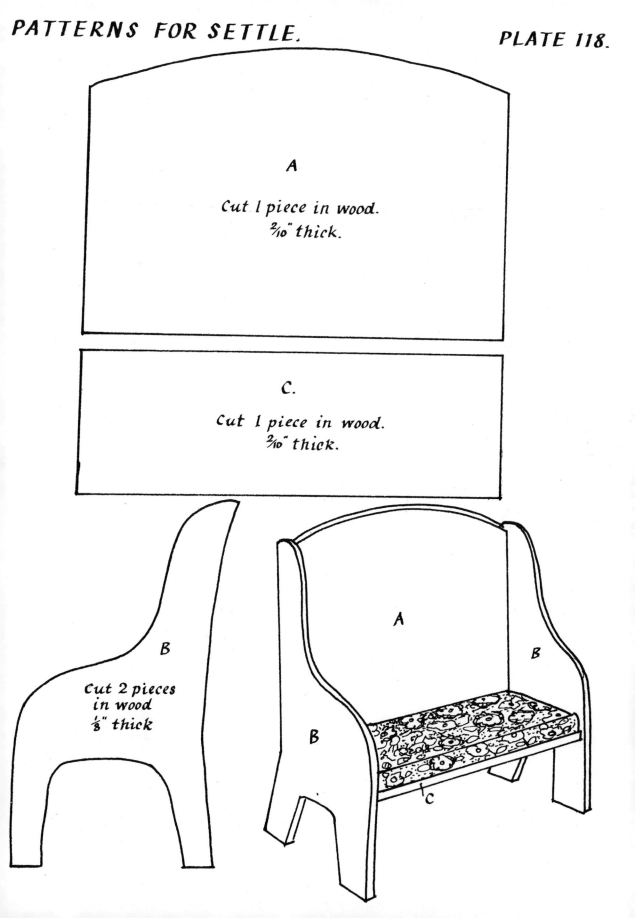

A

Cut 1 piece in wood.
²/₁₀" thick.

C.

Cut 1 piece in wood.
²/₁₀" thick.

B

Cut 2 pieces
in wood
⅛" thick

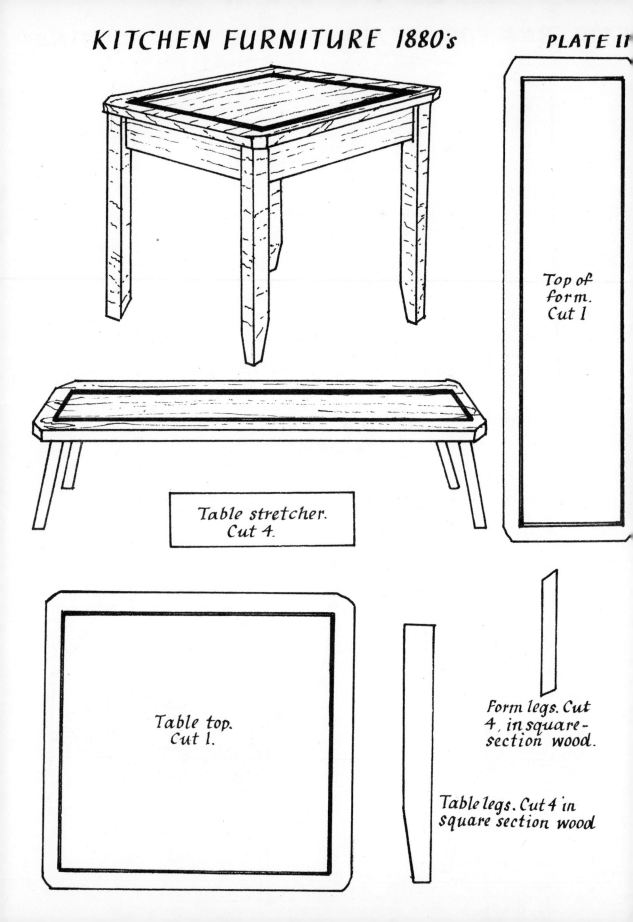

Top of
form.
Cut 1

Table stretcher.
Cut 4.

Table top.
Cut 1.

Form legs. Cut
4, in square-
section wood.

Table legs. Cut 4 in
square section wood

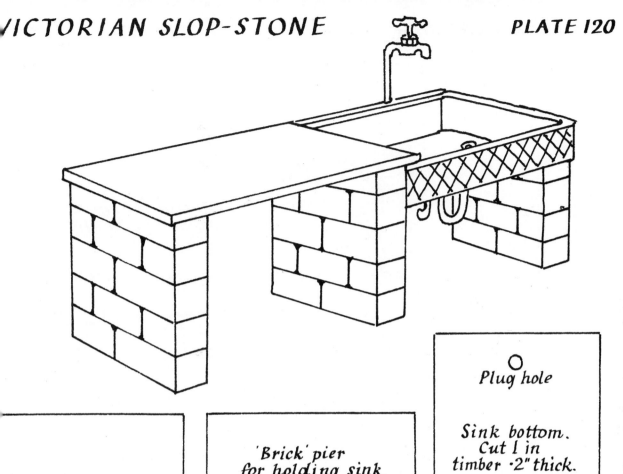

O

Plug hole

Sink bottom.
Cut 1 in
timber ·2" thick.

'Brick' pier
for holding sink.
Cut 1 in
timber ·4" thick.

'Brick' piers for
holding draining board.
Cut 1 in
timber ·4" thick.

Long side of sink
Cut 2 in
timber ·2" thick.

Short side of sink. Cut 2
in timber ·2" thick.

'Stone' draining board.
Cut 1
in timber ·2" thick.

Cut 1.

Piece of wood to
be glued to middle
brick pier to
support sink.

KITCHEN CABINET & SINK OF THE 20th. CENTURY. PL. 1

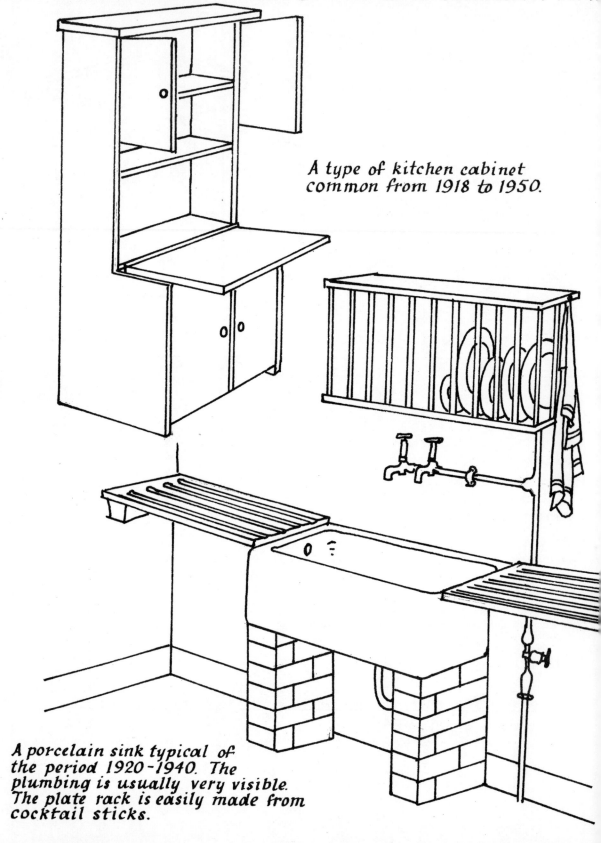

A type of kitchen cabinet common from 1918 to 1950.

A porcelain sink typical of the period 1920-1940. The plumbing is usually very visible. The plate rack is easily made from cocktail sticks.

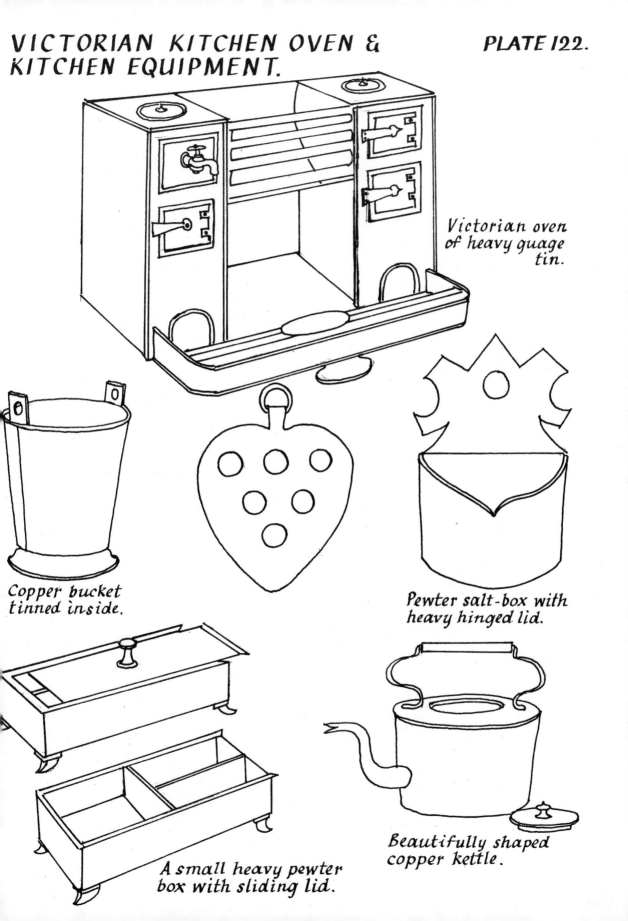

Victorian oven of heavy guage tin.

Copper bucket tinned inside.

Pewter salt-box with heavy hinged lid.

A small heavy pewter box with sliding lid.

Beautifully shaped copper kettle.

PLATE 123.

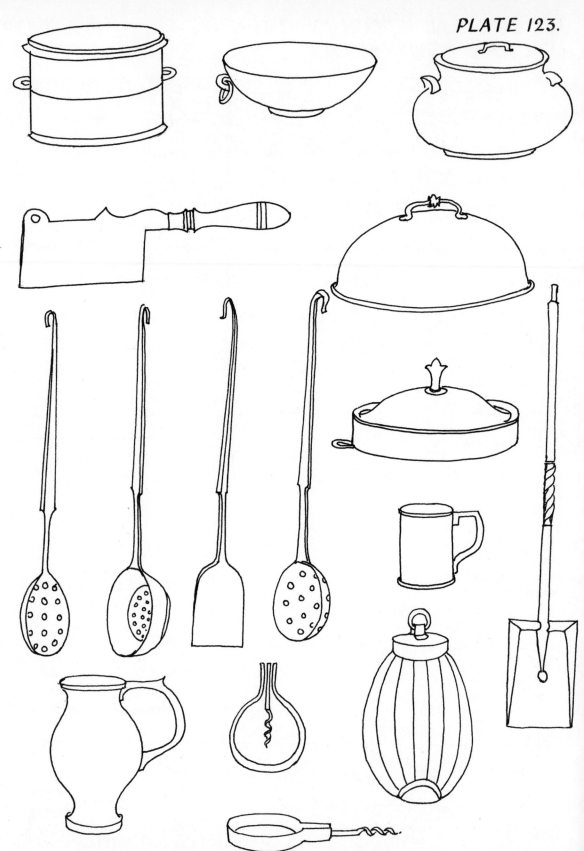

A set of Victorian kitchen utensils of brass, copper, pewter iron & tin

KITCHEN EQUIPMENT.

PLATE 124.

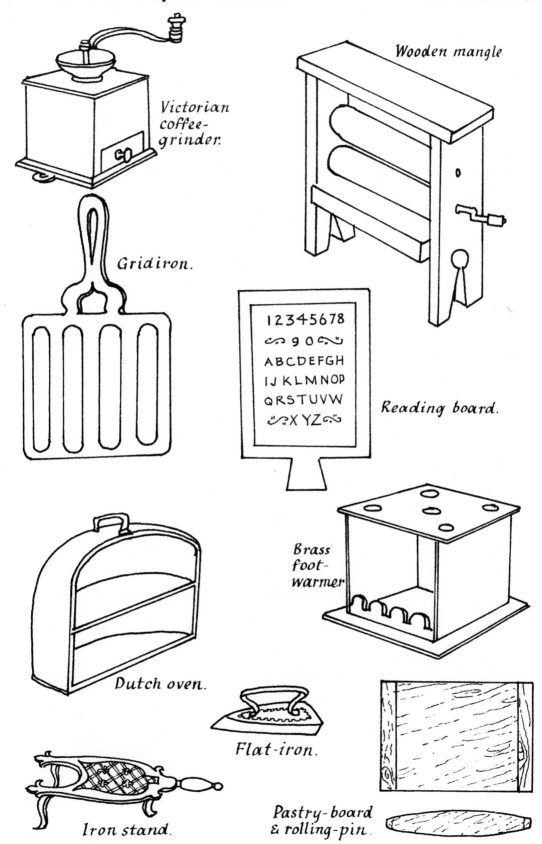

Victorian coffee-grinder.

Wooden mangle

Gridiron.

1 2 3 4 5 6 7 8
9 0
A B C D E F G H
I J K L M N O P
Q R S T U V W
X Y Z

Reading board.

Brass foot-warmer

Dutch oven.

Flat-iron.

Iron stand.

Pastry-board & rolling-pin.

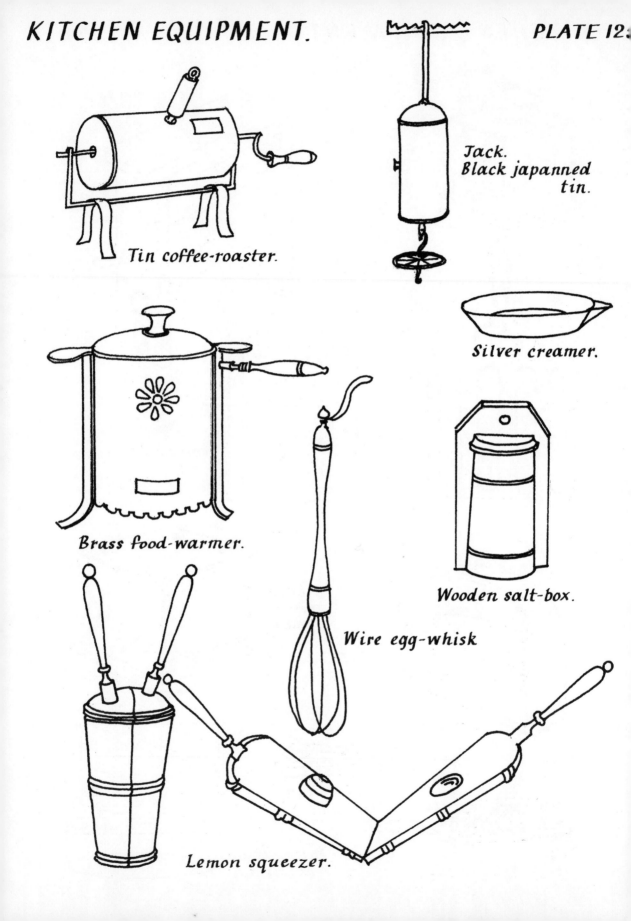

KITCHEN EQUIPMENT.

Tin coffee-roaster.

Jack.
Black japanned
tin.

Silver creamer.

Brass food-warmer.

Wooden salt-box.

Wire egg-whisk

Lemon squeezer.

Food (Plates 126, 127)

Little dolls' house food remains from before the nineteenth century. Perhaps it was rarely made.

Mrs. Vivien Greene writes that the only 18th-Century food she has seen was a tongue and a chicken made of wax, so maybe the nature of the material accounts for its disappearance.

I have seen old dolls' house food in the Utrecht dolls' house that dates from 1674–90. There is a 300-year-old duck and some equally ancient fruit and there is food in preserving bottles and barrels of dried fish, peas, rice and groats. By the beginning of the 19th Century, model food was quite plentiful although it was at first rather large in scale. It was made of plaster, bisque and wood, decorated with plaster cream and icing. The early Victorian, and especially the European manufacturers, seemed very fond of large pieces of raw meat which furnished the popular butchers' shops of the eighteen-forties.

You can now buy very well made cakes and vegetables, sold separately or arranged on produce stalls. The fruit and vegetables are good and the Christmas cake, with its miniature paper frill and ribbon is excellent. I feel that naturalism at all costs is the first consideration if you are making dolls' house food. It should be easily recognisable so there is little point in trying to imitate stews and porridge. Quickly recognised shapes such as those of fish, eggs and sausages are more appropriate. It should be remembered that there are fashions in food. A pig's head with an orange in its mouth is not today found in many private homes.

There are paintings of still life in the 17th and 18th Centuries that depict food of the times, such as Oudrey's beautiful white hedgehog pudding, and there are blancmanges, sorbets, cottage loaves, large cheeses, trifles and raised pies. Present-day foods that can readily be imitated are: plates of fish and chips, sliced loaves, tomatoes, grape-fruit, bottles of milk and basin-shaped Christmas puddings instead of the football-shaped ones of the past. This all makes modern food sound rather dreary, which I do not believe to be the case, quite the reverse, but 'convenience' foods are newly invented and appropriate for a modern dolls' house.

The coloured illustrations in Mrs. Beeton's Cookery Book are a help when making late Victorian food. They can be amusingly horrifying, as are the two suckling pigs lying head to tail on a single dish with their decapitated heads alongside, and all the ducks, hens, rabbits and hares sit in naturalistic positions complete with heads.

When making food for a modern dolls' house, it can be copied directly from life or from mouth-watering illustrations in glossy magazines.

Such food can be made from several materials. There is a self-hardening clay called Plastone and a clay that can be fired at home called Sculpy. The latter is sold in the U.S.A., but I have not seen it yet in England. Food can be carved from plaster of paris or cast in a mould. A dolls' house kitchen usually contains some sort of pattypan or bowl that will serve as a mould. The tin lids from packets of herbs and spices will make moulds for round cakes and the china pots for watercolour paints make moulds for square cakes. Another useful modelling material is made by mixing equal quantities of salt and flour, moistened with water. This makes good bread, scones, cakes and pastries for when baked hard in a slow oven it has the right colour and texture. A light wash of milk or egg yolk on top of each piece before baking gives them a nice shiny brown surface.

Another recipe for a modelling material is easy to use and cheap to make and it is called cornstarch clay. It can be used instead of Plastone or Barbola paste. It is very white and has a rather crunchy texture. Heat 1 cup of salt with $\frac{1}{3}$rd cup of water until it begins to boil. Remove it from the heat and mix in half a cup of cornstarch. (Cornflour in England, not ordinary flour.) Stir until it has the consistency of stiff dough and if it does not thicken return it to the heat until it does. Knead this dough until it is malleable. Small objects made of this material will harden in one or two days, depending on their bulk and the temperature of the room. They can then be painted. This cornstarch clay will keep for some time if it is sealed in a plastic bag with the air excluded, or put in a sealed container. This material can be modelled, or moulded by pressing it into a suitably shaped container. The possibilities are endless, for if this material is rolled into a length of half an inch diameter and then cut into slices it can be pricked with a knitting needle to make crumpets. The quality of the imitation lies in the perfection of the final painting and I would recommend a wide range of paints; watercolours, tempera, matt oil, gloss paint, varnish and so on, because food has so many varied textures. For example, I made a dish of clear soup by pouring brown varnish into a dish and leaving it to harden. Sausages, bacon and fruit might well be modelled in coloured wax, because of the texture. Once you have embarked on this manufacture of food, you will find yourself carried away by the possibilities. There are the lovely well-risen cakes baked in tin lids with the salt and flour mixture, decorated with almonds (grains of rice) and the sacks of potatoes made from Plastone rolled in cocoa. There are miniature eggs in a straw-lined basket, and strings of onions modelled in Plastone with a piece of cotton thread through each onion so that they can be tied to the central piece of string. There are wax cherries with brown linen thread for stems, plates of spaghetti made this time with the real thing, the very thinnest vermicelli, relaxed in boiling water, coiled on to a miniature dish, left to harden and topped with red plaster meat sauce. These thin strands of vermicelli will also serve as drinking straws.

I particularly enjoy seeing such an excess of food displayed along the front of the kitchen floor of a doll's house, or even arranged outside on lovely dishes as they are in the London Museum outside Maude Mary Landsdowne's dolls' house. This has a magnificent collection of food; sirloins, lobsters, fish of all kinds, a chicken complete with its head tucked under its wing, cakes and vegetables, and a half section of a pig's head painted in a most decorative manner, rather like a painting by Paul Klee. All this is on white china plates with green and gold rims.

VICTORIAN DOLLS' HOUSE FOOD.

19th. century German bisque pie.

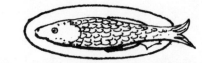

19th. century German bisque Food.

Almond cake.

Edwardian bread.

German 19th. century.

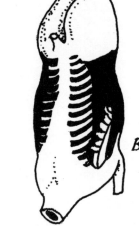

Butchers' meat. 1840

Eggs in a basket.

Victorian glass dome.

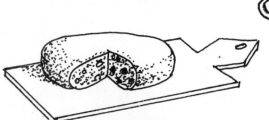

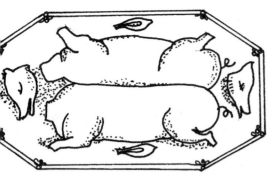

Sucking pig.

Cake frill.

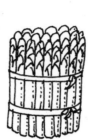

Asparagus

Pineapple.

Plaster leg of lamb.

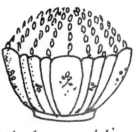

Sausages

Cod's head.

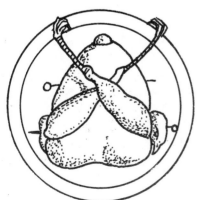

Trussed woodcock.

String of onions.

Hedgehog pudding.

Until the end of the 18th Century most beds were four-posters, heavily curtained to keep out the draughts. These curtains were often elaborate, fringed and tasselled, and the finest beds had canopies topped with angels, crowns, eagles and ostrich feathers. The most splendid beds were made at the end of the 17th and the beginning of the 18th Centuries.

Some of the beds in the early Nuremburg dolls' houses were placed along the walls and they were very high, requiring a stepladder to get into them. The mattresses were thick and filled with down and they had enormous embroidered pillows and heavy curtains. English dolls' house beds are much lower and there is a fine one made in 1760 which still has its original ivory silk draperies and laced sacking base. It has oak posts with urn shaped finials.

During the eighteen-thirties and 'forties, the field bed became fashionable. At first these beds had curved canopies with curtains that hid the supports, but soon the posts were abandoned and rods to support the curtains were fixed to the wall. At the same time, we find the first of the half-testers appearing in dolls' houses. These eventually became the standard dolls' house bed and although the low-ended metal beds became fashionable after the Great Exhibition of 1851, dolls' houses usually remained faithful to the half-tester.

Similarly, the most popular French dolls' house beds were in the style of the Second Empire, placed lengthways to the wall with draperies falling from a single central rod. By the end of the 19th Century, metal framed beds were practically universal, made of iron or brass, and some still retained small side-wings. Edwardian beds were usually of wood, elaborately constructed, but by the 'twenties they were of lighter weight and usually railed at the ends. Panelled head boards were fashionable from the 'thirties until after the Second World War, when the foot board was abandoned, and finally the head board followed it, to leave us with that most basic of objects, the divan. Needless to say, this ultimate in simplicity has been followed by a vogue for padded head boards, canopied beds and four-posters.

A Victorian Half-tester Bed (Plates 131, 132)

Among my bits and pieces, I had a broken Victorian letter rack made of papiermâché and I used the pieces from this to make a half-tester bed. From the shaped back piece I cut the foot of the bed as shown in plate 131. There was a hole near the top and I covered this on both sides with domed buttons and painted them black to match the papiermâché. The sides of the bed I cut from the sides of the letter rack. The base is cut from a solid piece of wood, $5\frac{1}{2}'' \times 4'' \times \frac{1}{2}''$ deep. This I wrapped in a piece of old pillow case ticking, padding it slightly on the top and sides to make it look like a mattress. I cut very small circles of red paper and pinned these to the top of the mattress. The red paper should be only very slightly larger than the pin heads. The bed head is made from a piece of wood, $4'' \times 6'' \times \frac{1}{4}''$, covered in silk. The canopy is built up from $\frac{1}{4}$ inch thick pieces of wood glued and nailed to the bed head, which in turn is glued to the base of the bed. The foot of the bed and the two side pieces are now glued into place. I covered the canopy with a pelmet made from braid 1 inch deep and I made small tassels to hang from the braid. The side curtains are hung from the inside of the canopy and they hang better if they are tied back with a ribbon. The legs are made from four pieces of wood $\frac{1}{4}$ inch square and $\frac{3}{10}$ inch long and these are glued to the corners of the bed and painted. On to the bottom of each leg I glued a collar stud.

Bedding

It is said that medieval mattresses were made of bedstraw, which is the beautiful white climbing plant that trails through our hedges, and that Christ was born on a bed of this plant, which is now called Ladies Bedstraw. However, ordinary straw was used for bedding for centuries, sewn into a bag and emptied and burnt when it was foul. By the 14th Century, feathers had come into use as well, mainly goose feathers, and these remained in general use until curled horsehair, flock and coconut fibre were introduced in late Victorian times. Such materials were packed firmly into palliasses and buttoned at intervals to hold the stuffing in place. These 'buttons' were round pieces of leather with a string between the top one and the bottom one.

In this century, spring mattresses are the most widely used and their covers are no longer made from the traditional striped ticking but from all kinds of patterned and flowery textiles.

Sheets and pillow cases have been used by the upper classes since medieval times. The early ones were usually of homespun linen. Bedding was always white until very recently when coloured and patterned sets came into vogue. I usually use old cotton or linen handkerchiefs for making sheets and pillow cases. They are the right weight and have a nicely finished hem. It is very rare to find a dolls' house bed with two pillows, whether it is a single or a double bed, but if you are making bedclothes perfect in every detail, then you should have two pillows and a bolster for a Victorian double bed.

The first reference to a blanket used as we would use them today was in the 14th Century. The word means white cloth and they remained white until modern times. The hems were usually finished off in blanket stitch, with red or white wool, and sometimes they had two coloured stripes at either end. Today blankets are still usually made from wool but they are brightly coloured and the hems are bound with satin ribbon. Blanket material is too thick to use for a dolls' house bed and I use pieces of well washed woollen vest for mine.

Counterpanes, bedspreads and quilts keep changing their names and appearance over the years. Early beds had covers of fur and there is a white fur one on an 1830 dolls' house bed in the Bethnal Green Museum, but I do not think very many were used on beds in those times. At the end of the 17th Century, there were many embroidered silk and linen covers. Patchwork quilts are perhaps the most decorative of all home made furnishings ever invented. Some of the American ones are outstandingly beautiful. I will describe several ways of making these for dolls' houses (plate 147).

They can be made in exactly the same way as full size quilts are made, and there is one in Kay Smith's dolls' house where the patches were cut from a template drawn from the end of a hexagonal pencil, and it is exquisitely made. For anyone looking for an easier method, the patches can be painted on to a white cloth with rather dry watercolour or poster colour, or for a larger design the pattern can be stencilled. When complete, it should be backed with a piece of cotton material and quilted by hand or sewing machine.

Victorian beds were often covered with knitted or crocheted quilts of white cotton and these can be made on a miniature scale and they are improved by the addition of a deep knotted fringe.

About 1900, eiderdowns became the status symbol of bedding. It seems that feathers moved from underneath to on top, as had long been the practice in Europe. These eiderdowns were covered in rich materials such as silks and satins and they were kept on top of the other bedding so that they could be seen and admired. Later bedspreads were made to match the eiderdowns and gradually they became the more decorative of the two covers and lay on top.

The more opulent houses of the early 20th Century had bedspreads of silk or satin, in crimson, rose pink, or green, frilled, ruched and machine embroidered More austere dwellings had folkweave bedcovers in neutral shades.

Candlewick bedspreads have been very popular for the past twenty years and pale coloured corduroy velvet can be used to make these for a dolls' house.

Recently there has been a return to more exotic coverings such as the heavy quilts sold by Casa Pupa. This type of bold pattern can be stencilled on to woollen material and the design copied from one of the commercial advertisements.

A small extra furnishing for a Victorian bed is one of the velvet and bead embroidered pockets that were hung on the bed head. I had always thought that they were for the owner to put his false teeth into when he went to bed, but I find they were only to hold his pocket watch.

There are also the heating aids, from warming pans to electric blankets. A warming pan is rather difficult to imitate, but stone hot-water bottles can be carved from an inch of blackboard chalk, suitable painted and topped with a little stopper (plate 148). A rubber hot-water bottle can be made from part of a plastic glove . . . plastic rather than rubber because of the easily glued interlock lining. The simplest way is to start with a thin card pattern for the bottle to either side of which you glue the plastic. The neck can be held open by inserting a bead. A cover can be made of flannel or winceyette. You can make an electric blanket for a modern dolls' house from two pieces of pink or blue winceyette. Between these pieces stitch or glue a length of very narrow electric flex in the correct pattern, leaving one end hanging free. Two beads can be threaded on to this to make the switch and the plug. The edges should be bound with satin baby ribbon (plate 148).

In early times, men wore nightshirts and women nightdresses and both sexes wore nightcaps which were tied or buttoned under their chins. During the 17th Century, the nightclothes for both men and women became more elaborate and were trimmed with lace, and when the family was in mourning they also wore black nightclothes. The usual material for night attire was linen, but there were alternatives such as silk or flannel. In the 19th Century, the jelly-bag nightcap was worn by men whilst women wore a cap similar to a baby's bonnet. In the late 1860s nightcaps went out of fashion and about the same time nightdresses became much more elaborate. Pyjamas came into fashion in the 1890s for both men and women, but although these were rapidly adopted by the men it took about twenty years before they were accepted by women.

A tester bed from a
house of 1830-1840.
It has a gilt pediment,
birds-eye maple
columns, a fur quilt
& cream silk curtains.

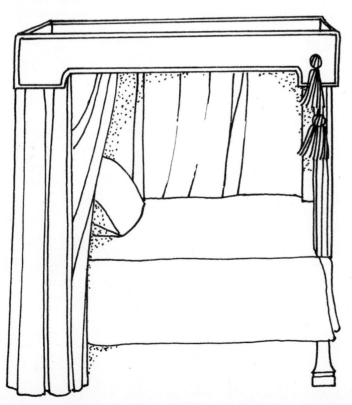

This is the four-poster
from the Blacketts'
Dolls House of 1740. It
has fluted columns,
pale blue silk curtains
& bedspread. Also a
very plump embroid-
ered cushion.

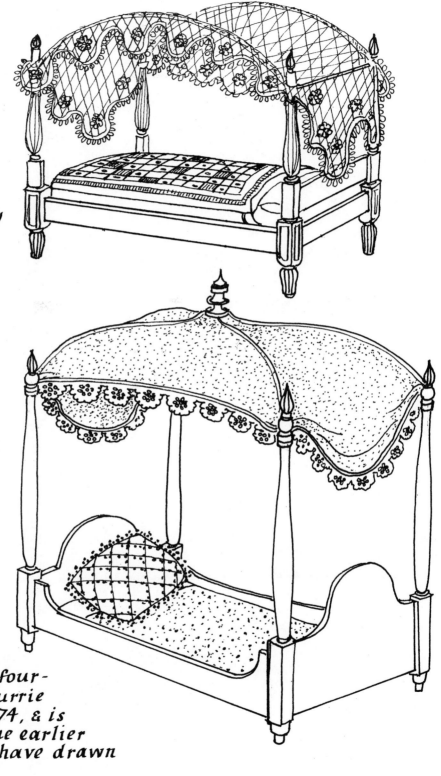

This American
ed is doll-sized
 was beautifully
 made in mahogany
 n Regency times.

This dolls' house four-
poster is in the Currie
olls' house of 1874, & is
ery similar to the earlier
 merican one I have drawn
bove.

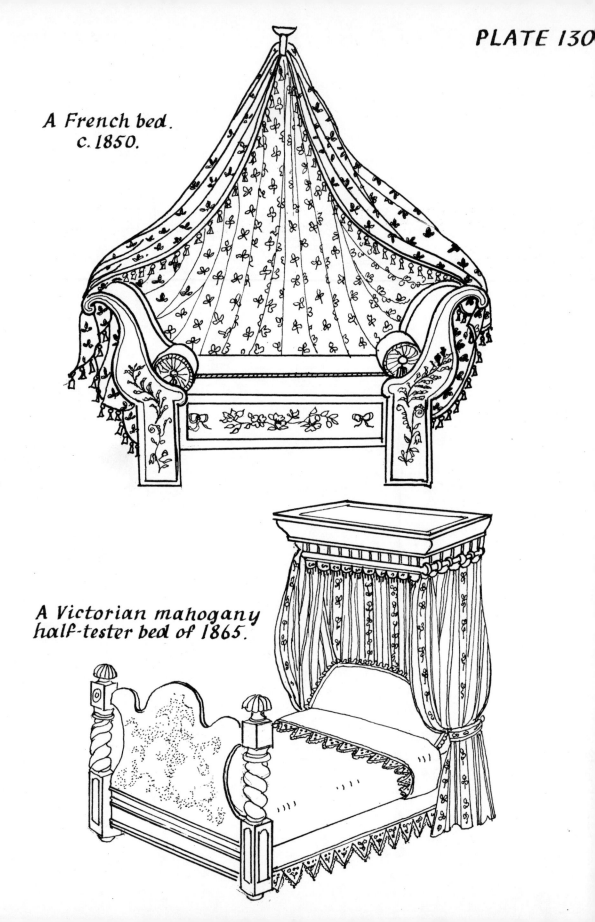

PLATE 130

A French bed.
c. 1850.

A Victorian mahogany
half-tester bed of 1865.

A VICTORIAN HALF-TESTER BED

PLATE 131.

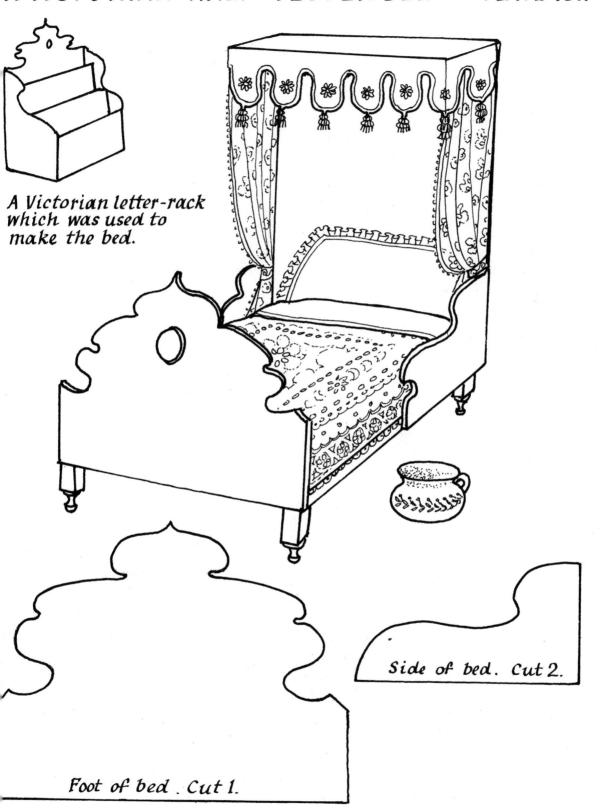

A Victorian letter-rack which was used to make the bed.

Side of bed. Cut 2.

Foot of bed. Cut 1.

Front of canopy.
Cut 1 in ⅛" wood.
A piece of braid 7" long will cover the canopy.

Side of canopy.
Cut 2 in
⅛" wood.

Base of bed.
Cut 1 in ½" wood.

Use a piece of thin wadding 4" x 5½" to pad the base of the bed.
Use a piece of ticking 5½" x 9½" to cover the base of the bed.

Bed-head.
Cut 1 in ¼" wood.

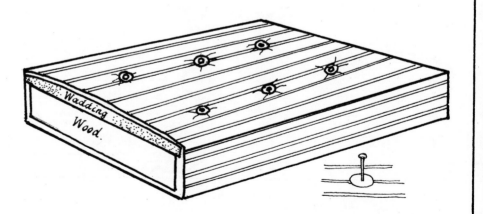

Use a piece of silk 6" x 8¾" to cover the bed-head.

MID 19th CENTURY BEDROOM SUITE.

PLATE 133.

Mid 19th century
bedroom furniture
of satin-wood with
excellent royal blue
decoration.

VICTORIAN BED & WARDROBE.

Bedroom furniture from Ursula
Somervell's dolls' house of 1860.

The half-tester bed is of brown-
painted metal. The white curtains
have a pattern of pink seaweed.

The bright mahogany wardrobe
is decorated with a gold line.

BEDROOM SUITE.

PLATE 135.

Bedroom suite of 1875-1880.
Made of wood painted black
& decorated with yellow
lines, stuck-on "scraps" of
full-blown flowers, cupids &
tigers. It was varnished &
had plain brass knobs.

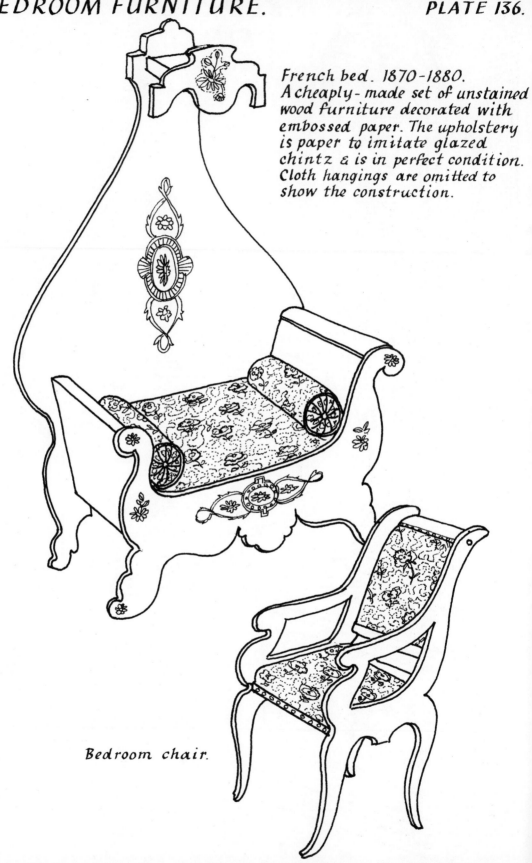

French bed. 1870-1880.
A cheaply-made set of unstained
wood furniture decorated with
embossed paper. The upholstery
is paper to imitate glazed
chintz & is in perfect condition.
Cloth hangings are omitted to
show the construction.

Bedroom chair.

A black & gold bedroom suite c.1880. Small in scale, it is finely decorated & has an inset mirror in the dressing-table.

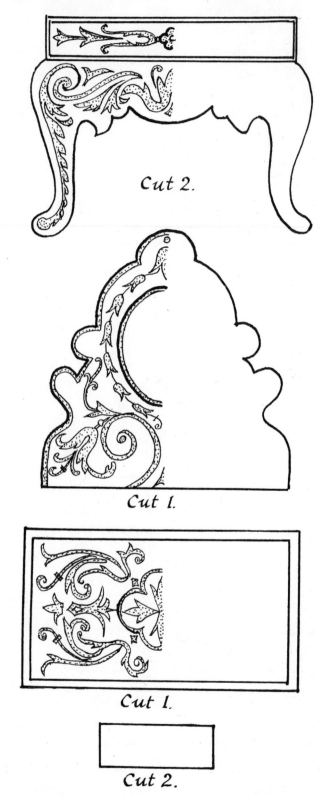

Cut 2.

Cut 1.

Cut 1.

Cut 2.

Plans for the black & gold dressing-table on plate 137.

PLATE 139.

A bedroom suite of c. 1890.

Made of unstained, unpolished
wood with spotted muslin
draperies.

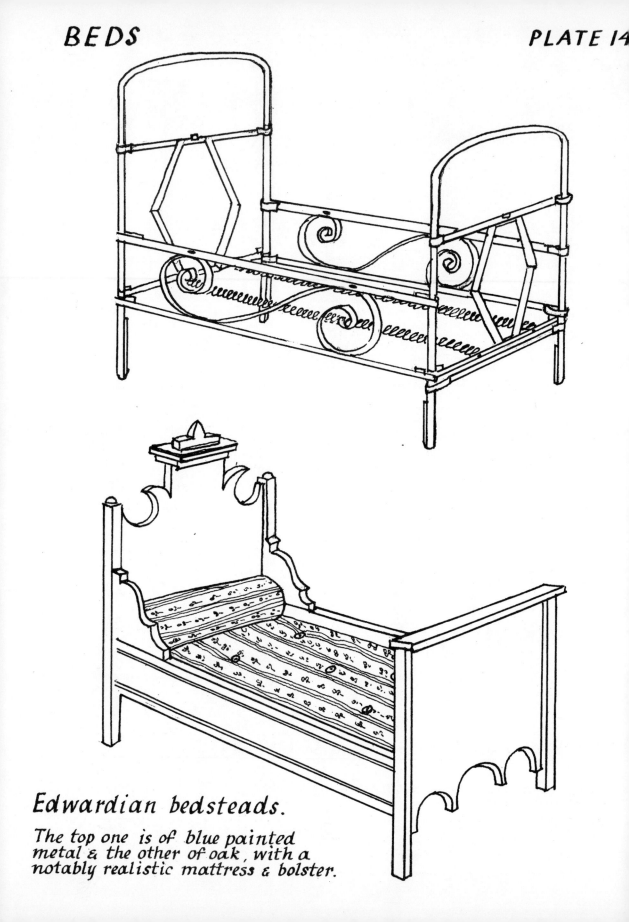

Edwardian bedsteads.

The top one is of blue painted
metal & the other of oak, with a
notably realistic mattress & bolster.

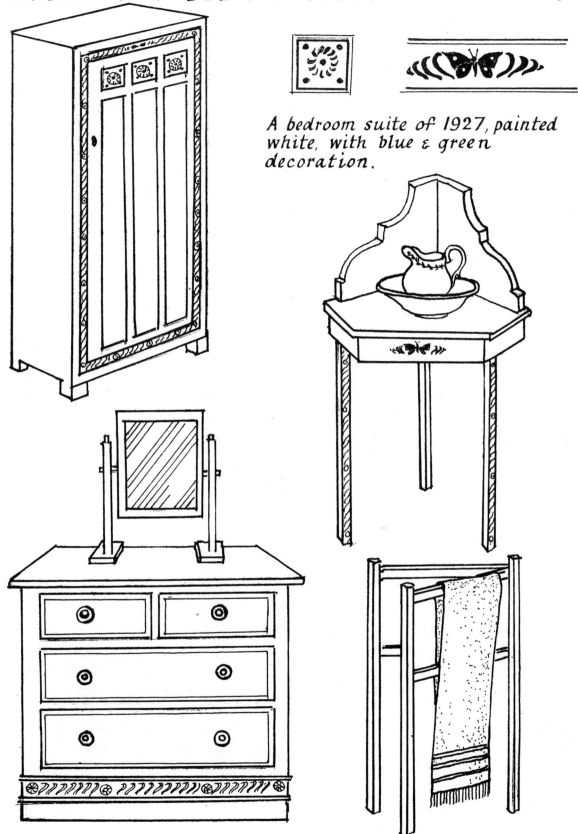

A bedroom suite of 1927, painted white, with blue & green decoration.

WASHSTANDS.

PLATE 14

This Victorian washstand is very light in weight & is stained to reresent mahogany. It has a pleasant shape, & there is a fitted pâpier-maché bowl.

On the back of this late Victorian washstand is written "For Dora for not crying when Mac tried on, 6½ years old," & the companion piece to this is inscribed "To Effie for leaving to suck her thumb at 7½ years old, from her Mother, Nov./94." Poor Dora & Effie!

This washstand was sold in Cheyne Walk, Chelsea, probably in the early 20th. century. It is well made & lacquered in red, which gives it a very oriental look.

EDWARDIAN DRESSING-TABLE

PLATE 143

Typical of the era, this
dressing-table is wildly
over-complicated & made
of an unsuitable wood,
oak; but because it is so
typical I have made plans
for several such pieces.
The dressing-table stands
5¼" high x 3" wide x
2¼" deep.

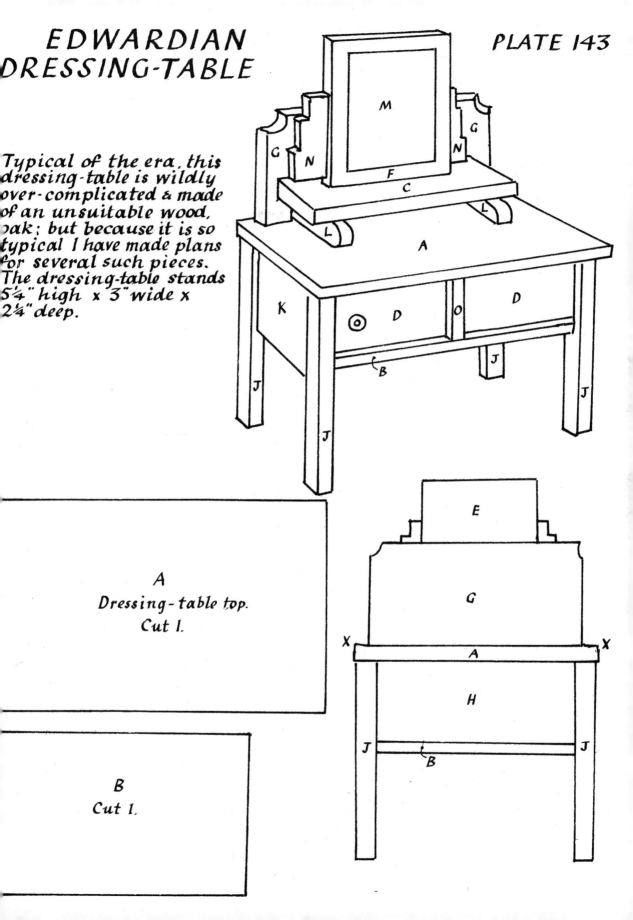

A
Dressing-table top.
Cut 1.

B
Cut 1.

EDWARDIAN DRESSING-TABLE

PLATE I

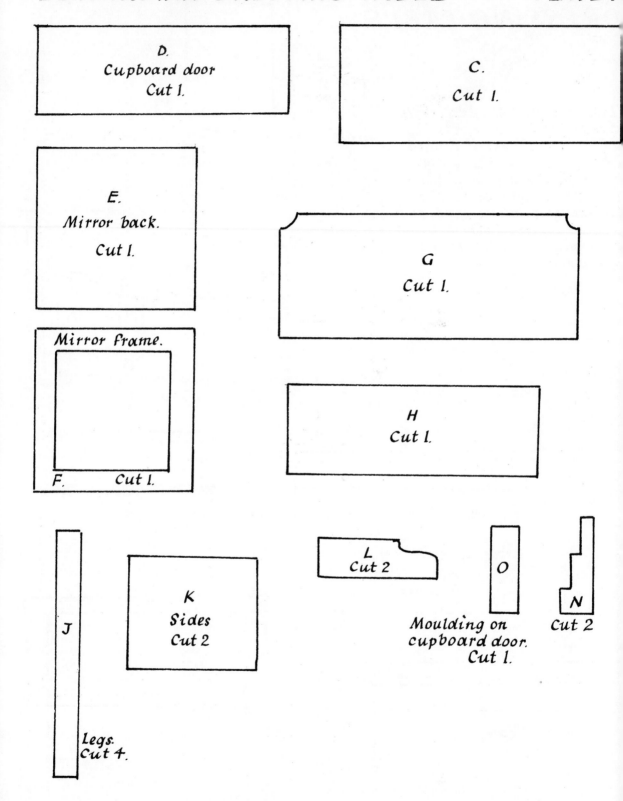

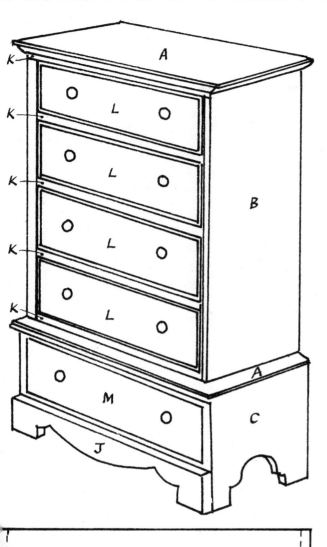

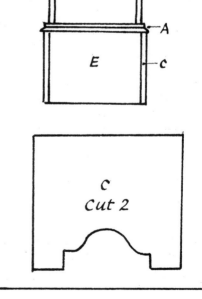

Tallboy, early 20th. century. In 18th. century style, it is painted deep cream, with black metal knobs. The pieces marked A are the top & middle horizontals & to give them extra thickness should have an added layer, ⅒ smaller, shown by dotted lines. It is 5″ high, 3³⁄₁₀″ wide & 1⁹⁄₁₀″ deep.

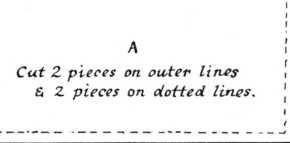

A
Cut 2 pieces on outer lines
& 2 pieces on dotted lines.

C
Cut 2

B
Cut 2

Base. Cut 1.

D
Cut 1

K
Cut 5

L
Cut 4

M
Cut 1

E
Cut 1.

N
Cut 4

F
Base for bottom drawer.
Cut 1.

O
Cut 4

P
Cut 1.

G
Cut 8

H
Cut 2

J

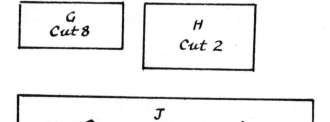

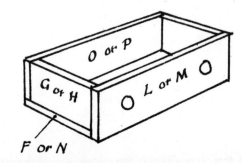

O or P

G or H

L or M

F or N

Early 19th. century.

1848

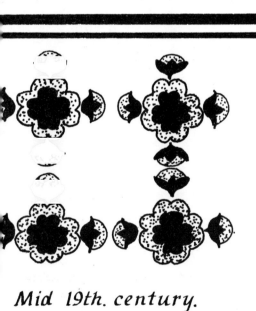

Mid 19th. century.

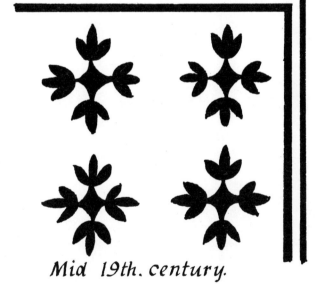

Mid 19th. century.

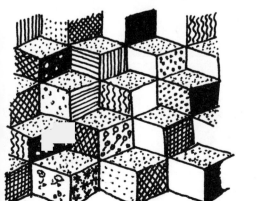

Mid 19th. century box patchwork.

1839.

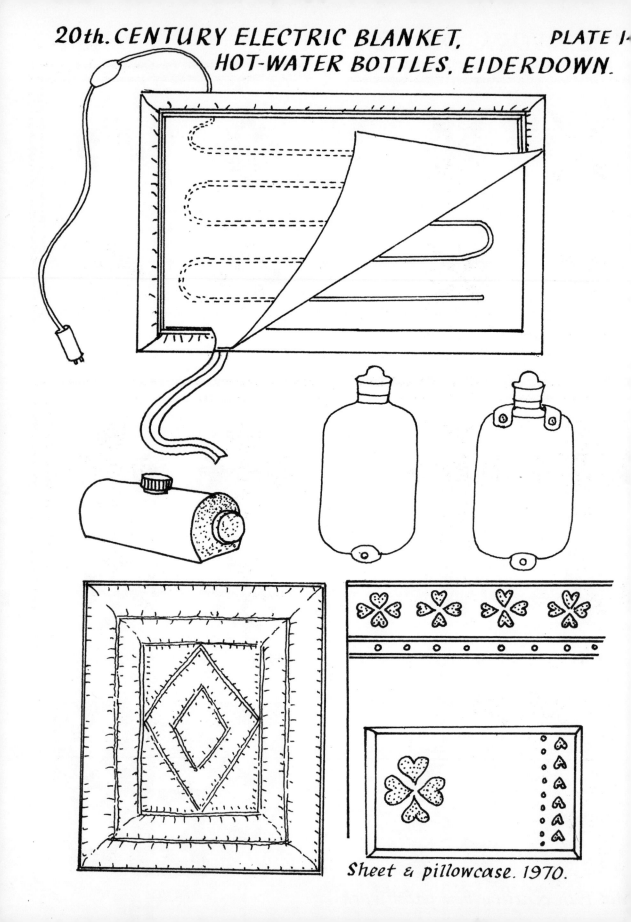

Sheet & pillowcase. 1970.

Fixed baths, directly connected to a water system and therefore demanding a new room of their own, only came into general use towards the end of the 19th Century and then the room was often a converted bedroom or a peculiar annexe. For some years, wealthy customers and the trade ran riot with every conceivable refinement and embellishment. There were baths of marble, lavatories and bowls of decorated earthenware, and fine mahogany and brass fittings. With the demand for bathrooms in less extravagant homes, the manufacturers began to make the more simply shaped, undecorated baths of enamelled iron or porcelain that are most familiar to us.

Washstands, together with sets of jugs and bowls, have been used from about 1740 until this century and of course they follow the current fashions of the day. Hip baths were used early in the 19th Century, slipper baths followed in the mid-19th Century and full sized baths from 1860 onwards. There were also showerbaths in the last century (plate 151). Dolls' house washstands continue to be made until the nineteen-twenties of wood, metal and papiermâché, and the more elaborate had real marble tops. The baths and lavatories for dolls' houses were either of porcelain or metal and the latter are painted, sometimes to imitate wood or even marble. Others were just painted in attractive colours—rose pink with a gold line or pale turquoise with a white decoration. By comparison dolls' washbasins are rather dull. Even cheaper sets had taps that ran with water and lavatories that flushed (plate 152). There are few home-made items of bathroom furniture, although I have seen carved wooden ones where the white enamel has yellowed with age.

Plate 151 shows a Victorian soapdish which I used for a bath in a late Victorian dolls' house. It only needed the addition of four feet. It is made of white pottery, decorated with deep blue flowers and leaves.

Late Victorian tin bath.

PLATE 150

Late Victorian & Edwardian
bathroom fittings.

PLATE 151

A Victorian showerbath & wood & porcelain bathroom furniture.

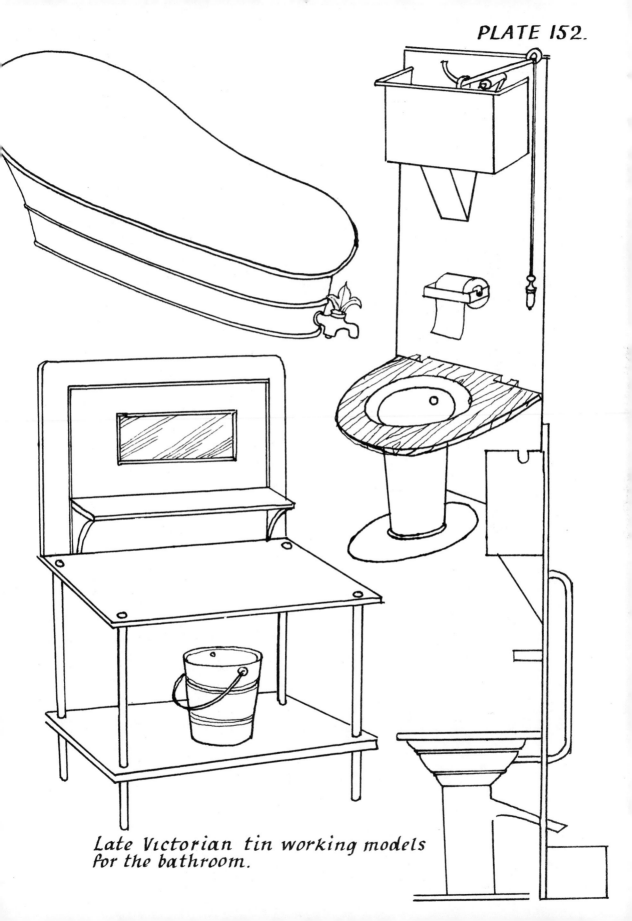

PLATE 152.

Late Victorian tin working models
for the bathroom.

PLATE 153

BATH
WINK TOY SERIES

A marbled basin, washstand
& mat, c.1920, & a modern plastic
bath, basin, stool & cupboard.

I have often found the furniture in the dolls' house nursery to be older than that in the other rooms, presumably moved there as the main rooms were refurnished with more elaborate acquisitions, as indeed happens in reality.

In every nursery I have seen, there have been two essential pieces of furniture, a toy cupboard and a round table covered with oilcloth or plush bobble-edged cloth.

Having a nursery in a dolls' house certainly allows for the most imaginative accessories, such as very small toys and the dolls' own dolls' house (plate 158). The nursery will always take the odd wickerwork chairs that are difficult to place elsewhere, and the many cradles. My experience of collecting dolls' furniture is that one ends up with more cradles and fewer beds than a normal house would hold.

The fireplace of a nursery can be an area of particular interest, with a fire-guard, and clothes warming, a tin bath and a frozen Charlotte on the rug, and toy cats and dogs everywhere. An enrichment would be to decorate the nursery as for Christmas, with paper chains and a Christmas tree, miniature cards on the chimneypiece and a stocking full of toys in the fireplace. Of course many of these things are a mid-Victorian development and should not go into an earlier house.

COTS

PLATE 13

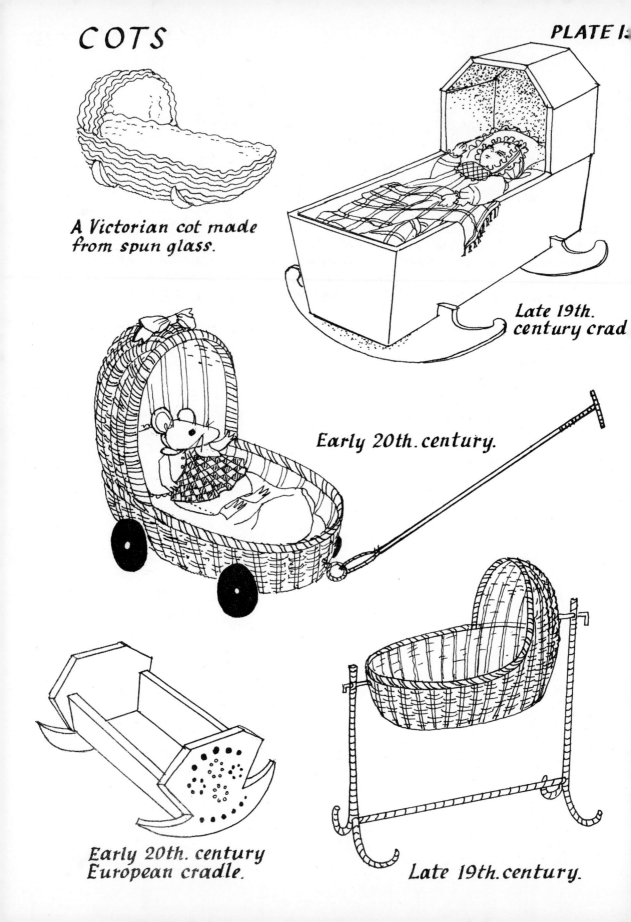

A Victorian cot made from spun glass.

Late 19th. century crad

Early 20th. century.

Early 20th. century European cradle.

Late 19th. century.

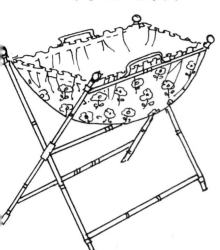

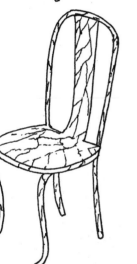

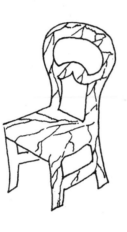

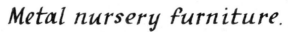

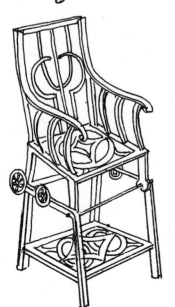

Metal nursery furniture.

The twisted-metal chair is bright gold with photographs of Windsor Castle on the seat & back, c.1950. The other two chairs are of tin rather than wood & painted to imitate marble, mysteriously enough! The sewing machine is bright painted tin, the high chair silver-type metal & the horn gramophone & the sewing basket are bright gilt.

A set of early 20th.
century wicker-work furniture, & a metal vacuum flask.

The Christmas Tree (Plate 157)

It is possible to buy small artificial Christmas trees, made for cake decoration, and these can be trimmed with gold and silver balls. It might be interesting to make a tree all of silver and gold and I show a drawing of one where the trunk is made from an artists watercolour brush $4\frac{1}{2}$ inches high, covered with silver paper. The branches are of fine flexible wire wound around with silver tinsel. The strands of the tinsel are trimmed until they are about $\frac{1}{4}$ inch long. The branches are then fastened round the trunk at regular intervals. From them hang, on nylon thread, silver and gold sequins of varied size and shape, about four to a branch. To the end of each branch, a candle about $\frac{1}{2}$ inch high is glued and these are made of newspaper edging. The paper is cut into $\frac{1}{2}$ inch square pieces and one edge is moistened and rolled between the finger and thumb. The damp edge enables it to be rolled easily and tightly. A needle and thread with rather a large knot is threaded through the candle and pulled tight. This forces the rolled paper into a peak at the top and the thread is cut off to show as a wick. Before it is cut, the candle can be dipped into wax and the result is a perfect wax candle.

The tree can be set in Polyfilla in a container appropriate to the house and the time. Gifts can be wrapped in gold and silver paper and put around the foot of the tree. It is possible to find in magazines very tiny coloured pictures and these can be stuck to folded cartridge paper to make Christmas cards, with silk cords and tassels.

The manufacture of paper chains defeated me until I cut an $\frac{1}{8}$ inch strip of soft flexible coloured metal foil and fastened it to the corners of the room. It twists into rather sharp angles that catch the light and look like the genuine article.

As early as 1760 we find 'kissing rings' garlanded with ribbons, candles and rosy apples, and they hang like chandeliers from the ceiling. Plate 157 shows one made from two interlacing metal rings trimmed with tiny artificial leaves sold for wedding cakes. The second ring is made from the brass ring from an old electric table lamp. For the modern house, I have drawn the up-to-date equivalent, the mobile of cut out paper birds fastened to fine wire.

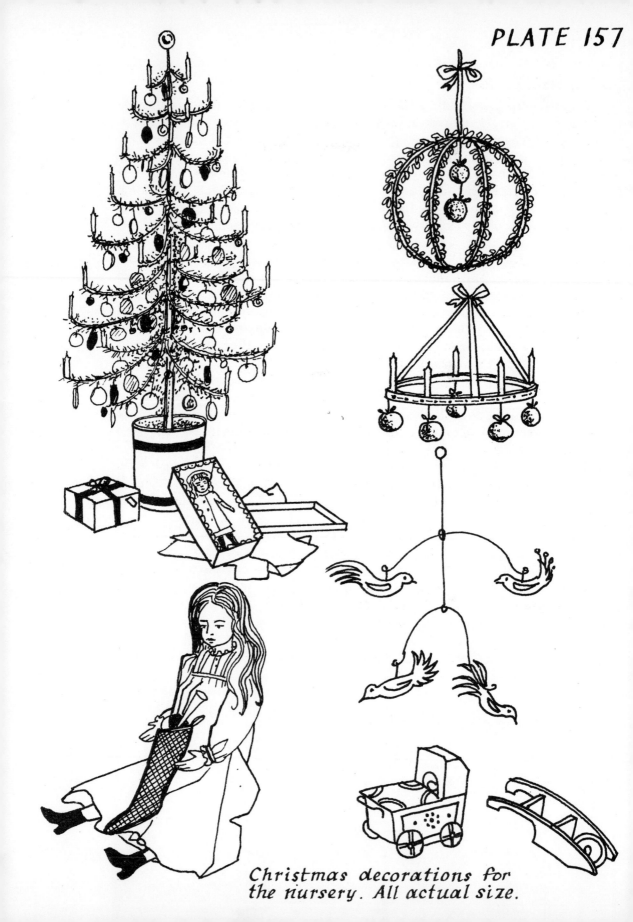

PLATE 157

Christmas decorations for
the nursery. All actual size.

The Dolls' Dolls' House (Plate 158)

This tiny house is $2\frac{1}{2}$ inches wide, $1\frac{2}{10}$ inches deep and $2\frac{1}{2}$ inches high to the roof ridge. It is made of thin card built up on two rectangles of wood $\frac{2}{10}$ inch thick. One of these forms the base of the house and the other supports the roof. The windows are cut out of the front piece of card and thin plastic is glued across the holes for glass. The glazing bars are painted. The door is cut on two sides only and then folded along the dotted line to make a hinge and a pin head is used for the door knob. When the four sides are glued together they are reinforced at the inside corners with gumstrip and glued to the wooden rectangles. The roof is now glued into position and the chimney is folded to form a box that is glued to the roof. Thin strips of card are glued around the edges of the roof to form coping stones and the steps are added. The house needs to be carefully painted, with poster colour and a fine brush. The brick work should be a purple brown shading to brick red in patches and the pointing is done with the very finest white lines. The roof is almost black. To give a more perfect finish I glued very narrow strips of brown gummed paper round the edges of the windows.

Screens (Plates 160, 161)

The scrap screen inevitably comes to mind when screens are mentioned. These popular 'folk art', do-it-yourself objects have recently caught the imagination, partly because of the interesting collage of old pictures and partly because of the rich golden patina of the varnish.

I have drawn a plain four fold screen (plate 160) which could be made from pieces of wood or card fastened together with $\frac{3}{8}$ inch hinges. These hinges can be fixed with wire rather than screws (plate 161). This wire is twisted together on the back and hidden by the scraps.

The scraps should be small in scale, on thin paper, brightly coloured and of such a nature that they will recall the period they seek to represent. They should be glued to each side of the screen and a decorative edging, possibly of gilt, glued round all the edges. A coat of paper varnish stained a warm deep yellow completes the effect.

Another very simple screen is the one with arched tops (plate 160). This is made of four pieces of cardboard covered in material and sewn together. The shape gives nothing away and the period can be indicated purely by the age of the fabric. Plate 161 gives the size of the card and eight pieces of material should be cut $\frac{1}{2}$ inch bigger all round. The shape of the card should be drawn on four of the pieces and these should be machined to the other four pieces. Turnings are cut away and the cloth is turned right side out and slipped over the cardboard shape and sewn by hand along the bottom edge. These four panels are sewn together.

The more elaborate screen of the eighteen-nineties (plate 161) is made of fretwork and must have been very tricky to cut. It is something of a hybrid because of the Art Nouveau fret and the romantic Victorian forget-me-nots and ribbons on the panels below.

The small fire screen is drawn actual size (plate 160), and is made up of religious texts. I saw this in a dolls' house of about 1820. Pole screens for shading the heat of the fire were very popular in Regency times and are often to be found in dolls' houses. The one I have drawn was in the same 1820 dolls' house.

The circular screen was of card covered with cream silk and edged with lace. A print of a rose is glued to the centre. The screen is fastened on to a brass rod that fits into a shaped wooden base. These pole screens are not difficult to make and small prints of flowers and rural scenes can be used to decorate them.

PLATE 158

A DOLL'S DOLLS' HOUSE.

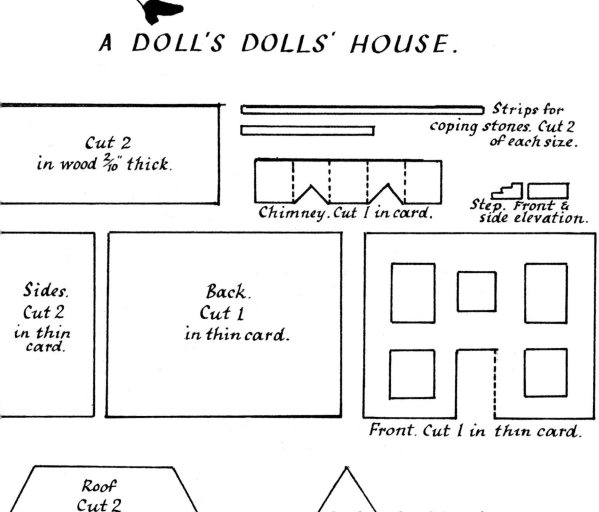

Cut 2 in wood 2/10" thick.

Strips for coping stones. Cut 2 of each size.

Chimney. Cut 1 in card.

Step. Front & side elevation.

Sides. Cut 2 in thin card.

Back. Cut 1 in thin card.

Front. Cut 1 in thin card.

Roof Cut 2 in thin card.

Roof. Cut 2 in thin card.

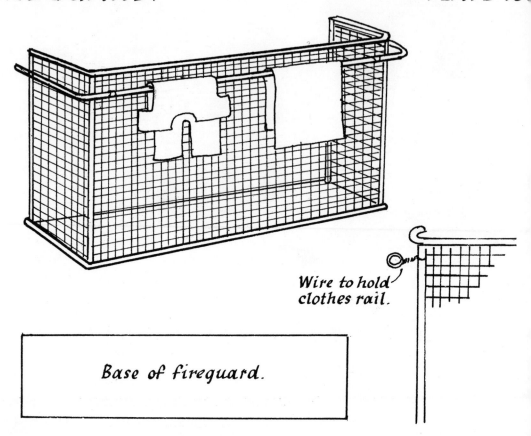

Wire to hold
clothes rail.

Base of fireguard.

This fireguard is very well made, probably at the beginning of this century. The materials are well chosen. The top & bottom edges, the extra clothes rail & the four uprights are all made from copper wire which is easily bent & the joints can be soldered together.

The floor of the fireguard is made from black card & it is glued & wired into place with thin fuse wire.

Round the inside of this wire framework is glued square mesh net which is painted with black enamel until it is quite rigid.

The rail which holds the clothes is an extra refinement. It is rather difficult to fix neatly, but worth the extra effort. It can be fixed to the guard with wire twisted to hold it 3/10" in front of the main structure.

The sleeping suit is made from two pieces of material cut out flat in the characteristic shape of the garment, & the neck & edges of the sleeves are finished with buttonhole stitching.

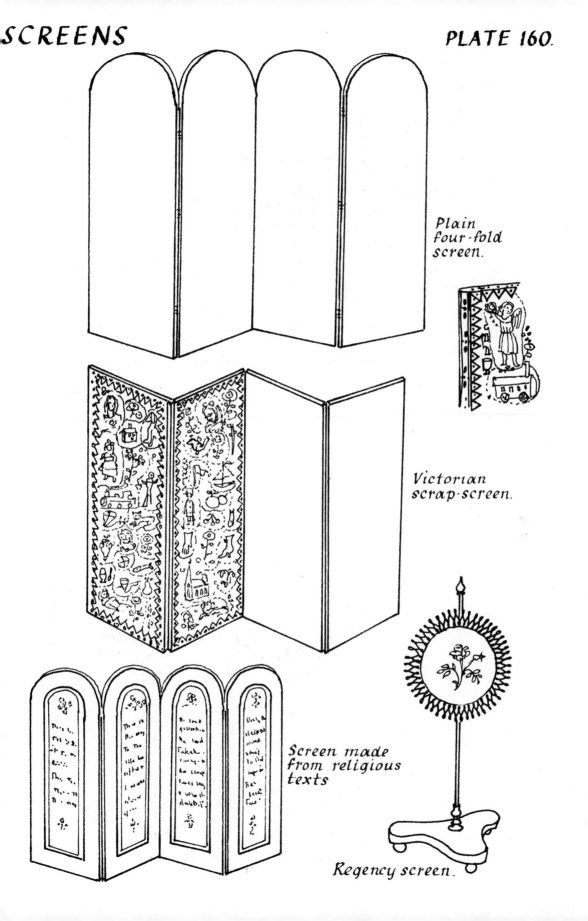

Plain four-fold screen.

Victorian scrap-screen.

Screen made from religious texts

Regency screen.

SCREENS

PLATE 161

Late Victorian fretwork screen.

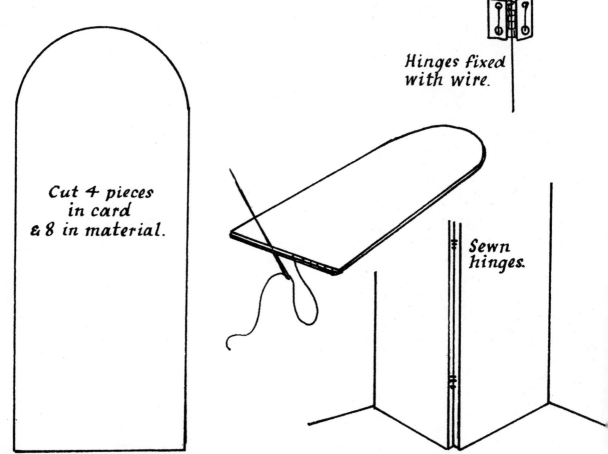

Hinges fixed with wire.

Cut 4 pieces in card & 8 in material.

Sewn hinges.

Construction of the four-fold screen.

Hall and Staircase (Plates 162–165)

I have a Victorian dolls' house of typical design in that it has three openings on the front that reveal six rooms.

The centre opens to show two small rooms that would rationally be the hall and landing but there has never been any stairs. I decided to build a staircase and to make the upper room into a bathroom.

The hall is $10\frac{1}{2}$ inches wide, 18 inches deep and 16 inches high and I built two partitions, the larger to enclose the stairs and the smaller one at right angles to make a cloakroom at the back of the hall. The smaller one has a door opening inwards on to a cloakroom with a handbasin and lavatory. The partitions were cut from $\frac{1}{2}$-inch thick wood, the largest $16'' \times 13''$ and the smaller $16'' \times 8''$. I have drawn plans $\frac{1}{4}$ inch to 1 inch in scale to show the door and an optional extra door on the half landing. I papered the ceiling, walls and floor and the two partitions, and made the staircase from seven blocks of wood 3 inches wide by $1\frac{3}{4}$ inches deep by 1 inch high. These blocks were glued so that each block was attached to the back half of the lower one. A piece of wood $5'' \times 3''$ was added to the top stair to make the half-way landing. To hold them firmly in place against the partition I glued and nailed two extra blocks of wood underneath the stairs. I had a length of Victorian woven tapestry 3 inches wide, a floral pattern on a grey ground, and this I glued to the stairs and half landing. I made brass stair rods of cocktail sticks covered in gold foil, with gilt beads at each end. The clips I cut from thin metal. The cloakroom door was made from a piece of wood $\frac{2}{10}$ inch thick with thin strips of balsa wood to outline the panels.

I made the architrave for the door from wedge-shaped moulding sold by the Hobbies shops. The door was stained dark mahogany colour. The whole was assembled with glue and small nails and reinforced by screws through the bathroom floor.

Because I wished to have a bathroom I allowed the stairs to disappear out of sight above the cloakroom, but if a full flight were required they could of course be repeated on the other side of the partition, using the optional doorway marked on the pattern.

A good touch is a rope handrail made from a carefully plaited silk cord, hung through two brass screw eyes.

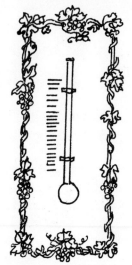

Thermometer on card with
metal edging. Mid 19th. century.

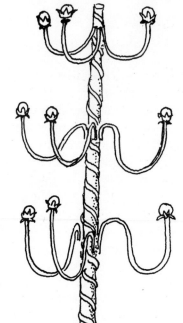

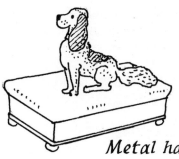

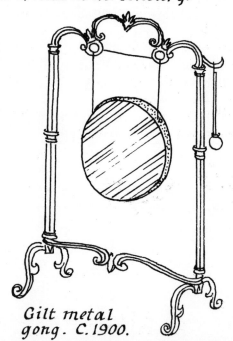

Metal hall furniture. Mid 19th. century.

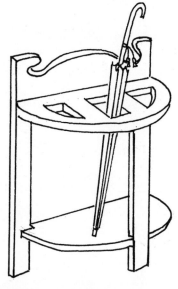

Wooden Edwardian
umbrella-stand.

Gilt metal
gong. C. 1900.

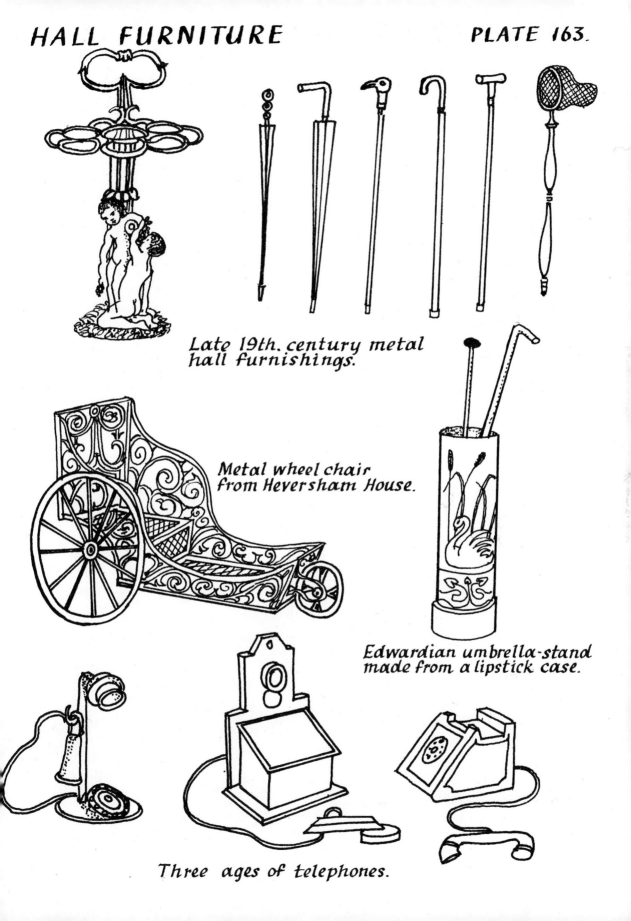

Late 19th. century metal hall furnishings.

Metal wheel chair from Heversham House.

Edwardian umbrella-stand made from a lipstick case.

Three ages of telephones.

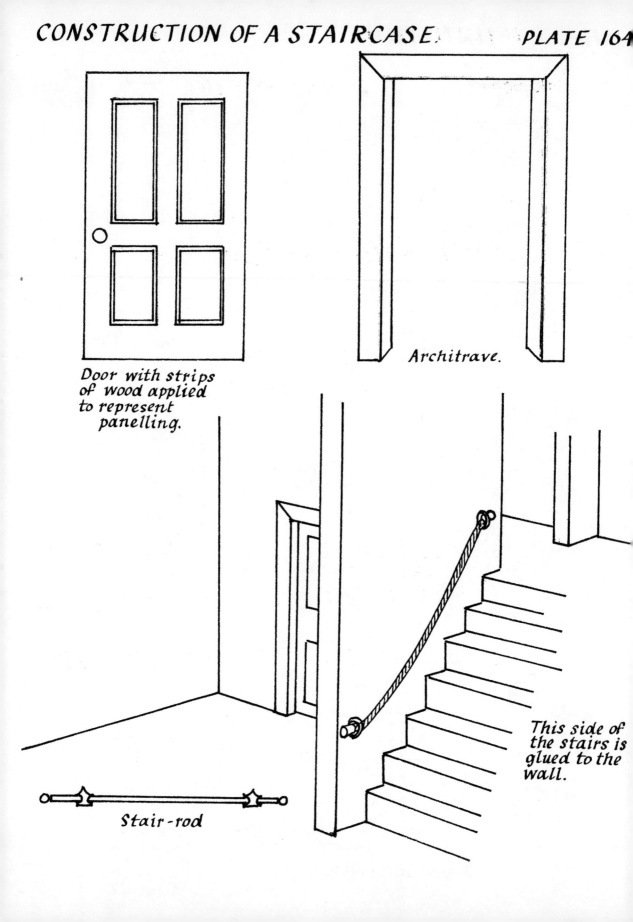

Door with strips
of wood applied
to represent
panelling.

Architrave.

This side of
the stairs is
glued to the
wall.

Stair-rod

CONSTRUCTION OF A STAIRCASE PLATE 165

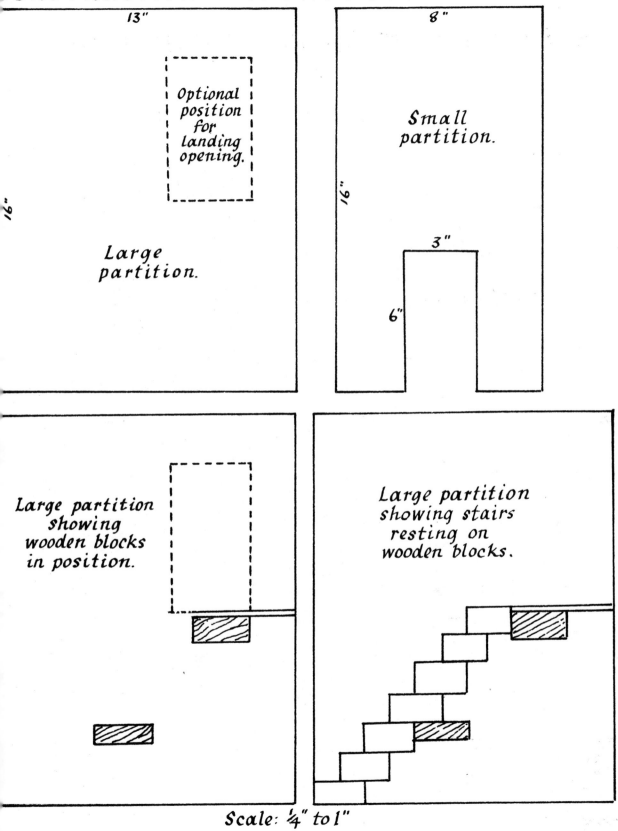

Scale: ¼" to 1"

PLATE 16

TRADITIONAL HOME-MADE FURNITURE.

☆ TRADITIONAL HOME-MADE FURNITURE ☆

For a long time there has existed a tradition for certain pieces of furniture to be made by members of the family, to entertain and instruct the children and, more probably, to entertain themselves. The scarcity of good antique pieces of dolls' furniture and their rising cost makes this tradition into a valuable opportunity for those who wish to make more things for their old dolls' house.

There were most probably written instructions, in popular magazines, for making things from cardboard and bobbins, for such pieces are to be seen in the majority of old dolls' houses.

A MID-VICTORIAN ARMCHAIR AND SOFA

The method of making these chairs and sofas remained unchanged for generations. They are made by covering a cotton reel with material and adding a little wadding on the top of the seat for padding. A piece of card is then cut into a suitable shape for the chair back, padded and covered in the same material and stitched to the cotton reel. A frill is then sewn round the base of the chair seat (plate 169).

This method can be elaborated upon and some very interesting furniture can be made using the same basic principles, and I have drawn patterns and given instructions for making a chair and sofa of the mid-Victorian period. The chair is $2\frac{1}{2}$ inches wide and $4\frac{1}{4}$ inches high and the sofa is $5\frac{1}{2}$ inches wide by $3\frac{1}{2}$ inches high, which is rather large for some dolls' houses but the patterns can be reduced in scale. The choice of material is very important; it should be thin and if possible it should be old material, but if this is impossible then it should be material which is reminiscent of the period. I used a piece of old pale blue silk for mine and I trimmed it with pale pink. Sateen is a suitable material to use because it was often used in the past.

To make the armchair, cut two pieces of balsa wood to the size shown in plate 168, for the chair seat. One piece should be $\frac{1}{4}$ inch thick and the other $\frac{3}{4}$ inch thick. They should be sandpapered smooth and the front edge of the thinner piece should be sanded until it is slightly rounded. Now cut a piece of firm but flexible card from the pattern on plate 168 for the chair back. Two pieces of wadding are needed for padding the chair back and the chair seat and these can be glued into position. If the material used to cover the chair and sofa is cut on the cross it will be easier to get it to fit well. First, take one piece of the fabric for the chair back and run a gathering thread round the outside edge. Now place the chair back (wadding side down) on to this and draw the gathering thread tight. Then, with a double thread, stitch the material from edge to edge to hold it firm (plate 169). Mark a set of dots on the front of the chair $\frac{1}{2}$ inch apart and with some thick thread make french knots at these points to give the Victorian 'buttoned' effect. The french knots should be quite large with the thread wrapped round the needle five or six times. Now sew the second piece of material on the back of the chair, leaving the bottom edge open. If the covering material is very thin, it may be necessary to line it so that the criss-cross threads do not show through the back. The chair seat should now be covered, the loose edge at the bottom of the chair turned back and, with dressmakers' pins, the back of the chair should be attached to the chair seat by putting the pins through the card and into the balsa wood. The flap of material is then pulled down over the bottom edge and the pins are hidden by it.

The second piece of balsa wood is now covered in the upholstery material and the feet are nailed into place.

The base of the chair is now glued to the rest and a frill or a piece of material cut on the cross is stretched on to the chair. The chair can be enhanced by the addition of a shaped cushion (plate 168), which fits the chair seat and is 'buttoned' with french knots and has an edging cord of pale pink silk and two miniature tassels. An extra length of cord can be sewn round the edges of the chair and sofa to cover the stitches if this is found to be necessary.

PLATE 167.

A home-made mid-Victorian armchair & sofa.

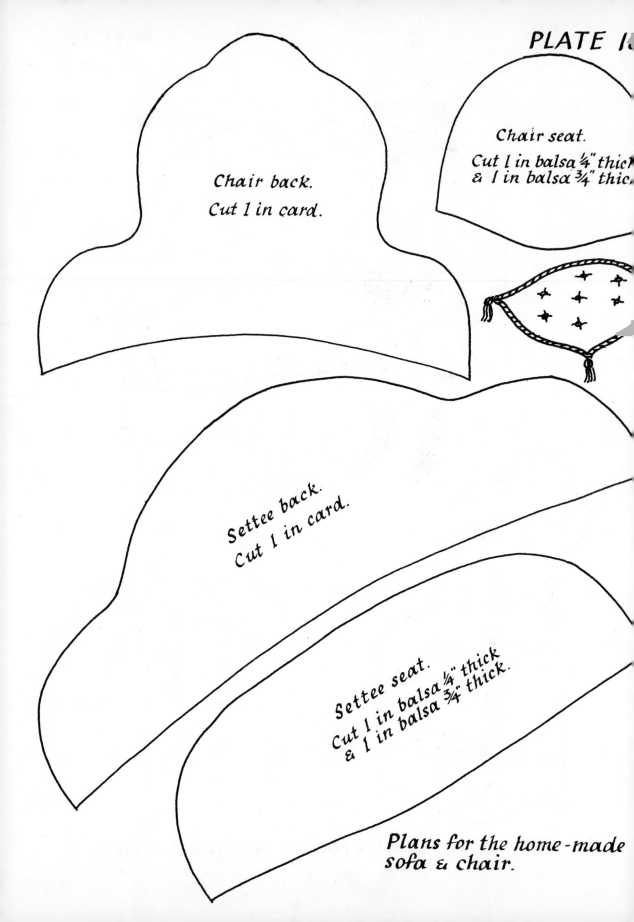

PLATE 15

Chair back.
Cut 1 in card.

Chair seat.
Cut 1 in balsa ¼" thick
& 1 in balsa ¾" thick.

Settee back.
Cut 1 in card.

Settee seat.
Cut 1 in balsa ¼" thick
& 1 in balsa ¾" thick.

Plans for the home-made
sofa & chair.

PLATE 169.

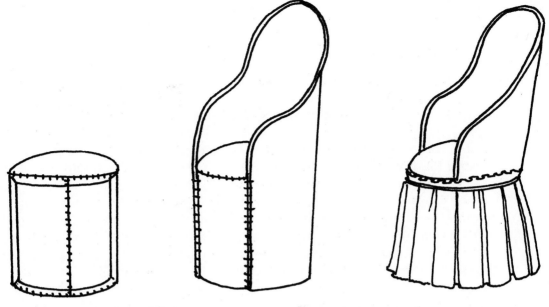

A chair made from card & a bobbin.

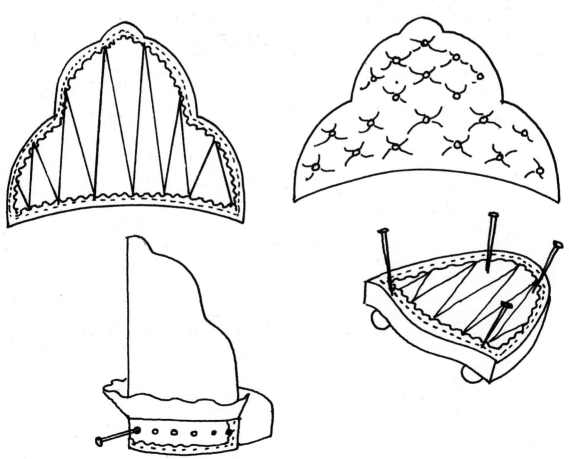

Construction of the mid-Victorian armchair.

About 1920, probably as a result of the much publicised dolls' house made for Queen Mary, there was a renewed interest in making dolls' house furniture for yourself. I have seen many examples from this period made from wire and card and they are all painstakingly made, with surprising skill and attention to detail, yet none of them have the look of mass production.

I have given plans for making three such pieces, a bed, a cabinet and a settee. Plastic-covered electrician's wire can be used and it should be about the thickness of an ordinary piece of string. Where the wire is used to form the legs of the furniture, it is used double and the two pieces should be pressed together as tightly as possible, and the loop formed at the bend can be hammered flat. The two wires are bent to the correct shape and covered with either a self-hardening clay or a thin layer of paper to disguise their origin. The pieces of card are attached to the wire structure with fuse wire. Thin card should be used, no more than $\frac{1}{16}$ inch thick and when a thicker piece is needed it should be built up with layers of thin card for this will give it greater strength. The success of this furniture depends on the accuracy of the cutting and the neatness of finish.

These pieces were mainly made during the period when black and gold lacquered furniture was fashionable and all those that I have drawn are painted in this manner. The painting should be carefully executed and I would use poster colour, giving several coats until the surface is quite even. I would then add the gold decoration before giving the piece a coat of water-colour varnish.

The base of the bed and the seat of the settee were made from thin white cotton stitched to the wires and the bed clothes were exquisitely made; two sheets, one pillow, one blanket, a very delicate silk bedspread and a cream silk eiderdown. The squab of the settee was well shaped and lightly padded and the canework was made from tapestry canvas glued to the wires and painted black.

I have also seen settees made in the same way, where the wire framework is thickly padded to make chesterfield settees.

In the Russell dolls' house, which was made in 1921, there are several sets of this kind of furniture. There is a four-poster bed with a canework head and foot and the four posts were made from two thicknesses of wire with a third wire wound round these to give the effect of oak twists. There is also a bobbin twist settee made from very fine wire threaded with wooden beads. It has a canework back and a very authentic looking tapestry seat.

The drawing-room set in the same house (plate 173) is really marvellously made from laminated card painted ivory and decorated with thin gold lines. The loose cushions are covered with ivory watered silk.

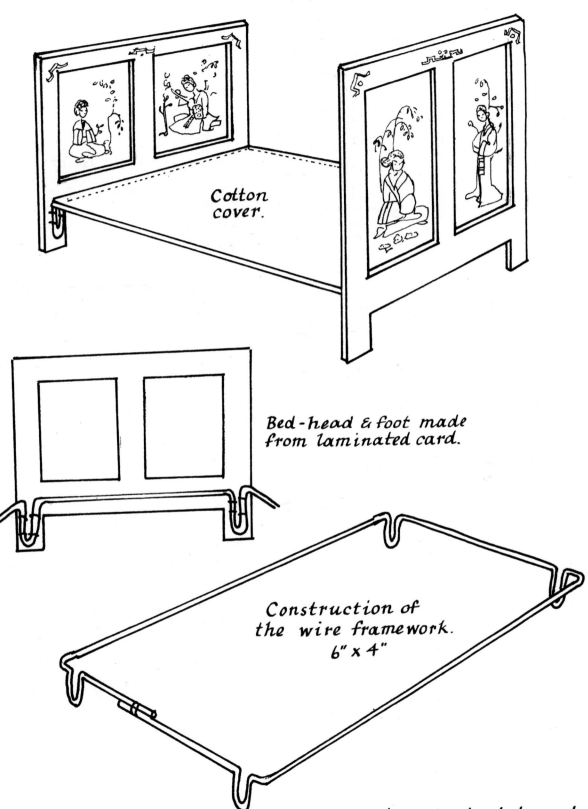

PLATE 170

Cotton cover.

Bed-head & foot made from laminated card.

Construction of the wire framework.
6" x 4"

black & gold "Chinese" bed c.1920 made of wire & laminated card.

A 'LACQUERED' CABINET c.1920.

Made from laminated card.

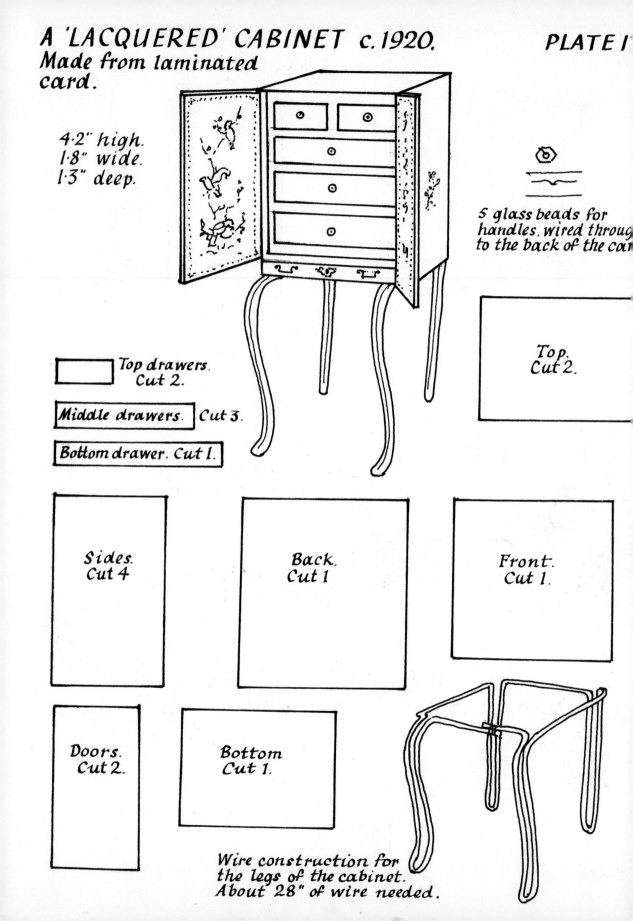

4·2" high.
1·8" wide.
1·3" deep.

PLATE I

5 glass beads for handles, wired throug to the back of the cab

Top drawers.
Cut 2.

Middle drawers. Cut 3.

Bottom drawer. Cut 1.

Top.
Cut 2.

Sides.
Cut 4

Back.
Cut 1

Front.
Cut 1.

Doors.
Cut 2.

Bottom
Cut 1.

Wire construction for the legs of the cabinet. About 28" of wire needed.

A SETTEE OF WIRE & CANVAS 'BASKET-WORK' WITH A PADDED SQUAB. 1920-1930.

PLATE 172.

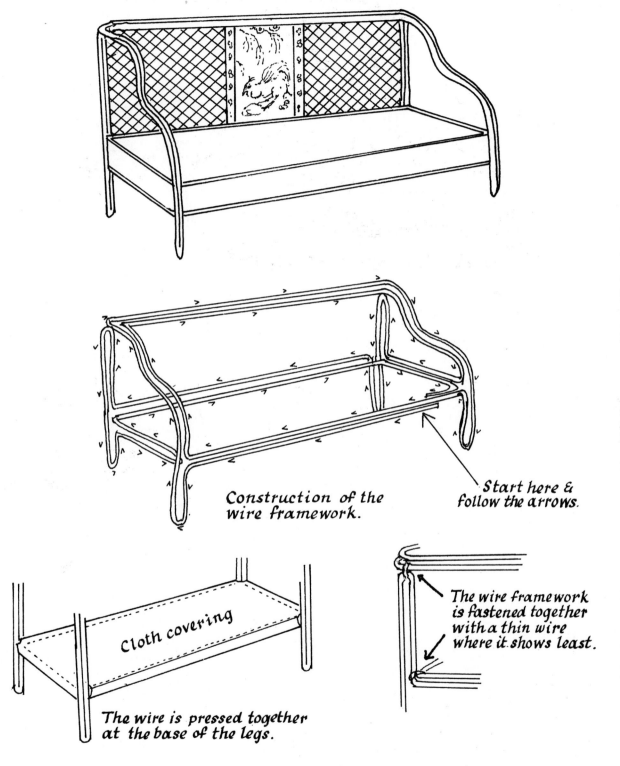

Construction of the wire framework.

Start here & follow the arrows.

Cloth covering

The wire is pressed together at the base of the legs.

The wire framework is fastened together with a thin wire where it shows least.

DRAWING-ROOM FURNITURE MADE FROM LAMINATETED CARD IN 1921.

PLATE 173

Cork & Pin and Conker & Pin Furniture

This is very typical of the sort of furniture that has been made by children in the nursery for generations.

In the autumn this furniture was made from horse chestnuts, but during the rest of the year it was made from corks. The largest horse chestnuts were always used and they were polished until they shone like antique mahogany. Unfortunately they dried up and withered and the pieces made from cork are the ones that have survived.

The table is made by cutting a slice of cork for the centre of the table top and putting about twenty glass-headed berry pins round the edge. Four more pins are stuck in at an angle for the legs. The weaving is done with a thick linen thread which is woven over and under the pins and pressed close as each row is completed. The legs are also covered with linen thread.

I have drawn a set of Victorian cork and pin furniture. There are two chairs, a settee, a table and a stool. The cork which formed the seat of the settee was cut in half longitudinally and covered in green velvet. White linen thread was used for the weaving.

Sometimes this type of furniture was woven with silver tinsel thread which turned it into a poor dolls' silver filigree set.

RK, PIN & CONKER FURNITURE.   *PLATE 174.*

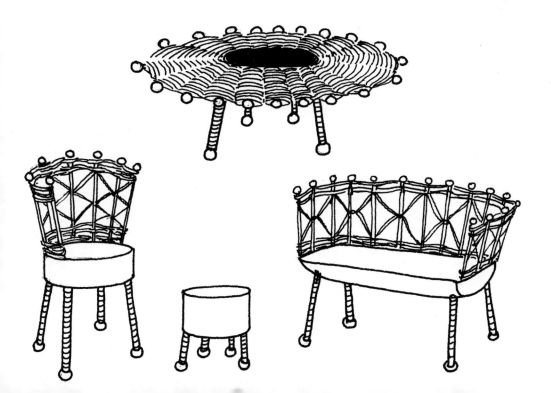

PLATE 17

Cot.

FURNITURE MADE FROM BOXES
& MATCHBOXES.

The most basic of all home-made dolls' house furniture is that made from cardboard boxes. As children, we must all have made dozens of beds and cots by up-ending the lid of the box to form a canopy (plate 175). This seemed a very natural shape for a bed, although few of us knew the half-tester that was represented. Despite the simplicity of these pieces, they can be quite beautiful if the right materials are used. These simple structures should be elaborately decorated and no pains should be spared to smother them in ribbons, laces, frills and beads.

First I will describe a cot which is the piece most often made and I have drawn diagrams (plates 176, 177) for a cot $3\frac{1}{4}$ inches long, $1\frac{3}{4}$ inches wide and $3\frac{1}{2}$ inches high. For the covering I used a very beautiful piece of ivory-coloured satin. I trimmed it with old lace, only half an inch wide, forming this into swags and rosettes, and I set a pearl in the centre of each rosette. The canopy I hung with very delicate floral net trimmed with lace and decorated with a satin bow. I also made a pillow from the same ivory coloured satin, but the bedclothes I made from a thinner cream silk.

Plates 176 and 177 give the size of the cardboard needed for the cot. After cutting this out with a sharp knife, I scored the fold lines. I then cut two thicknesses of paper handkerchief the same size as the card to act as padding, and also a piece of satin $\frac{1}{2}$ inch bigger all round (plate 177). The paper handkerchiefs were laid on the card and the satin laid on these, right side up, and the edges glued to the back of the card. The card is now bent up at the dotted lines to form the shape of the cot and the sides are sewn together at the corners. I then covered a piece of stiff wire 5 inches long with a strip of material. I bent the top $1\frac{1}{2}$ inches of the wire at a right angle to hold the canopy and I stitched this to the back of the cot.

The outside of the cot I covered with a piece of the material $10\frac{1}{2}$ inches long by $2\frac{1}{2}$ inches wide, which allows $\frac{1}{2}$ inch on the length for the join and 1 inch on the width for the hem at the top and bottom. I turned the hem on the lower edge of this strip and, keeping the materials wrong side outwards, I glued this strip to the upper edge of the cot, and made a seam at one of the back corners (plate 176). I then folded the satin on to the right side and the cot was ready for trimming.

Last of all, I made the canopy from the net 7 inches long by $1\frac{1}{2}$ inches wide and I sewed this to the top of the wire, inserting a triangle of net, $1\frac{1}{2}$ inches at the base by $3\frac{1}{2}$ inches high, into the canopy, which I trimmed with lace and ribbons.

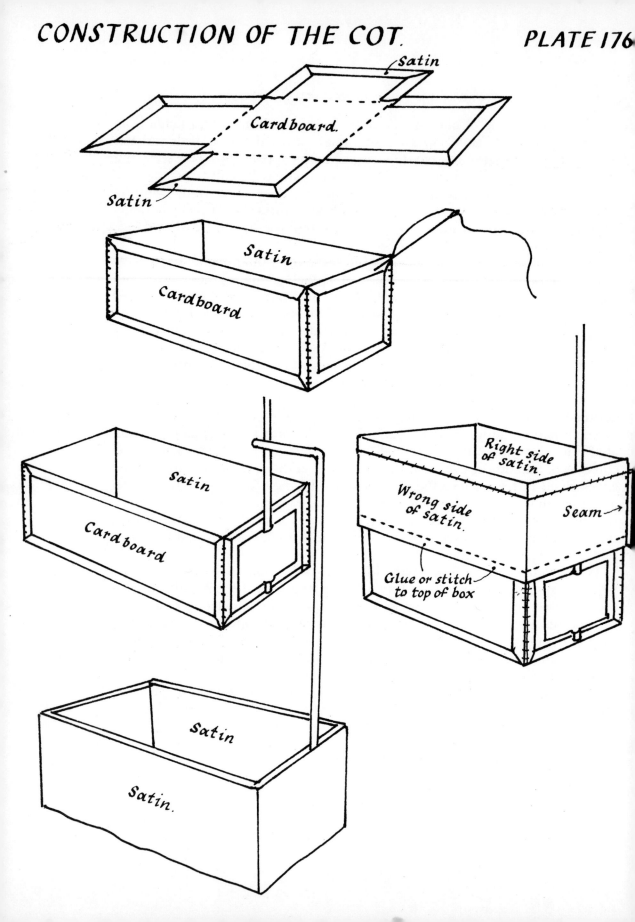

Satin

Cardboard.

Satin

Satin

Cardboard

Satin

Cardboard

Right side of satin.

Wrong side of satin.

Seam →

Glue or stitch to top of box

Satin

Satin.

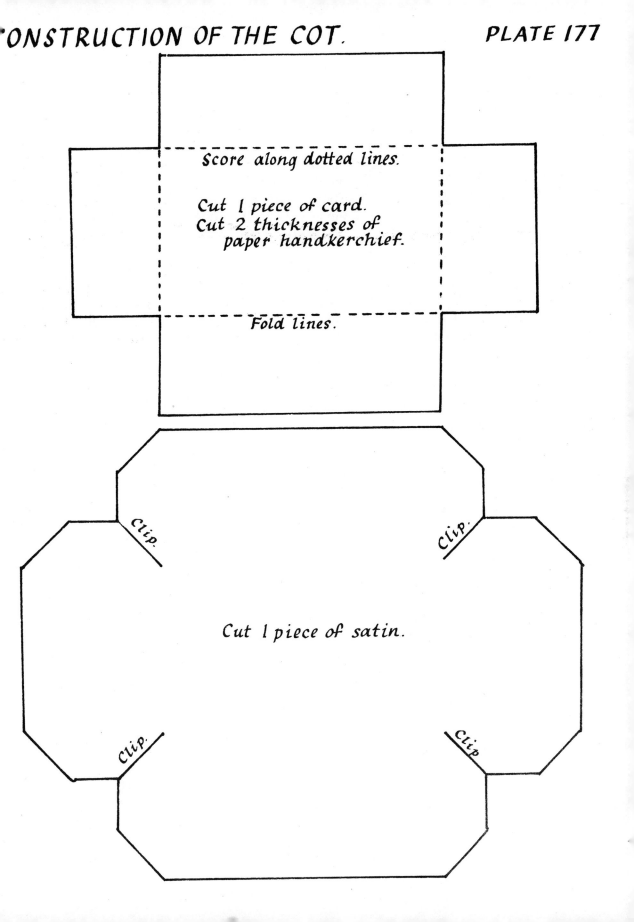

Score along dotted lines.

Cut 1 piece of card.
Cut 2 thicknesses of
    paper handkerchief.

Fold lines.

Clip.   Clip.

Cut 1 piece of satin.

Clip.   Clip.

The Half-tester Bed (Plate *178, 179*)

Using the same method it is possible to make a half-tester bed. Instead of a net canopy, a head board is incorporated into the main structure and covered wires are used to hold the side curtains. The bed head is improved with padding and a very thin layer of cottonwool can be laid on to the card under the satin and this can be 'buttoned' with small pearls.

Net curtains are hung on the projecting wires and a bead is used as a decorative finial on each wire. Four feet should be added to raise the bed from the ground. They need not be elaborate for they will be hidden by the lace frill.

The Chair (Plates *178, 180*)

A piece of satin $\frac{1}{2}$ inch bigger than the card is cut and glued to it. The card is then folded to form a box which is the seat of the chair. The top section of the chair back is padded, covered and buttoned before being glued to the chair seat. The back of the chair is then covered and a fine cord is used to cover the joins.

The Dressing Table (Plates *178, 181*)

Apart from the difference in proportion, the dressing table is essentially the same as the chair. A small mirror can be glued to the back, or a larger one hung on the wall.

BEDROOM FURNITURE MADE FROM BOXES.

PLATE 178.

Half-tester bed.

Dressing-table & bedroom chair.

CONSTRUCTION OF THE HALF-TESTER BED.

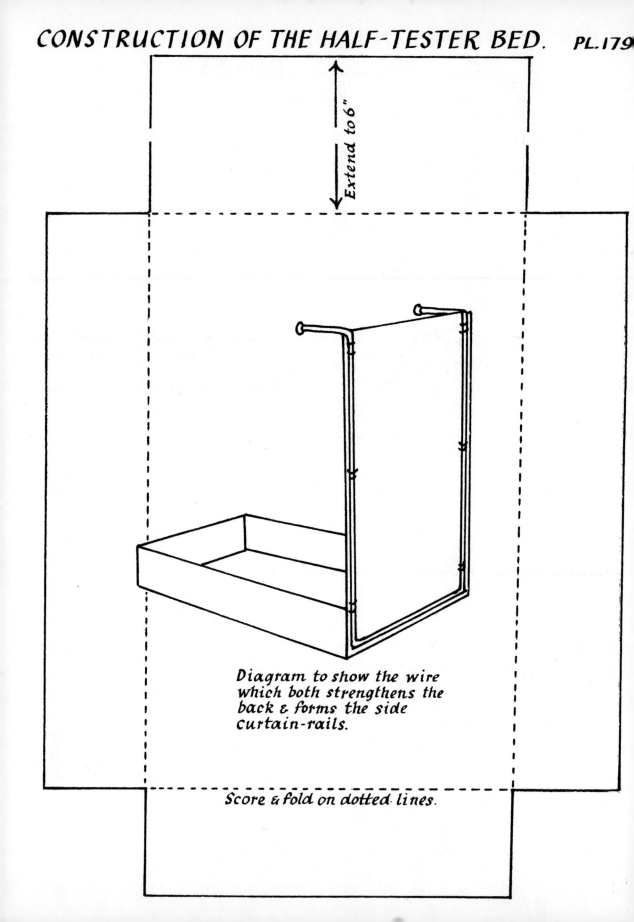

Extend to 6"

Diagram to show the wire
which both strengthens the
back & forms the side
curtain-rails.

Score & fold on dotted lines.

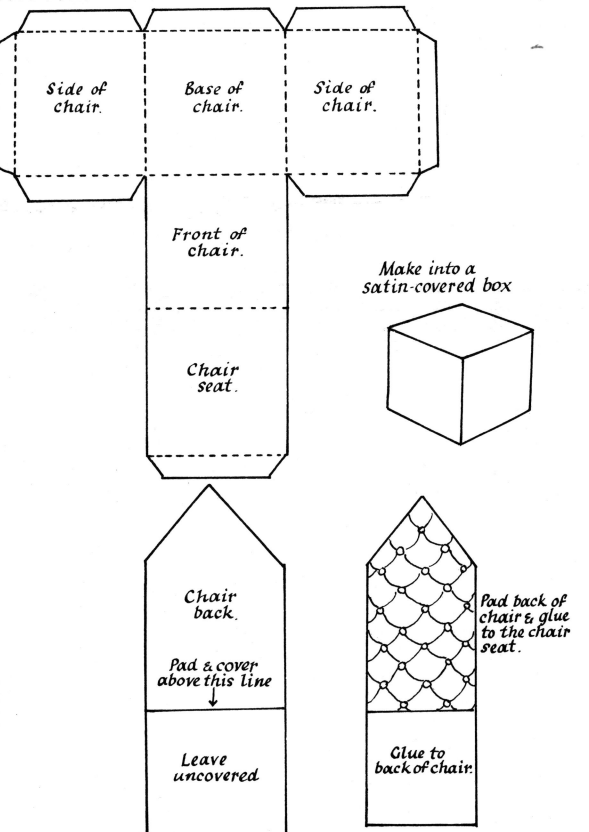

Side of
chair.

Base of
chair.

Side of
chair.

Front of
chair.

Chair
seat.

Make into a
satin-covered box

Chair
back.

Pad & cover
above this line

Leave
uncovered

Pad back of
chair & glue
to the chair
seat.

Glue to
back of chair.

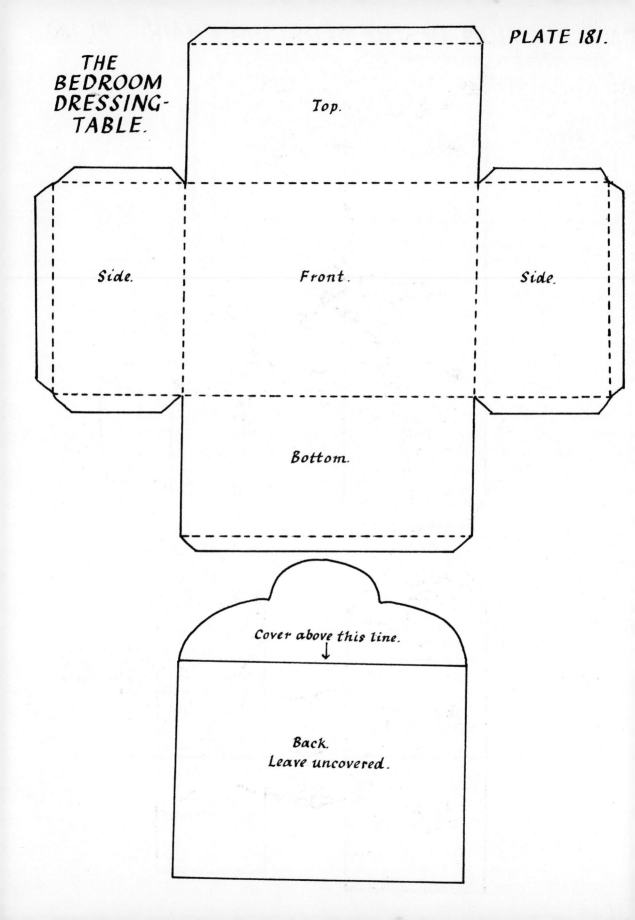

THE
BEDROOM
DRESSING-
TABLE.

PLATE 181.

Top.

Side.

Front.

Side.

Bottom.

Cover above this line.

Back.
Leave uncovered.

Furniture made from Matchboxes

I have heard of a booklet which was published some years ago by Bryant & May Ltd., but I have not seen it. It gave detailed instructions for making not only dolls' house furniture from matchboxes, but dolls' houses, not to mention town halls and cathedrals! Apparently this leaflet was sold for 1*d.* and it contained 32 pages of ideas.

Most children have made furniture from matchboxes and I think that it is surprising how few remain. I have seldom come across any in the dolls' houses that I have seen.

I have given one page of drawings (plate 182) of ideas for using the type of matchbox that is made of thin wood and measures 2·1 inches long by 1·4 inches wide by 0·7 inches deep. All are very simple to make.

The Chest of Drawers is made by glueing together six matchboxes and then covering the outside of the chest with a thin piece of card to hide the joins. The card should be 2·1″ × 7·2″ and it should be scored with a knife before it is folded, to give good sharp edges.

The chest of drawers can be painted at this stage with poster or tempera colour and varnished.

These pieces of furniture made from matchboxes have an ageless quality and the type of finish which is applied gives the feeling of the period. Instead of painting the furniture, some pieces could be covered with a decorative paper. The type of paper that covered Victorian exercise books would look very well, or, for a more modern piece, a small floral pattern would be suitable.

The Sink Unit, which is only suitable for a modern house, can be painted and the sink and draining board can be covered with silver foil to imitate stainless steel.

Stairs can be made by glueing matchboxes together with each box overlapping the last by half the width of the box. They will need a prop under the top stair but they make a very strong staircase. This type of matchbox makes a rather narrow, steep, plebeian type of staircase, but Swan Vestas, with their added width and lower depth, give a much grander effect. It is easier to paint or cover the stairs before they are fixed into the room.

There are, of course, many more ideas for using matchboxes in dolls' houses and combinations of different sized boxes increases the scope; and the matches themselves can be used to make all sorts of interesting extras.

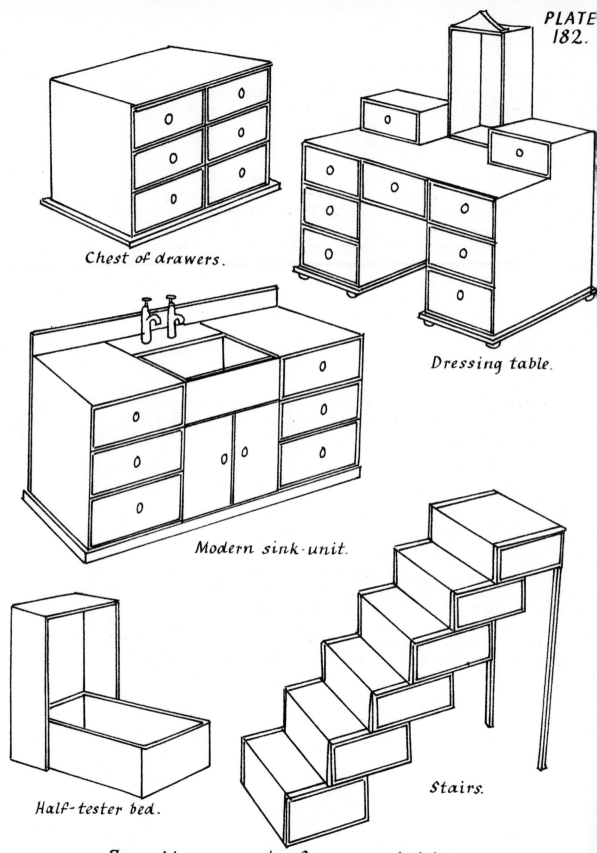

PLATE
182.

Chest of drawers.

Dressing table.

Modern sink-unit.

Half-tester bed.

Stairs.

Furniture made from matchboxes.

The construction of these two types of furniture is identical and both of them are interesting pieces to own. The feather furniture has a certain novelty value and the straw furniture can be very beautiful because of its delicate construction and colour.

I had wrongly assumed that feather furniture was one of the traditional kinds that was always home made, but I saw in a sale at Christies' in 1970 a set of nine ladder-backed rocking chairs in their original box that were obviously intended to be sold commercially. They were beautifully made and very elaborate and they sold for £6.

The only straw furniture that I have seen is in Dingley Hall. It is a set made in Japan in the 1870s and I am sure that the Japanese were so skilled that they would make such furniture in a few minutes, but it is an exacting job and takes a little while to acquire the skill for yourself. I found that it was easier to assemble the pieces a few at a time, fixing them with both pins and a quick drying glue. The best pins to use are the small ones, $\frac{1}{2}$ inch long, called 'Lillikin' pins. The fault to avoid is getting the pieces of furniture twisted and this is caused by not getting the pins quite horizontal.

The bends on the chair arms should be made at the joints on the straw for they bend easily at these points without breaking.

Some furniture is disappointing when it is drawn and this applies particularly to straw and feather furniture, but I can recommend the finished results.

It is necessary to collect considerably more straw and feathers than one would expect to need for a few small pieces of furniture, for there is a great deal of wastage in choosing just the right thickness of straw, and each feather only makes one strut.

Any kind of feather of the right size is suitable to use. I used some very pretty tail feathers from white fantail pigeons, but hen, duck and seagull feathers are just as good.

It is an advantage to keep feather furniture small in size so the discrepancies in the widths of the quills and the natural curves are minimal. A stool $1\frac{1}{4}$ inches high and a chair $2\frac{1}{2}$ inches high are about the right size.

The easiest piece to make is probably the stool illustrated on plate 183 and for this you will need four pieces, $1\frac{1}{4}$ inches long, from the ends of the quills, for the legs of the stool, always using the rounded end of the quill for the base of the legs. Four pieces of quill with the feathers left on one side form the top of the stool; two of the pieces should be $1\frac{3}{4}$ inches long and the other two pieces $1\frac{1}{4}$ inches in length. These are pinned and glued to the legs with the two larger pieces overlapping the shorter ones. The feathered ends do not present the difficulties that one might expect, for the feathers grow on the quill curved in both directions, both upwards and over, and they fold into each other very neatly. Four more pieces are needed for the spindles. Measure the lengths exactly on your stool. These spindles are not just for decoration. They help to keep the stool rigid and the more struts and spindles that are added, the stronger the furniture will be. Both feather and straw furniture are remarkably strong and long lasting. The materials themselves keep their colour and resilience and there seems little difference in appearance between furniture made in the 1830s and that made at a much later date.

When the basic skill has been acquired by making the stool, it is easy to progress to the more complicated pieces; and the more complicated they are, the more beautiful they become. It is the arrangements of the spindles and the design of the chair backs that indicate the period of the furniture.

There are also pieces of quill furniture where the feathers are not used and the seats and chair backs are upholstered on to the stripped quills.

PLATE 183

Furniture made from feathers, from 1830 on.

PLATE 184.

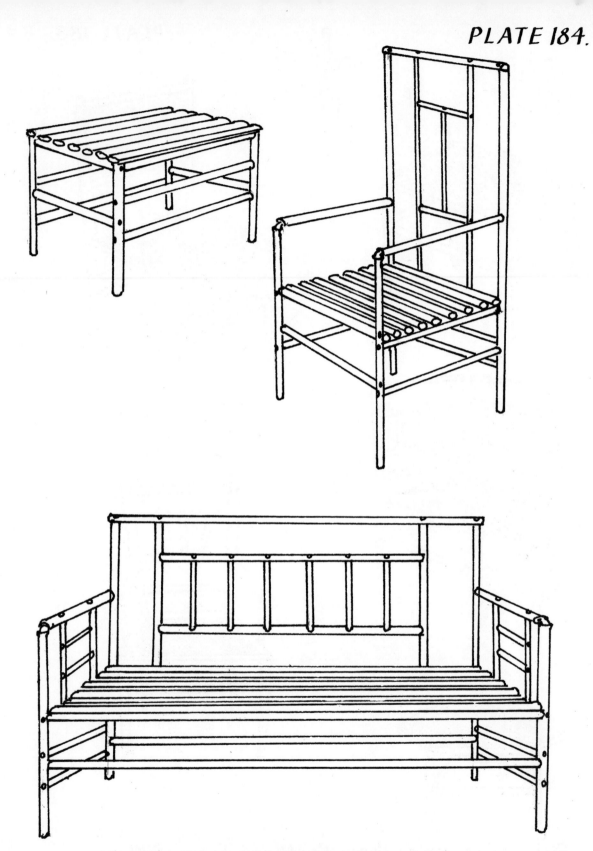

Furniture made from straws.

An Edwardian Bed made from Rushes (Plate 185)

This bed is made from the dried stems of the tall rushes that grow on the edges of lakes and tarns. It is similar to straw, but when the outer husk is peeled away the stem is cream in colour instead of golden. It makes a pretty bed, and although it is quite firm when it is finished and it will not break if it is dropped, it is too delicate for a dolls' house intended as a child's plaything.

The following lengths of stem are needed to make the bed. The upright posts and the two long side pieces are made from thicker stems than the rest of the bed.

THE BED HEAD
    2 uprights $4\frac{1}{2}$ inches long
    2 pieces for the cross struts $3\frac{1}{2}$ inches long
    4 pieces for the centre uprights $2\frac{1}{2}$ inches long
    2 thinner pieces for the small cross struts 1 inch long.

THE FOOT OF THE BED:
    2 uprights $3\frac{1}{2}$ inches long
    2 pieces for the cross struts $3\frac{1}{2}$ inches long
    4 pieces for the centre uprights 2·2 inches long.

THE BASE OF THE BED:
    2 side pieces $5\frac{1}{2}$ inches long
    3 pieces for the cross struts $3\frac{1}{2}$ inches long.

The base of the bed measures $4'' \times 5\cdot2''$. This bed is put together in the same way as the feather and straw furniture, using the small pins and dabs of glue at each joint.

A Brass Bedstead

A very impressive brass bedstead can be made in exactly the same way and to the same sizes as the one described above, but it can be made from plastic drinking straws covered with gold paper. The narrow drinking straws are the ones to use, and the ends should be plugged with a self-hardening clay to give the pins a firm hold.

Small gold-coloured glass beads can be used for the knobs.

PLATE 185.

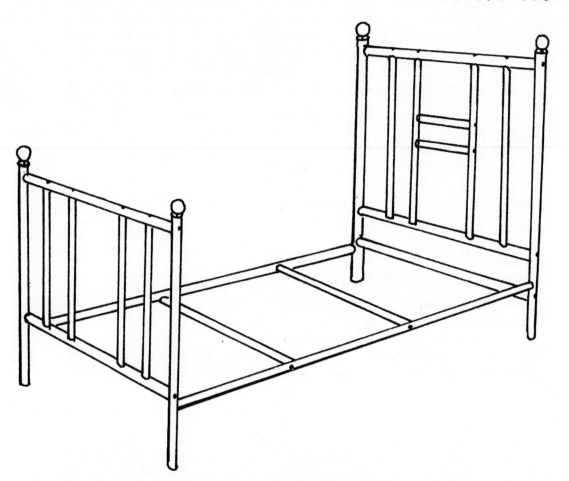

An Edwardian bed made from rushes.

Such exquisite objects as shells are always a temptation to craftsmen, often with disastrous results, but some of the Georgian and Victorian shell flower arrangements were so delicate and so beautiful that one keeps on trying to use them.

Shells for use in a dolls' house need to be very small, and tweezers are often necessary to make up some of these decorations, otherwise they can look crude. I think that one piece decorated with shells in a dolls' house is probably sufficient. Sometimes Victorian dolls' house furniture manufacturers used shell decoration, but most of the pieces I have seen have been clumsy with over-large iridescent shells coupled with magenta satin. One can imagine the same object, more delicately handled, looking quite lovely.

Frames for mirrors or pictures could be made up from small shells.

I have, in the past, decorated the roofs of dolls' houses with shells of many kinds arranged in patterns; and small shells can also be used to make a cobbled path to a house. There are many other uses—a fireplace can be decorated with a single shell, or the fine pale pink shells that resemble toe-nails can serve as dishes or as wall lights, or, as in real houses, they can be used for decorations under glass domes with stuffed fish, birds and dried flowers.

Shells can be attached to objects by laying a thin layer of Polyfilla and pressing the shells into this before it dries. Such a layer will take about ten minutes to harden on a normally absorbent surface, so only a small area of Polyfilla should be laid at one time. It is not necessary to mix new Polyfilla for each area for a pile kept on a non-absorbent surface and covered with a damp cloth will keep soft for an hour or so.

If both the size of the shells and the area to be decorated are small, then a glue such as Durofix can be used instead; and again it is necessary to spread only a small area at a time.

I think that shells look their best on a light, delicate background—white or pale pink—for they loose their fresh appearance if they are put on to a dark or brightly coloured ground.

If desired, shell work can be varnished. This brings out the colours of the shells, but a high gloss can look too harsh.

A Victorian Settee Decorated with Shells (Plates 186–188)

I have drawn a simplified version of a mid-Victorian settee. The construction should not be too elaborate when using shells or the whole effect can be confusing.

The shaped pieces can be cut from wood or card about ⅛ inch thick.

The seat and the two wedge-shaped pieces for the sides and the extra piece for the settee back should be padded into a good shape and upholstered with thin material before all the pieces are glued together. A few small nails will ensure a good firm piece of furniture and the nail heads can be covered with the shell decoration.

Wall Mirror

This mirror is made from a handbag mirror with paper glued to the edges to form an absorbent surface for the shell work. This paper can be spread with glue or a very thin layer of Polyfilla and the design is made up with a few shells, but the background is filled in with grains of rice and lentils.

After trying this, I could see that rice holds many possibilities, for the shape is good and the texture splendid.

A Dolls' House Roof Decorated with Shells

When covering a dolls' house roof, or making a path, the shells can be more varied in type and size and this also means that the Polyfilla can be spread more thickly.

The surface of the roof should be sandpapered with a very coarse sandpaper or scored with a rasp to give it a good tooth. When this is done thoroughly the shells will not fall off. The corner shells are always vulnerable but if they are knocked off they can quite easily be glued back into their moulds.

PLATE 186.

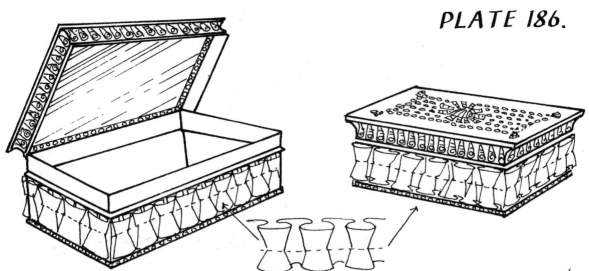

An Ottoman from a dolls' house of 1850. Shell decoration on the lid.

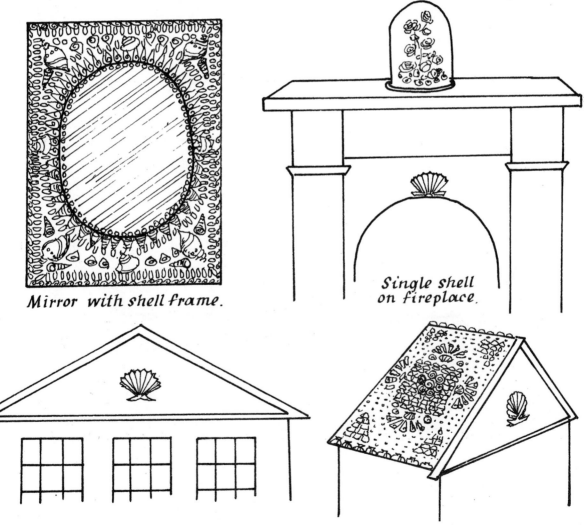

Mirror with shell frame.

Single shell on fireplace.

Sea-shells used as decoration.

PLATE 187

A Victorian settee decorated with shells.

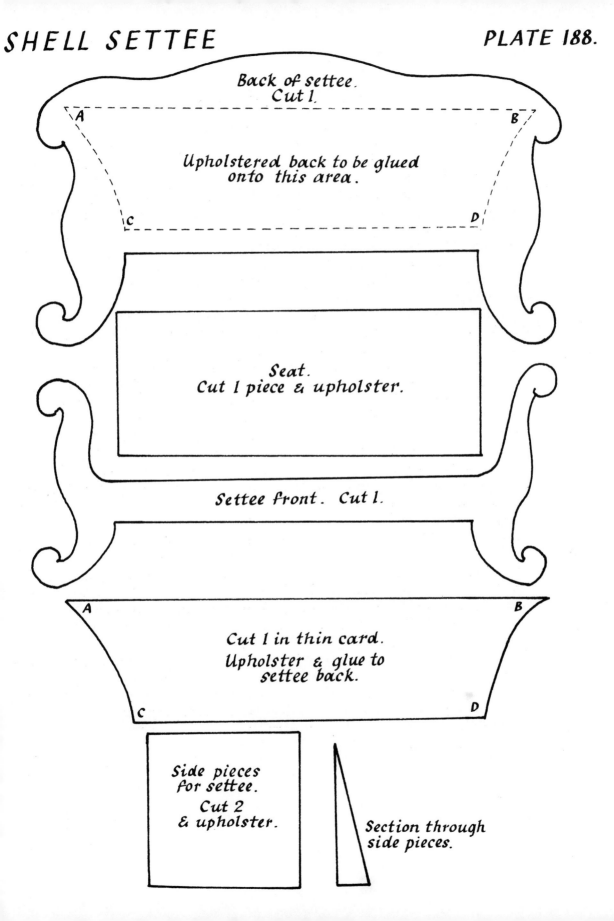

SHELL SETTEE

PLATE 188.

Back of settee.
Cut 1.

A   B

Upholstered back to be glued
onto this area.

C   D

Seat.
Cut 1 piece & upholster.

Settee front. Cut 1.

A   B

Cut 1 in thin card.
Upholster & glue to
settee back.

C   D

Side pieces
for settee.
Cut 2
& upholster.

Section through
side pieces.

WIRE AND RAFFIA FURNITURE

This furniture is made in Spain from wire bound with raffia, and seats and table tops are woven from strands of raffia to resemble canework. I tried making this kind of furniture, covering the wires in several different kinds of thread, but in the end I still liked the raffia covering best. One piece which I tried with natural-coloured linen thread was quite pleasant and it seemed to me that natural, rather than synthetic fibres, gave a quality to the furniture that would make it acceptable to all of the different periods, and that it is the shaping of the wire that determines the era. After copying one chair it became quite easy to start inventing all sorts of furniture.

The wire chosen should be easy to bend and of a kind that will hold its shape quite firmly, and copper wire has both of these properties. Whenever possible, it is better to bend the wire round a curved object of the right size and shape, for it is too difficult to get a good form in any other way. The wire should be shaped before it is covered.

It can be covered either by using a simple buttonhole stitch or by using a double buttonhole stitch (plate 190). This stitch is made by using two pieces of thread, working one buttonhole stitch with the loop on the inside of the circle and the other stitch with the loop on the outside, making each stitch alternately until the whole wire is covered. The advantage of the double buttonhole stitch is that it gives a rather nice edging on the outside of the wire and loops on the inner edge to take the strands of thread for the 'canework'.

The method of making the 'canework' is shown on plate 190. I have exaggerated the thickness of the wire and the stitches to make the diagram easier to read, but the effect is much better when it is carried out with a fine thread. Plate 190 A shows the horizontal threads and plate 190 B shows the vertical threads which are laid on top of the horizontal ones. Plate 190 C shows the diagonal stitch which is worked from the bottom right to the top left, picking up the horizontal stitches and putting the thread over the vertical ones. It is easier to start this diagonal stitch in the centre and work to the bottom left and then start again in the centre and work to the top right-hand side.

When all of the wires are covered and the canework complete, the pieces should be firmly stitched together, and where there is an overlap the wires can be buttonholed together, which will give a stronger and neater finish. The decorative patterns on the chair and settee backs can be made as varied as you wish.

PLATE 189.

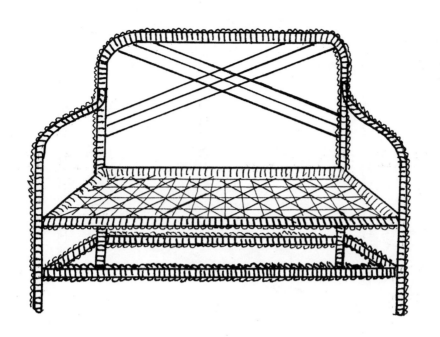

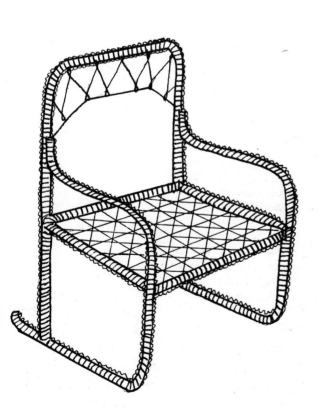

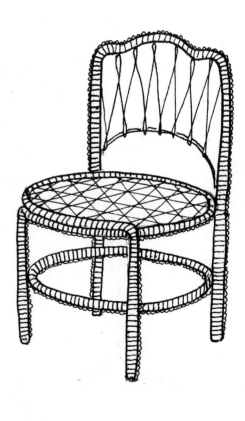

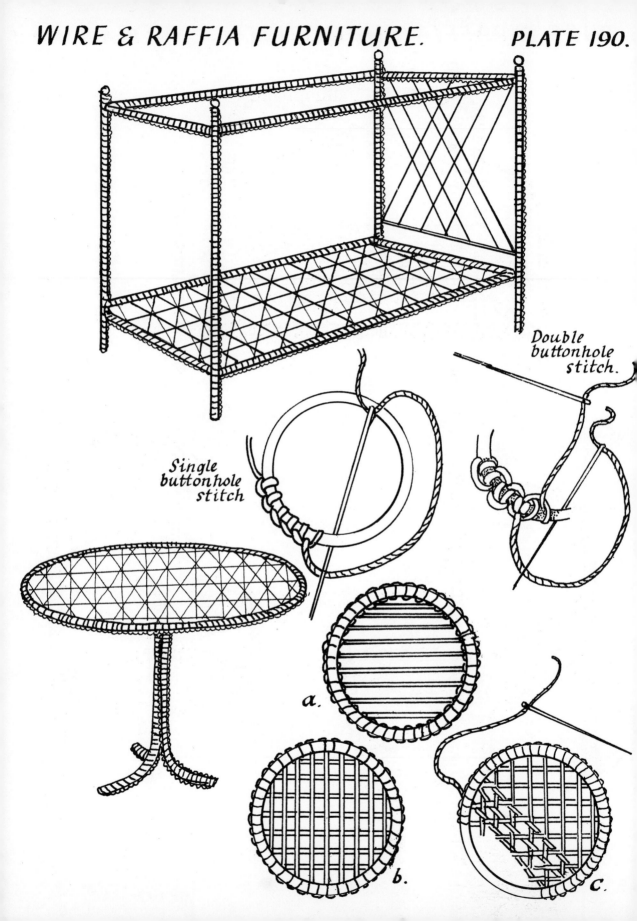

WIRE & RAFFIA FURNITURE.

PLATE 190.

Single buttonhole stitch

Double buttonhole stitch.

a.

b.

c.

GLASS OBJECTS

There are many delicate and beautiful objects in old dolls' houses that are made from glass, and apart from the obvious ones that represent glass objects, there are also things which are traditionally made from glass only in dolls' houses. Glass plant pots were at one time very popular. Each had a single stem with three or four leaves and two flowers made from stiffened linen and because the pots were made of solid glass many of them have survived. Glass bird cages holding glass birds were made in early Victorian times, and so were glass chandeliers, made either from blown glass or from glass beads (plates 191, 194). I have also seen a glass cradle, barely 2 inches long, and the glass looked as if it had been piped into shape as one would pipe icing on to a cake (plate 154). It is still possible today to buy some glass objects for dolls' houses. There are decanters and glasses, although many of these are now being made from plastic.

As it is extremely difficult to make glass objects for ourselves we must fall back on adapting pieces which are available. Scent bottles are often small enough to double as decanters or as bases for oil lamps, and doctors and vets will gladly give you the small bottles left over from injections. They are the right scale and shape for bottles and jars in sweet shops and kitchens. Other small glass tubes, such as those containing sea-sickness preventative tablets, make useful beginnings.

It is possible to cut, or rather break, glass tubing and I have been able to replace the missing chimneys from my old dolls' house oil lamps. For this purpose, I used airlocks which are sold to winemakers (plate 191). To cut the glass, score it with a triangular file and then, holding it with a cloth, break it off with a quick sharp jerk. To give an even more realistic effect, submerge the glass almost to the top of the bulbous part in white emulsion paint so that the paint gets inside the glass. The paint can be wiped away from the outside.

More difficult, but still worth trying, is to break off the top of a test tube to use as a glass dome. The difficulty is to get a firm grip on the rounded end of the tube. I have heard that small glass domes can be bought in Catholic repositories but I have not found any small enough yet. Tin lids filled with self-hardening clay or Polyfilla can be used as bases for these glass domes and into these can be fixed the objects which are to be displayed—minute grasses, the seed heads from mosses, which are surprisingly bird-shaped, or small velvet artificial flowers. Fruit can be modelled for these displays and perhaps even a really small doll can be found. Of course, glass-fronted cases are easier to make and they look well with a tiny modelled wax doll surrounded with artificial flowers. The case should only be 2 inches high, at the most (plate 191).

These dolls in glass cases were fashionable during Victoria's reign and in a museum in Arles I even saw a Victorian doll in a glass bottle, a variation on the ship in a bottle theme.

Glazed wall cases can house stuffed birds, butterflies, fish, model ships or even a display of buildings in a landscape called a bocage, and nothing could look more Victorian than these. There is, in the Bethnal Green museum, an early Victorian dolls' house which contains German furniture, and in one of the rooms there is a really elegant glass-fronted box with a pinnacled roof and a three-dimensional cardboard stage set with two cardboard figures.

In the Barry Elder Doll Museum, there is a dolls' house made from glass. This must surely be very unusual, but it is disappointing for, although the description conjures up visions of a winter palace, it really is a very pedestrian Edwardian villa. The walls and roof are certainly made from glass, but they are backed with harshly coloured wallpaper bricks and slates, and as there is no way of opening it, it is merely a model house.

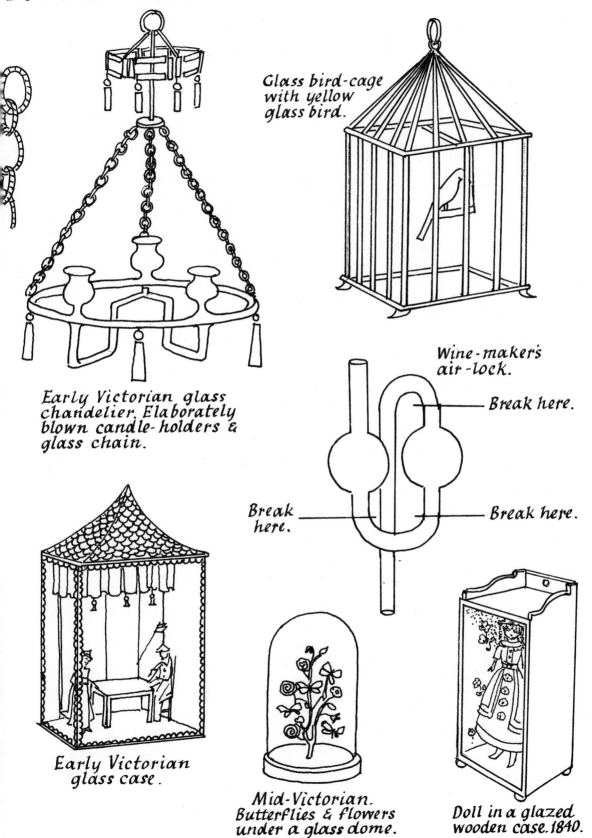

Glass bird-cage with yellow glass bird.

Early Victorian glass chandelier. Elaborately blown candle-holders & glass chain.

Wine-maker's air-lock.

Break here.

Break here.

Break here.

Early Victorian glass case.

Mid-Victorian. Butterflies & flowers under a glass dome.

Doll in a glazed wooden case. 1840.

Fascinating home-made dolls' house furniture can be made from beads, and drawings in black and white give a very poor impression of how nice it can look. I have done a drawing of a bentwood chair made from beads (plate 192) and this is a simple shape to try. I made it with beads which were roughly $\frac{1}{4}$ inch long. They were black and iridescent and shone like beetles' wings, and I used round blue beads for the feet and to decorate the back of the chair. This chair is 3 inches high and to make it you will require a piece of wire $7\frac{3}{4}$ inches long for the back, and another piece $4\frac{1}{4}$ inches long for the smaller back rest. Two pieces $5\frac{1}{4}$ inches long are needed to make the circles for the seat and the lower circle of beads. The two front legs are made from wire 2 inches long. Each of these pieces of wire is $\frac{1}{2}$ inch longer than required, to allow for the finishing off and fixing to the other pieces.

The wire must be thin enough to thread through the beads, but it must be as stiff as possible for its thickness.

Start to make the chair by fixing a small round blue bead on to the end of the longest piece of wire. Then thread the long beads on to the whole length, finishing off with another round bead. Bend this into shape to form the chair back. Now thread the beads on to one of the pieces of wire which is $5\frac{1}{4}$ inches long and form this into a circle for the seat, twisting the wires securely where the ends join. Join this to the chair back $1\frac{1}{2}$ inches from the bottom. Now make the two front legs, using the 2-inch long wires. These legs are joined to the front of the circle of beads which forms the seat. The second ring of beads is fixed $\frac{1}{2}$ inch below the top ring. The piece of wire $4\frac{1}{4}$ inches long is made into the smaller part of the chair back. When making a chair of this size, beads can also be used for the chair seat, but for a bigger or more elaborate piece a cushion would be better.

A Victorian Beaded Cushion (Plate 192)

These miniature beaded cushions must have been very popular in Victorian times, for one comes across them so often. Perhaps they were made for pin-cushions.

They should be made with the smallest beads and in two colours. The pad looks well in strong coloured satin.

For a cushion 2 inches square, cut a piece of material $4\frac{1}{2}'' \times 2\frac{1}{2}''$ and make this into a pad filled with wadding. The bead covering is easy enough to make but it takes a little time.

For the first row, thread 4 inches of beads, starting with a dark bead, followed by four white ones, then a dark one again, and so on. At the end of the 4 inches, and ending with a dark bead, turn back to form a second row of four white beads, one dark one, and four white ones again, but instead of adding a second dark bead, pick up the dark bead from the previous row (plate 192) and so on, picking up alternate dark beads until the end of the second row is reached. The third row is worked in the same way, picking up the alternate dark beads from the row above. This makes the diamond pattern.

When the beadwork is large enough, cover the pad by sewing the dark beads together along the join (plate 192). At each corner there are four loops of beads. Each of these is made from one length of beads, working $\frac{1}{2}$ inch of white beads, then $\frac{1}{2}$ inch of dark beads. Repeat this twice and then loop these and sew them into position so that the dark beads come on the outer edges of the loops.

The Beadwork Stool (Plate 193)

After seeing a dolls' house that I was busy furnishing, two small girls produced this beadwork stool for the drawing-room. They were just six and eight years old and it is very rich and lovely. They had bought the beads from a shop called Theatre Land Ltd., 14 Soho Street, London, W.1, who sell beads, 28 to the inch, for 25p for 2 ounces in one colour, but they had bought for $12\frac{1}{2}$p a bag of 'Sweepings' and so the beads were very varied—small pearls, minute gilt ones, long beads and round beads in reds, yellows and three different blues. They had used the tray from a small match box as a base and had sewn the beads in a geometrical pattern on to a piece of dark green material which they glued and stitched on to the box.

A Victorian Armchair (Plate 193)

This armchair is made from card, padded with wadding and covered in red satin. The legs are made from wood painted red, but are hidden by the bead fringe. The bead decoration on the back, arms and seat of the chair is worked with very small crystal beads to a floral pattern.

Bead Chandelier. Early Victorian (Plate 194)

This plate shows an early Victorian chandelier about $3\frac{1}{2}$ inches high and it is made from white, gold and sky-blue beads, threaded on to wire and hung from a metal chain. The smaller top circle is made from long white beads and round gold ones and this circle is wired to the metal chain. From this hang three lengths of white beads which are attached to the lower larger circle, which is $1\frac{3}{4}$ inches in diameter. This is made from long white beads threaded into diamond shapes, and round blue beads threaded into circles. The hanging beads are white and gold. Two pieces of wire are used at the same time to make this circle (plate 194). The beads are threaded on to each wire and the wires are twisted between each diamond and circle. The hanging beads are attached with thread to the base of the diamond shapes. From this circle hang six lengths of white beads which are joined at the base to form the bag.

Bead Chandelier from Modern Materials (Plate 194)

This chandelier, which is early Victorian in design, is made from modern materials. The brass bands used for the circles are drawn actual size and are beautifully made. These and several other types of edging that can be used on many pieces of furniture or as pelmets or fenders, can be bought from the American shop called The Pedler's Shop, 12408 E. 46th Terrace, Independence, Missouri. They stock a wealth of fascinating miniature decorations and objects that are impossible to buy in England.

To form this edging into circles, bend it round some cylindrical object, leaving a small overlap so that the ends can be wired together. The drawing, with plastic droppers, shows a decorative edging, one of many varieties sold in drapers' shops at the moment. It is composed of plastic droppers that look like glass and they are fused to a cotton braid. A length of this can be glued on to the inside of the brass circle. Eight lengths of glass beads are threaded on to wires to hang from this band and when joined at the base they form the bag of the chandelier. Each of the droppers has a small air bubble in it and, for a modern dolls' house on a small scale, these beads are very suitable for electric light bulbs.

The edging made from gilt plastic beads can be bought by the yard and is very useful when making chandeliers.

Other Uses for Beads

During the late Victorian era and until the 1920s, bead curtains were often used to hang in doorways or across alcoves. These were mainly imported from the East and they were often decorated with flowers such as chrysanthemums and roses. The only examples that I have seen in a dolls' house is the one in the hall of Mrs. Bessie Roberts' house, made in 1903. It is now in the Bethnal Green Museum and it has very deep rooms from back to front, with windows on the back walls. It is very pleasant to look at, but the deep rooms must be very difficult to play in.

These curtains are easily reproduced, by making a fringe of glass beads. It would be difficult to use coloured beads to form the decorations, as they are in the full sized curtains, but quite simple to make the fringe of clear crystal beads and then apply the decorations with coloured inks. The Edwardians used beaded fringe for the shades on gas brackets and lampshades and in the 1920s carved oak circles hung with beaded fringes hid the glare of the electric light bulbs.

BEAD "BENTWOOD" CHAIR. Actual size.   PLATE 192.

Seat
fixed here.

Lower circle
fixed here.

Lower
back-rest.

Front legs
Cut 2.

Enlarged drawing of bead
wired to the end of each leg.

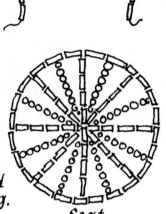

Seat.

Beads to
hold the
back-rests
together.

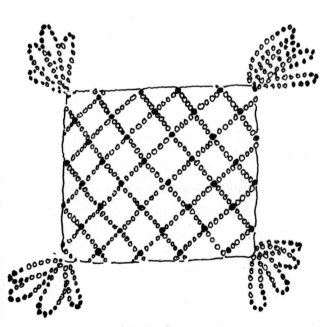

1st. row . 4" long.

2nd. row.

3rd. row.

Sew up the cushion by joining the dark beads.

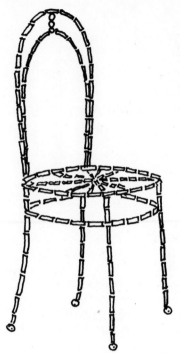

Bead 'bentwood' chair.

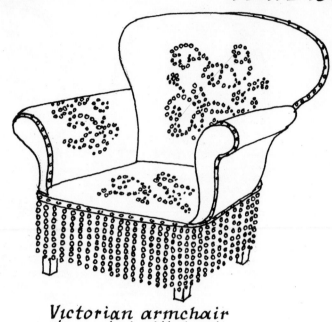

Victorian armchair
decorated with beads.

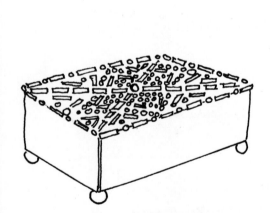

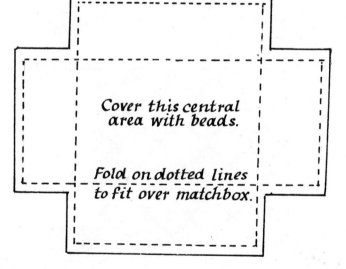

Cover this central
area with beads.

Fold on dotted lines
to fit over matchbox.

Stool decorated
with beads.

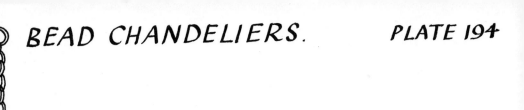

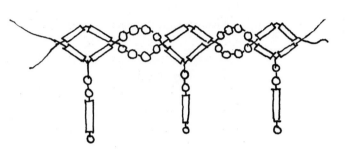

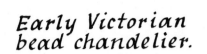

Early Victorian
bead chandelier.

Metal edging.

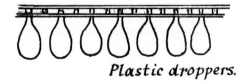

Plastic droppers.

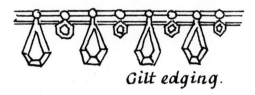

Gilt edging.

Regency style chandelier
made with modern materials.

It is always satisfying to make something from nothing and very often some of the best pieces in dolls' houses are made from useless odds and ends.

On plate 195 I have drawn three tables. The first one turned out very well. It was made from a miniature brass candlestick about $2\frac{1}{2}$ inches high, and a lid from a tin of scouring paste (Chemico). I plugged the hole on top of the candlestick with a piece of wooden dowelling which I glued into place with Araldite, and on to this I screwed a circle of wood slightly smaller in diameter than the tin lid. This was to provide as large a surface as possible to glue to the lid, which I later painted to represent marble.

The second table is intended for a modern dolls' house. It is rather chi-chi and is made from the lid of a Max Factor 'Creme Puff' container, which is 3 inches in diameter, of white plastic decorated with a gold design. The centre of the lid needed a piece of white plastic glueing over it to cover the lettering. The base of this table is made from a gilt lipstick case and a gold coloured lid from a talcum powder tin.

The third small table is intended for an 1820 dolls' house. For the table top I used a very chipped and battered pillbox of that period. The lid is white enamel, decorated with black line drawings and the inside and the base are a lovely sage green colour. The inside of the lid is mirror, tarnished with age. I divided the inside of the box into six compartments, using card painted green to match the enamel, and into these I put sewing materials, minute bobbins made from slices cut from a cocktail stick, painted black and wound with white cotton, and small cards wound with coloured silks. The shaped base of the table I cut from wood and stained and polished it to represent mahogany and I used glass-headed pins for the three feet.

Victorian table with 'marble'
top & brass pedestal.

Modern occasional
table.

Regency work-box.

The Deed Box

The final object to make for the dolls' house is a deed box. It should match the period of the rest of the furnishings and be as elaborate as possible, with plenty of metal clasps and hinges.

Inside, and tied with pink tapes, should be the deeds of the house and all the information that you have—the age, where it came from, who were the previous owners, and of course the name of the house and the name of the present owner. Also it should contain information about which pieces are original and which have been replaced, and whether the wallpaper, curtains and carpets are genuine.